# Where's Where in Dublin
# A directory of historic locations, 1913–1923

*The Great Lockout, The Easter Rising,*
*The War of Independence, The Irish Civil War*

Joseph E.A. Connell, Jnr

Dublin City
Baile Átha Cliath

First published 2006 by
Dublin City Council
Dublin City Library & Archive
138–144 Pearse Street
Dublin 2

A catalogue record is available for this book
from the British Library.

ISBN 0 946841 81 0 (Casebound)
0 946841 82 9 (Paperback)

Design and origination © Environmental Publications
Cover design: Conor Gallagher
All photographs courtesy Seamus Kearns Postcard Collection

Printed in Ireland

# Contents

*To Pam*

Grá mo chroí

# Acknowledgements

First, for everything, I must thank my parents; without them I would have had no such love for Ireland. And, of course, my brothers and sister, and their families .

I am grateful to Dublin City Council for including this book as part of its commemorative programme for the 90th anniversary of the 1916 Rising, and for financing its publication. The staff of Dublin City Library & Archive, especially Dr. Mary Clark and Alastair Smeaton, oversaw the publication process under the guidance of Dublin City Librarian Deirdre Ellis-King, while the superb illustrations are from the postcard collection of Seamus Kearns, and my sincere thanks go to him for his kindness in providing these.

Those who have helped and encouraged me are too numerous to mention and I thank them all; at the risk of offending someone I omit I must especially mention Pam Boyd, Bob Clarke, Lorcan Collins, Maureen Comber, Rev. Paul Connell, Bob Fuquea, Martina Crowley-Hayes, Barbara Hollandsworth, Peggy Keating, Desmond Long, Mary Macken, Rev. Anthony Mulderry, and Sean Spellissy.

And, always, Pam Brewster for all things.

# Foreword

As one walks down any street in and around central Dublin, one can look into the door-ways and up to the windows and feel the eyes of history looking back.

For many years I walked down Dublin streets and wondered, then discovered, just what secrets were held there, and within the buildings, rooms and halls that line those streets.

This work, then, is one of discovery. I hope it will humanise (as it did for me) those who participated in the 'revolutionary' years between 1913 and 1923 – the most momentous decade in Irish history.

Certainly there is hero-worship in such a compendium. I freely admit to beginning this work as a means of getting to know the participants of that time better. I wanted to know where they worked and dreamed, where they were successful and not, and where they lived and many died. What began as a study of their surroundings evolved into a complete account of the 'where' of that tumultuous time.

Each section is arranged alphabetically to allow the reader the easiest access to the information. The Address section is alphabetised by street, and then chronologically within an address. The Organisation and Garrison section is also arranged alphabetically and chronologically, so the reader can find a name and the location of participation in the Rising, for example, as easily as possible. One should freely use the Index to move from one location to another, and to place a participant in all the sites listed. Every effort has been made to place individuals in their most important positions, and any errors or omissions are mine alone.

It is not intended that the book should be read from cover to cover. It was not written that way, and I wish it to be an awakening for the reader as it has been for me.

My intention is that the reader will enter the book at any convenient spot – at that very address in Dublin, for instance, where one is standing if one is lucky enough to be visiting. If one is not so lucky, a 'walk' through the city may be undertaken using the maps and the addresses to give one a feel of just what those streets and buildings 'saw' during the period. This makes for a book one can read for just a few minutes or into which one can delve for hours. Any time spent will allow the reader to begin a process of getting to know those whose dedication, industry, and life's blood made modern Ireland.

The Rising and the War of Independence were, like all revolutionary endeavours, a gamble. Men and women who believed that any effort was better than none launched them, but their plan of operations had not been, and could not have been, fully worked out. All revolutionaries extemporise – it is only their determination to be revolutionaries that is fixed. The participants left few notes and still fewer 'minutes' of meetings.

A good illustration is found in the organisational meeting that led to the foundation of the Irish Volunteers, the central military unit of the Rising, as noted in the description of the meeting held in Wynn's Hotel, 35–37 Abbey Street Lower, on 11 November 1913. Even those most instrumental in calling that meeting – Bulmer Hobson and The O'Rahilly – could not agree either on those who attended or those who were invited. The history of those years is replete with stories such as that and this book is an attempt to give the reader the fullest information possible by noting where such meetings took place, and the circumstances and attendees.

Because of his special prominence during the War of Independence and the Civil War, there is a section devoted to locations used by Michael Collins. His presence was ubiquitous during those years and he often appears in the main body of addresses, but I believe his activities, offices, and the locations of those who were particularly connected with him merit a section of their own.

Hopefully, this book will bring to life all those locations that have such wonderful and historic tales to tell.

I am greatly indebted to all the authors of the sources listed, to those who left any notes of the period, and especially all who have given me their time in interviews and conversations. Without them I would have been 'lost'.

# Introduction

Between 1845 and 1850, Irish farmers suffered through successive crop failures due to potato blight – the fungus *Phytophthora infestans* – and the waves of emigration which followed led directly to the most convulsive decades in Irish history.

By 1851, the population of Ireland had been reduced by more than two million due to starvation, disease, and emigration to Britain and North America.

Some of those who emigrated to the United States founded revolutionary groups dedicated to the overthrow of British rule in Ireland. In March 1855, John O'Mahoney and Michael Doheny organised emigrants who had previously belonged to the Young Irelanders, and called themselves the Emmet Monument Association. The group immediately sent funds back to Ireland and communicated a greater nationalistic fervour, and this combined to create a new Irish patriotic movement. On St Patrick's Day 1858, with the financial and philosophical support of those exiled Young Irelanders in America, James Stephens formally established the Irish Republican Brotherhood (IRB) in Dublin. Stephens maintained contact with the Irish-American nationalist groups, including a sister organisation to the IRB that O'Mahoney called the Fenian Brotherhood. Following abortive raids on Canada by the Fenian Brotherhood in 1867, the organisation was outlawed in America, prompting another Irish emigrant, John Devoy, to establish Clan na Gael, and it was this organisation which provided much of the funding for further nationalist efforts in Ireland.

Many Irish Americans gained military experience during the American Civil War and following its conclusion they decided the time was ripe to break Ireland away from the British Empire by means of force. In 1867 militant leaders in Ireland led an uprising known as the Fenian Revolt, a reference to the ancient Irish legendary warrior band of the Fianna. Thereafter 'Fenians' became synonymous with underground Irish republicanism. The transient eclipse of the movement began when this attempt to establish an independent Irish republic failed, but those members of the secret society known as the IRB continued to plan and foment a military separation from Britain, albeit with no success.

For the remainder of the nineteenth century most efforts at improving the lot of the Irish were constitutional, led by Charles Stewart Parnell, 'The Chief' of the Irish Party in Britain's parliament. The Irish National Land League was founded in Dublin in 1879 with Parnell as president. The main objectives of the League were to provide tenants with a fair rent, fixed tenure and free sale. The long term aim was that farmers would own the land. The Land League became a hugely popular movement overnight, assisting Irish farmers to stand on their own feet and assert their rights.

Parnell always believed that solving the land question should be the first step on the road to Home Rule for Ireland. In December 1882, when the suppressed Land League was replaced by the Irish National League, he ensured that the new organisation was under the control of his party and that its primary objective was the winning of Home Rule. William Gladstone, several times Liberal prime minister in England in the latter half of the nineteenth century, convinced by Parnell's success, gave the Home Rule movement his support. Though the Home Rule Bill of 1886 met with fierce opposition, it was Parnell's affair with the married

Katherine O'Shea that was fatal to his leadership, and ultimately to Home Rule in his time.

Parnell's refusal to step down following Mrs O'Shea's sensational divorce case produced a bitter split in the party. Meetings of the Irish Parliamentary Party were held in December 1890, and after a long and acrimonious discussion whether the man (Parnell) was more important than the cause (Home Rule), the party split in two. Parnell lost the leadership of the Parliamentary Party.

By the 1890s, though, Home Rule was raised from a faint hope to the forefront of national politics. The land question had not yet been solved but Parnell's involvement in it was a vital factor and he helped future reforms to get underway.

Concurrently, there was a revival of both Irish games and Irish cultural studies throughout Ireland. In the 1880s many, including Archbishop T. W. Croke, maintained that 'ball-playing, hurling, football kicking according to Irish rules … may now be said to be not only dead and buried, but in several localities to be entirely forgotten. What the country needed was an Irish organisation to bring order and unity to sport on a nation-wide basis.'[1] In August 1884 Michael Cusack outlined to a group of local athletic enthusiasts his plans to establish a national organisation for Irish athletes and to revive hurling. On 1 November 1884 the Gaelic Athletic Association (GAA) was founded.

Similarly, the Gaelic League, the purpose of which was not only the revival of the Irish language but also to assist Irish speakers where Irish was still spoken, was founded by Douglas Hyde, Father Eugene O'Growney and Eoin MacNeill on 31 July 1893. Quickly the Gaelic League had a major impact on the social life of Ireland. It was responsible for giving the Irish language a prominent position in the national school system and it revived Irish poetry, drama and literature, and after 1903 St Patrick's Day became a national holiday. The Irish people began to recognise, and take pride in, their Irish culture.

This cultural renaissance around the turn of the century, advanced by both the GAA and the Gaelic League, led to an increased desire for Home Rule. Irish separatists at this time primarily promoted a 'constitutional' solution to their aspirations, not the 'physical force' solution fostered by the IRB and the members of its secret society. The IRB however utilised the meetings of the Gaelic League and the GAA as prime opportunities for recruitment. It was not to be the last time the Brotherhood would exploit other organisations to further its separatist aims.

As the new leader of the Irish Parliamentary Party, John Redmond, who supported Parnell in the later stages of the fallen leader's political career, was appointed the leader of the Home Rule Party in 1900. Redmond realised that the Liberal victory in Britain of 1906 gave the Home Rule Party its chance. The Liberals had been supportive of Home Rule since the time of Gladstone and the 1911 Parliament Act effectively ended the power of the House of Lords to veto legislation passed by the House of Commons: now the Lords could only delay legislation passed by the Commons. After 1911 Redmond and his party expected Home Rule to be proposed, and in 1912 a third Home Rule Bill was introduced. Redmond fully expected it to be approved, and the Commons passed this Third Home Rule Bill in the early summer of 1914. (In August 1914, however, the onset of World War I suspended enactment of Home Rule 'for the duration'.)

All of these movements in Ireland reflected other European social, economic, and cultural revolutions of the nineteenth century. Nineteenth-century Europe was the crucible

---

1. O'Dubghail, M., *Insurrection Fires at Eastertide,* 1966 p. 17.

for many of the ideas and institutions that now shape life in Ireland, including the industrial revolution (particularly in Ulster at that time), capitalism, democracy, socialism, unions, bureaucracy, and nationalism. Yet life was not changing for the average worker in Dublin even though new ways of life for the working classes brought change to the rest of European cities. Dublin's large popular press began to expand political awareness, and new values and ideas such as nationalism and socialism began to emerge. The tinder that lit the fire was an economy that left many of the poor starving. The city was a miserable place in the early 1900s, with overcrowded and dilapidated housing, acute poverty and tens of thousands unemployed. In these circumstances the appearance of three men in Dublin at the time provided the catalyst for the changes that were to come.

James (Big Jim) Larkin arrived in Ireland in 1907 to begin work as an organiser for the English National Union of Dock Labourers. In 1908, that union suspended Larkin from his post as organiser because of his concentration on specifically Irish problems. Thereafter the new arrival founded his own union, the Irish Transport Workers' Union, and the first members were enrolled and union cards issued on 20 January 1909. Later the name was changed to the Irish Transport and General Workers' Union (ITGWU).

The words 'and General' were formally added in 1912 under the influence of James Connolly who had returned from the United States and begun his syndicalist teaching in 1910, especially his 'One Big Union' concept and the promotion of his socialist ideals.

In 1883 Thomas Clarke (born on the Isle of Wight, but inculcated with Irish separatism as a member of Clan na Gael in the United States) was arrested as a member of an Irish separatist bombing campaign in England. He spent the next fifteen tortuous years as a prisoner in various English jails. Upon his release he returned to the United States. There he married Kathleen Daly from Limerick, the niece of John Daly, one of his cellmates in Pentonville Prison.

Upon his return to Ireland in 1907, Clarke set out to bring the IRB's 'physical force' ideals to a new generation of Irish patriots. He must be given credit for reviving the IRB, establishing its newspaper *Irish Freedom* (a militant anti-English paper), and bringing new blood into the IRB leadership, especially mentoring his protégé, Sean MacDermott.

With these three highly influential men in place – Larkin, Connolly and Clarke – as well as other leaders, the stage was set for both economic and nationalistic upheavals to begin.

On 25 August 1913, trams all over Dublin stopped in their tracks. Larkin's action was not only to shut down the tram system but to mobilise all Dublin's workers as well, and thus began the Great Lockout of 1913. Under the leadership of Larkin and Connolly, the Dublin workers made their first concerted effort to raise their living standards and improve their lives.

When Larkin was subsequently exiled to the United States, Connolly became a central figure in the workers' opposition to the Employers Federation. Connolly assumed leadership of the ITGWU, and he formed the Irish Citizen Army (ICA) following the Lockout. The ICA was created to protect the workers from any groups that might be used by the employers, including the Dublin Metropolitan Police, whose assaults on workers had killed three and injured hundreds during the Lockout. Connolly vowed that the workers would protect themselves in the future. It was also at this time that he revived a newspaper called *The Worker's Republic*, one of his many labour and radical publications.

Also in 1913 two other armed militias were established in Ireland.

In a direct reaction to the possibility of Home Rule for Ireland, Edward Carson and

James Craig founded the Ulster Volunteer Force. The intention was that Protestant Unionists in the north would prevent the enactment of Home Rule. Soon, the need for arms led the UVF to procure 20,000 rifles and two million rounds of ammunition from Spiro in Hamburg, acquire a transport steamer and bring the weapons back to Ulster. The gun-running was planned secretly and was meticulously accomplished. On 24 April 1914 the port of Larne was taken over by the UVF while the steamer docked there and unloaded.

As so often happened during the period, the perception grew that with armed men in Ulster threatening force to counter Home Rule, a similar force would be prudent and necessary to pressure Britain in the other direction. To this end Eoin MacNeill published an article, *The North Began*, arguing for the necessity of such a force, and on 11 November 1913 prominent nationalists met in Dublin to plan the formation of the Irish Volunteers. Padraig Pearse summed up the feeling at the time: 'An Ulsterman with a gun is not as ridiculous as a Nationalist without one'.[2]

Though the importation of arms had been prohibited by the British government, the landing of arms at Larne prompted the Irish Volunteers to purchase and bring ashore their own arms shipment. The O'Rahilly directed Darrell Figgis and Erskine Childers to a firm in Hamburg where they purchased 1,500 rifles and 45,000 rounds of ammunition. Childers' yacht, *The Asgard*, landed 900 rifles and 26,000 rounds of ammunition in the small port of Howth, just north of Dublin on 26 July 1914, and the remainder were landed in Kilcoole. While the 'Howth Mausers' were obsolete, they were the basis of arms for the Irish Volunteers, and about 800 Volunteers mustered and marched out to Howth on the day of the landing. The British sent contingents of the Dublin Metropolitan Police and the army to prevent the landing, and upon the soldiers return to Dublin there was a confrontation with civilians at Bachelor's Walk. Three civilians were killed and more than thirty-five were seriously injured during firing by soldiers of the King's Own Scottish Borderers.

Within a fortnight, the Archduke Ferdinand had been assassinated in Sarajevo, World War I had erupted across the continent, Home Rule was shelved, and the time the IRB had been anticipating was at hand. Quickly thereafter, John Redmond, as leader of the Irish Parliamentary Party, made a political calculation that in time would backfire. He encouraged Irishmen to join the British Army in the belief that by showing Irish solidarity with Britain, England would not renege on its Home Rule commitments.

Theobold Wolfe Tone's declaration in 1798 that 'England's difficulty is Ireland's opportunity' became the bywords of the IRB. The movement's Supreme Council determined that with England engaged in World War I, a Rising should be planned and undertaken in Ireland.

P. S. O'Hegarty, a chronicler of the times, wrote: 'The Insurrection of 1916 came because the Supreme Council of the Irish Republican Brotherhood decided that it would come ... It was the Supreme Council of the IRB which decided the Insurrection, planned it, organised it, led it and financed it.'[3] Thomas Clarke, Padraig Pearse, Joseph Plunkett along with Eamonn Ceannt, Thomas MacDonagh, Sean MacDermott and, later James Connolly, all of whom were IRB members, comprised the Military Council of the Irish Volunteers. Without informing the Commandant of the Volunteers, Eoin MacNeill, they planned the Easter Rising to take advantage of 'England's difficulty'.

---

2. Edwards, Ruth Dudley, *Patrick Pearse: The Triumph of Failure*, 1977, p. 179, from an article by Patrick Pearse in *An Cladheamh Soluis*, November 1913.
3. O'Hegarty, P. S., *The Victory of Sinn Féin*, 1924, 1998, p. 2.

The Rising had been scheduled for Easter Sunday, but when MacNeill found he had been deceived about a Rising he cancelled the manoeuvers scheduled for that day. Though they knew their plans had been severely compromised by the loss of another ship loaded with weapons and the inevitable confusion which MacNeill's cancellation caused, the Rising leaders decided that to delay further would be fatal for their plans. The Rising was re-scheduled for Monday at noon.

On Easter Monday, 24 April 1916, approximately 800 Volunteers and 200 ICA members stormed buildings in central Dublin and declared an independent Irish Republic. Under the command of Pearse and Connolly, the Volunteers and ICA members were combined into what Connolly termed the Irish Republican Army (IRA). Joseph Plunkett was the primary planner, and the objective was that the Volunteers and ICA would seize strategic buildings throughout Dublin in order to cordon off the city and resist the coming attacks by units of the British Army.

After capturing the General Post Office (GPO) on Sackville Street, Pearse read the Proclamation of the Provisional Government of the Irish Republic on the steps of that landmark building. However, the few people assembled were more wary and confused than enthusiastic. The insurgents then barricaded their posts and awaited the inevitable British assaults. The British put their efforts into securing the approaches to their administrative headquarters at Dublin Castle and isolating the rebel headquarters at the GPO. Artillery was brought into Dublin from the British military establishment at Athlone and, along with a small gunboat, the *Helga*, the British shelled large parts of the city and destroyed by fire much of the center of Dublin.

The crown forces greatly outnumbered the rebels, marshalling almost 20,000 troops by week's end in opposition to about 1,800 rebels. The British plan was to outflank and isolate the rebel defences, and soon the shelling and fires left the rebels in untenable positions in virtually all the buildings they held. On Saturday, 29 April, 'In order to prevent the further slaughter of Dublin citizens, and in the hope of saving the lives of our followers, now surrounded and hopelessly outnumbered', Pearse gave the order to surrender, and shortly afterwards all the rebel positions were turned over to the British.

There was very little public support for the rebels during the Rising. Many civilians had been killed or lost their property in the fires. When the rebels were marched off to boats to take them to prisons in Britain, many were pelted with vegetables, bottles and even the contents of chamber pots! Nothing these men and women had done during the week led the public to take their side. Soon, however, that opinion would change and the public would increasingly support the position and objectives of their fellow countrymen.

Britain, still engaged in World War I, determined that the Rising was an act of 'treason,' and that the participants and leaders should suffer the fate of traitors in wartime. Further to that the rebels had enlisted German support, a move which prompted outright vilification. General Sir John Maxwell, the British commanding officer, ordained that all seven signatories of the Proclamation should be executed in Kilmainham Gaol. Those and several other prominent commanders of rebel positions were executed – a total of fourteen men in all. James Connolly, so badly wounded that he lay in a hospital bed in Dublin Castle from the time of his surrender, was taken from the hospital, tied to a chair and shot. The executions created a wave of protest and outrage in Ireland.

Over 3,000 men and women were imprisoned following the Rising, most in jails in England. Some were never charged, and there were certainly some who had not participated in the Rising.

By the end of 1916 the British authorities determined to release most of the rebels, and these were home in Ireland by Christmas. They returned to a tumultuous welcome, a complete turnaround from the send-off they had been given by the populace eight months earlier on the way to prison. The tide of public opinion had clearly changed, and there was yet to come another imperious decision that would harden attitudes against the British. Though about 210,000 men from Ireland served in the British army during World War I, of whom some 35,000 died, not one was conscripted. Most entered the army for financial reasons, because they were poverty stricken and employment opportunities were so few in Ireland. Others followed the recruiting promises of the British and believed that enlisting 'to fight for small nations' would lead to Home Rule.

However, in 1918 Westminster passed a compulsory conscription Act, a move that greatly solidified Irish public opinion against Britain. Though no Irishmen were in fact conscripted during the War, the threat of conscription was such that an Irish Conference was convened as a protest against its possibility and it issued the following pronouncement: 'The attempt to enforce conscription will be unwarrantable aggression which we call upon all true Irishmen to resist by the most effective means at their disposal'.[4] The Catholic hierarchy concurred at their annual meeting at Maynooth. In this fashion the plan to introduce conscription in Ireland led to widespread support for independence. It fueled support for the republican separatist movement and Sinn Féin, the political party that comprehensively defeated the Redmondite nationalists in the December 1918 general election, which led in turn to the formation of the first Dáil Éireann (Irish Parliament), which convened on 21 January 1919.

---

4. Kee, Robert, *The Green Flag* (combining three separate volumes entitled *The Most Distressful Country, The Bold Fenian Men* and *Ourselves Alone*), 1972, p. 619.

One of the members of that Dáil (a member was known as a Teachta Dála or TD) was Michael Collins. Born in Co Cork in 1890, he went to London at the age of fifteen to work in the British Post Office. In November 1909 he became a member of the IRB, and in 1914 enrolled in the Irish Volunteers. He returned to Ireland for the 1916 Rising, but did not make his mark on events until after his release from prison at the end of 1916. He then set about re-organising the Volunteer movement. During the War of Independence, as the Volunteer Director of Intelligence, he became the mastermind of an Irish intelligence network that successfully countered British intelligence in Ireland. Though he often walked and cycled throughout Dublin, he was never taken despite a British government offer of £10,000 for his capture.

The intelligence system established by Collins was a crucial asset in the Irish War of Independence between 1917 and 1921. But he was also a brilliant Minister of Finance. It was Collins who devised and oversaw the Dáil Loan that raised millions for the cause of Irish independence. The final Loan total, subscribed by over 135,000 Irish people, was £378,858 in Ireland alone. A sum of $5,123,640 was raised separately in the United States. The natural intelligence, organisational capability and sheer drive of Collins galvanised those who came in contact with him.

The War of Independence was a guerilla campaign mounted against the British government in Ireland by the Irish Republican Army from January 1919 until the truce in July 1921, under the proclaimed legitimacy of the First Dáil. Military operations remained limited during 1919, although raids for arms became a regular occurrence. The violence was at first deeply unpopular with the broader Irish population, but attitudes changed gradually in the face of the terror of the British government's campaign of widespread brutality, destruction of property, random arrests, reprisals, and unprovoked shootings. The small groups of IRA men on the run were extremely vulnerable. Their success could make or break the activity of the IRA in a particular district – losing them often meant the end of operations. In September 1919 the Dáil was banned by the British, which served to make it easier for members of the IRA to carry out attacks, because their politicians no longer had a public platform from which to restrain them.

Meanwhile, Eamon de Valera had been elected President of the Dáil while in prison in Lincoln in England. After his dramatic escape from prison he left for the United States to highlight British injustices in Ireland and drum up support for an Irish Republic. He was most successful in raising funds for the Dáil loan, but was unsuccessful in his attempts to get either of the US political parties to officially recognise the Irish Republic in their 1920 election programmes.

For the remainder of 1919 and into 1920 the level of violence throughout Ireland increased. The British had to exert effective control over much of the countryside or lose the war. The IRA benefited from the widespread support given to it by the general Irish population, which regularly refused to pass information to the British. Much of the IRA's popularity was due to the excessive reaction of British forces to insurgent activity. An unofficial government policy of reprisals began in September 1919 in Fermoy, Co Cork, when 200 British soldiers looted and burned the main businesses of the town after a soldier was killed when he refused to surrender his weapon to the local IRA. Actions such as these increased local support for the IRA and international support for Irish independence.

The arrival of the Black and Tans (the Tans) in March 1920 changed the entire complexion of the war. These 'irregulars' were established as a section of the Royal Irish

Constabulary (RIC) and first appeared in the village of Upper Church, Co Tipperary. The British government needed more troops in Ireland to maintain its position, and turned to demobilised soldiers from World War I who were unemployed. The name came from their uniforms which were khaki tunics and dark green or black trousers, some with civilian hats, but most with green caps and black leather belts of the RIC. The name was given to them by Christopher O'Sullivan, editor of the *Limerick Echo*, who wrote that they reminded him of a pack of hunting dogs in Limerick: 'Judging by their attire, they resembled something one would associate with the Scarteen Hunt'.[5] The Scarteen Black and Tans were well known for their savagery, as were the soldiers.

The second British force to augment the regular army forces were the 'Auxiliaries' (the Auxies), who arrived in September 1920. Auxiliary to the RIC, they were originally called the Temporary Cadets – they were ranked as 'cadets' but were 'graded as RIC sergeants for the purpose of discipline'. By the end of the War of Independence in 1921 there would be over 10,000 Black and Tans and 1,500 Auxiliaries in the country.

Neither the Tans nor the Auxies exhibited much in the way of military discipline and the levels of violence and reprisals mounted daily. Their arrival and the brutality of their tactics drove many to support the IRA. The Irish, ruled by the British for so long, now began to think of their resistance as patriotism. The Dublin execution of an eighteen-year-old medical student, Kevin Barry, for killing a British soldier, the shooting of the Lord Mayor of Cork, Thomas MacCurtain, in front of his wife and children, and the arrest and death on hunger strike of the succeeding Lord Mayor of Cork, Terence MacSwiney, were events that made the British position in Ireland ever more untenable.

In response to the growing violence, the British government introduced the Restoration of Order in Ireland Act. This Act, passed in August 1920, allowed for the internment and court-martial of civilians and led to the arrest of a large number of IRA officers. The level of public support for the IRA, however, continued to rise. By the end of 1920, 182 policemen and 50 soldiers had been shot by the IRA. The British government initially asserted that it was dealing with civil disorder rather than with war, but by this stage it realised otherwise. The struggle was embittered by successive acts of violence and terror, and the reprisals and counter-reprisals which followed.

In an effort to placate those in the North who were still opposed to any movement in the direction of Home Rule in Ireland, on 11 November 1920 the Government of Ireland Bill was passed in the British House of Commons, proposing separate home rule parliaments for Southern Ireland and for Northern Ireland. A Council of Ireland was to be set up with members from each parliament in a move to one day remove partition and potentially reunite the two entities. Both parliaments would be subject to Westminster. This action again backfired on the British government because it infuriated the IRA, but it did establish the partition that exists to this day.

Later that month, the single most damaging event in relation to the British intelligence organisation in Ireland occurred. On Sunday morning, 21 November 1920, the special squad controlled by Collins executed fourteen British intelligence agents, known as the 'Cairo Gang,' who had been poised to eliminate him and other important leaders. In response, Auxiliaries drove in armoured cars into Croke Park during a football match,

---

5. *Limerick Echo*

shooting into the crowd at random. Thirteen unarmed people were killed and sixty-five wounded. Later that day three republican prisoners were 'shot while trying to escape' in Dublin Castle. This day became known as Bloody Sunday.

Dave Neligan, a Collins spy in Dublin Castle, reported that the killing of the intelligence personnel 'caused complete panic in the Castle'. Later Michael Collins, when asked how he felt about the episode, stated: 'For myself, my conscience is clear. There is no crime in detecting and destroying, in wartime, the spy and the informer. They have destroyed without trial. I have paid them back in their own coin.'[6]

By 1921 the IRA had become a force in Dublin and its 'flying columns' had become feared throughout the counties of Cork, Kerry and Clare. The flying columns were mobile units of from ten to one hundred men that could strike in devastating ambushes and then melt into a hinterland that they knew far better than the British soldiers who were deployed to fight them. Most IRA units however were chronically short of both weapons and ammunition. By the end of the spring of 1921, though a formidable opponent, the IRA had not been able to dislodge the British forces, and it became clear that it could not defeat those forces in the field.

De Valera returned to Ireland in December 1920, and the continued British references to the IRA as 'murderers' led him to press for a full scale engagement with the British as opposed to the guerrilla tactics used by the IRA. In Dublin on 25 May 1921 the IRA burned down the Custom House, a center of British administrative rule in Ireland. As a military operation it was a disaster for the IRA, with over eighty of its best men captured, and five killed. As a propaganda feat it was a huge success, demonstrating to the wider world how strong the IRA was and how weak the British position now was in Ireland. That 'strength' however, was illusory and most IRA leaders, and especially Collins, recognised that the organisation's desperate shortage of weapons and ammunition would soon allow the British to wear it down.

As British hopes faded, they began to wonder whether Ireland was worth the price. Ireland now cost more to defend and control than it was worth. Progressively throughout the first half of 1921 'peace' feelers were extended, and in July 1921 a truce was agreed. On 9 July terms were agreed upon and the truce went into effect at noon on 11 July 1921.

Following the truce, de Valera and British Prime Minister Lloyd George engaged in a correspondence to determine how negotiations should proceed. On 30 September de Valera was able to write: 'Our respective positions have been stated and are understood and we agree that conference, not correspondence, is the most practical and hopeful way to an understanding. We accept the invitation, and our Delegates will meet you in London on the date mentioned "to explore every possibility of settlement by personal discussion".' The 'date mentioned' was 11 October, and on that date treaty negotiations began in London. The Irish were represented by Arthur Griffith, Michael Collins, George Gavan Duffy, Robert Barton and Eamonn Duggan, as plenipotentiaries.

On 6 December 1921 a treaty was signed by the plenipotentiaries and returned to Ireland for ratification. De Valera was much opposed to the treaty, though it has been said that he was greatly affronted he had not been consulted on the final day before signature. At an acrimonious Cabinet meeting, the Treaty was approved by a four-to-three vote majority. It was then presented to the Dáil for ratification.

---

6.  Gleeson, James, *Bloody Sunday*, 1962, p. 191.

The 'Treaty Debates' in the Dáil took place between 14 December 1921 and 7 January 1922, when the Dáil voted 64–57 in favour of the treaty. The Treaty Debates were the most vituperative in Irish history. Invective was hurled at and by both sides, personality conflicts that had simmered for many years degenerated into name calling and insults, and the vote was considered a 'betrayal of the ideals of 1916' by those who felt the only acceptable treaty would be one recognising an Irish Republic. In addition, the treaty called for an oath of allegiance to the English crown, and that was considered traitorous by Republicans. Finally, the treaty called for partition of the North, and although partition was an established fact after 1920, the conflict in the South only served to further undermine any possibility of reunification.

Following the Dáil vote, the treaty was sent to the people for ratification and an election was scheduled for 16 June 1922, when it was approved by the people and the Irish Free State was established. The election did not represent a vote of confidence in the provisional government, and still less an expression of resistance to republican ideals. It represented a popular realisation of the need for stable government, and the acceptance of a realistic compromise with regard to Anglo-Irish relations. The desire for settled conditions was more important to the electorate than the endless debate over constitutional authority. The election had an important role in legitimising the treaty and the status of the provisional government. Although it did not prevent the Civil War which was shortly to follow, it greatly helped to facilitate the establishment of the Free State government during and after the War.

The most 'Republican' members of the IRA, the Dáil and the public still refused to accept the treaty or the establishment of the Free State, and initiated an insurrection against the new Free State government, which they accused of betraying the Irish Republic. On 13 April 1922, Dublin's Four Courts were occupied by Republicans/IRA troops led by Rory O'Connor. Upon taking it over, they issued the following proclamation:

> *Fellow citizens of the Irish Republic. The fateful hour has come. At the direction of the hereditary enemy our rightful cause is being treacherously assailed by recreant Irishmen. Gallant soldiers of the Irish Republic stand rigorously firm in its defence. The sacred spirits of the Illustrious Dead are with us in this great struggle. 'Death Before Dishonour'. We especially appeal to our former comrades of the Irish Republic to return to that allegiance and thus guard the Nation's honour.*

At 3.40 am on 28 June 1922, the insurgents were given an ultimatum to surrender by troops of the Free State under the command of Michael Collins, and when firing commenced twenty minutes later the Irish Civil War had begun.

The Civil War lasted until mid-1923 and cost an estimated 3,000 lives, including some of the leaders of the independence movement, notably Free State President Arthur Griffith, Michael Collins, as well as anti-Treaty republicans Cathal Brugha, Harry Boland, Liam Mellows, Liam Lynch, Joe McKelvey, Dick Barnett, Erskine Childers and Rory O'Connor.

The Civil War was the lowest point in recent Irish history. Perhaps Desmond Williams encapsulated the national tragedy best: 'When friends fall out, the daggers stay sharp. Families devour each other; the nearer in blood the bloodier. The causes of civil, as of other types of war, lie to some extent in the immediate past, and responsibilities for action, or lack thereof, are seldom clear cut. The participants rarely acknowledge this. But it cannot be repeated too often that no one person or party is ever wholly to blame for anything. Here again the Irish Civil War was no exception.' [7]

---

7. Williams, Desmond, *The Irish Struggle, 1916–1926*, 1966, p. 118.

# Baile Átha Cliath – Town of the Hurdle Ford: Directory of Historic Locations, 1913–1923

**Abbey Street Lower**: forty-five buildings were burned or damaged during the Rising, including Mooney's Pub, Daily Express, Union Chapel, Methodist Chapel, Peacock Theatre

**1 Abbey Street Lower**: Young and Co Ltd, wine and spirit merchants

**2 Abbey Street Lower**: J. J. Kelly and Co, cycle agents

**3 Abbey Street Lower**: Keating's cycle shop; the bicycles were used for barricades during the Rising

**4 Abbey Street Lower**: reserve printing offices of *The Irish Times*, a very Unionist paper. During the Rising George Plunkett led the Volunteers who took newsprint rolls for barricades, which greatly contributed to fires started on Thursday afternoon.

**5 Abbey Street Lower**: Ship Hotel and Tavern. Occupied by Frank Thornton's and George Plunkett's men during the Rising. It was a hangout of Oliver St John Gogarty when a medical student at Trinity.

**26 Abbey Street Lower** (at Marlborough St): Abbey Theatre. On the site of the former Mechanics' Institute Building, and there was a Mechanics' Institute Theatre. The name was changed in 1904, and the first performance as the Abbey was on 27 December 1904.
*15 October 1908:* Thomas MacDonagh's play *When The Dawn Is Come* opened. This was his only full-length play.
*25 October 1914:* First Convention of the Irish Volunteers. This was the first 'Convention' of the Volunteers after Redmond's Woodenbridge, Co Wicklow, speech (20 September 1914) pledging the 'Irish Volunteers' to fight for the English. This was the 'reconstitution' meeting. In his Woodenbridge speech, Redmond declared:

> *The duty of the manhood of Ireland is twofold. Its duty is at all costs to defend the shores of Ireland against foreign invasion; it is the duty more than that of taking care that Irish valour proves itself on the field of war [as] it has always proved itself in the past. The interests of Ireland, of the whole of Ireland, are at stake in this war. This war is undertaken in the defence of the highest principles of religion and morality and right, and it would be a disgrace forever to our country, and a reproach to her manhood, and a denial of the lessons of our history, if young Ireland confined her efforts to remaining at home to defend the shores of Ireland from an unlikely invasion and to shrink from the duty of approval on the field of battle, that gallantry and courage which has distinguished our race through its history.[8]*

Redmond's encouragement to support Britain's war effort was vigorously opposed by the founding members of the Volunteers. Immediately after this speech, Redmond's supporters split into the 'Irish National Volunteers' whereas a minority continued

---

8.   *Freeman's Journal*, 21 September, 1914

*After the insurrection – Sackville Street from Eden Quay to Abbey Street.*

under the leadership of Eoin MacNeill, reverted to their former name, 'Irish Volunteers', and called for Irish neutrality in the War. The 'National Volunteers' numbered about 175,000 at the time, while the 'Irish Volunteers' were reduced to about 13,500 men and women. The split proved most advantageous to the IRB, whose leaders were firmly in control of the Irish Volunteers.

A new alliance with the ICA, resulting from the split with Redmond, was frustrated by the refusal of the Volunteers to include two ICA members on the Provisional Committee or to affiliate with the ICA as a whole. The Provisional Committee consisted of: Eoin MacNeill (Chairman), The O'Rahilly (Joint Treasurer), Padraig Pearse (Press Secretary), Sean MacDermott, M. J. Judge, Thomas MacDonagh, Bulmer Hobson (General Secretary), Piaras Béaslaí, Sean O'Connor (Musketry Training Officer), Eamonn Martin, Padraig Ryan (Publications Secretary), Con Colbert, Joseph Plunkett (Joint Treasurer), P. Macken, Sean Fitzgibbon, Eamonn Ceannt (Financial Secretary), C. O'Laughlin, P. White, Liam Mellowes.

J. J. O'Connor and Eimer O'Duffy were appointed 'Volunteer Military Strategists'.

*31 October 1915:* Second Convention of the Irish Volunteers. This established a Declaration of Policy:

*To resist any attempt to force the men of Ireland into military service under any Government until a free National Government is empowered by the Irish people themselves to deal with it.*

Author St John Ervine was the manager of the Abbey in 1916. He was an anti-Nationalist and a 'revolt' by the theatre's actors on 29 April 1916 led to their dismissal. The play scheduled for the night of 24 April 1916 was *Cáitlín Ní hUallacháin*.

Though very close to the fires of the Rising, the theatre suffered no damage – not even a window was broken.

**32, 33 Abbey Street Lower**: Office of *The Leader*. D.P. Moran, editor, was founder of the 'Buy Irish' campaign –'Irish Ireland'.

**32 Abbey Street Lower**: a general strike was called here for 13 April 1920 by Thomas Farren, Chairman, and Thomas Johnson, Acting Secretary, of the National Executive of Trade Unions.

*To the Workers of Ireland. You are called upon to act swiftly to save a hundred dauntless men. These men, our comrades, have been forcibly taken from their homes, imprisoned without charge or trial for alleged offences of a political character in outrageous defiance of every canon of justice. They are suspected of loving Ireland and hating her oppressors – a heinous crime in the sight of tyrants but one which hundreds of thousands of Irish working men and women proudly acclaim as their birthright.*

In combination with the hunger strike which started about ten days earlier, this general strike resulted in the release of the prisoners at Mountjoy Prison.

**32 Abbey Street Lower**: meeting rooms of the Celtic Literary Society. Used by Maud Gonne MacBride for the founding meeting of *Inghinidhe na hÉireann* (Daughters of Ireland) in 1900.

**33, 34 Abbey Street Lower**: Royal Hibernian Academy. Burned during the Rising, and many great works of art were lost.

**35–37 Abbey Street Lower**: Wynn's Hotel (often written 'Wynne's,' but photos clearly show the name without an 'e'). The Irish Volunteers first met here as a group on 11 November 1913. The following attended according to *both* The O'Rahilly and Bulmer Hobson: Piaras Béaslaí*, Joseph Campbell, Eamonn Ceannt*, James Deakin, Sean Fitzgibbon*, Bulmer Hobson, Eoin MacNeill*, Sean McDermott*, The O'Rahilly*, Padraig Pearse*, W. J. Ryan (*became members of the Provisional Committee).
The O'Rahilly noted that D. P. Moran was invited but did not attend, but Hobson did not recall this. Hobson noted that Seamus O'Connor, Colm O'Laughlin and Robert Page *could* have attended. Others noted that Michael Judge, Eamonn Martin, and Colonel Maurice Moore attended.
Cumann na mBan (The League of Women) first met here in April 1914: Agnes O'Farrelly (Chairwoman), Áine Ceannt, Winifred Carney, Louise Gavan Duffy, Mrs Laurence Kettle, Agnes MacNeill, Nancie O'Rahilly, Mrs Wyse-Power.

**Abbey Street Middle**: In the early twentieth century, William Rooney taught Irish in his school in this street. The Celtic Literary Society met in the same premises and was frequented by Arthur Griffith, Sean T. O'Kelly and John MacBride.

**42 Abbey Street Middle**: The Gael Co-op Society Ltd, publishers

**49 Abbey Street Middle**: Sinn Féin Company, publishers of *Sinn Féin*. Devereaux, Neuth & Co, printers; printed *Sinn Féin*, replaced by *Scissors and Paste* in late 1914 after *Sinn Féin* was suppressed. Irish Industrial Printing & Publishing, printed *Fianna*.

**50 Abbey Street Middle**: Irish Photo Engraving Co

**53 Abbey Street Middle**: *The Irish Catholic* newspaper, owned by William Martin Murphy. This newspaper was also violently opposed to the ICA and the Volunteers as was Murphy's *Irish Independent*. In early May 1916, it wrote of the Rising and the leaders:

*Pearse was a man of ill-balanced mind, if not actually insane, and the idea of selecting him as chief magistrate of the Irish Republic is quite enough to create serious doubts as to the sanity of*

*those who approved of it …. Only the other day when the so-called Republic of Ireland was proclaimed … no better President could be proposed … than a crazy and insolent schoolmaster. This extraordinary combination of rogues and fools … to find anything like a parallel for what has occurred it is necessary to have recourse to the bloodstained annals of the Paris Commune.*

On 20 May it opined: 'What was attempted was an act of brigandage pure and simple, and there is no reason to lament that its perpetrators have met the fate which from the very dawn of history has been universally reserved for traitors …. We need say no more, but to say less would be traitorous to the highest and holiest interests of Ireland.'

**64 Abbey Street Middle**: Harry Boland's tailor shop

**67 Abbey Street Middle**: *Scissors and Paste*; Arthur Griffith, editor; suppressed in March 1915; attempted to get around Dublin Castle censorship by printing only items that had already appeared in mainstream publications.

**68 Abbey Street Middle**: Hayden and Company, tax experts

**72 Abbey Street Middle**: Catholic Boys' Home

**74, 75 Abbey Street Middle**: Gaynor & Son

**76 Abbey Street Middle**: YMCA for Sailors and Soldiers

**79, 80 Abbey Street Middle**: Eason and Son Ltd, wholesale newsagents

**83 Abbey Street Middle**: *Evening Telegraph* office

**84 Abbey Street Middle**: *The Freeman's Journal* (main entrance), owned by William Freeman, it was the only newspaper that seemed to accept that the responsibility for the riots associated with the Lockout of 1913 could not be laid primarily on the shoulders of Dublin's hooligan element or its socialists.

*The Freeman's Journal* was the voice of John Redmond's Nationalist Party. It had opposed Irish independence more bitterly than any other newspaper. Its circulation dropped greatly and it became a weekly after Redmond's recruiting speech to Parliament.

The proprietor in 1920 was Martin Fitzgerald. He was arrested and imprisoned and the paper fined £3,000 because of a report on ill-treatment of a prisoner by the Black and Tans. The building also housed the office of *Sport*.

*30 March 1922*, the IRA wrecked the office in retaliation for publishing the names of the Executive chosen on 26 March.

**85–89 Abbey Street Middle**: Alex Thom and Company

**91–93 Abbey Street Middle**: Fitzgerald and Son; tea, wine and spirits merchants

**96 Abbey Street Middle**: Maunsel & Co Ltd, publishers; burned during the Rising

**98, 99 Abbey Street Middle**: William Curtis and Sons

**102, 103, 104 Abbey Street Middle**: National Reserve Headquarters

**105, 106 Abbey Street Middle**: Perfect Dairy Co

**111 Abbey Street Middle**: Situated in this street and at 3-4 Liffey Street stood Independent House, the offices of the *Irish Independent*, owned by William Martin Murphy. A major newspaper, very pro-English, that tried to break up the ITGWU strike of 1913 and the Union itself.

Connolly suffered a serious leg/ankle wound emerging from the back entrance of this building while returning to the GPO late on Thursday afternoon (he had been wounded in the arm earlier that afternoon). He crawled down Prince's Street and was carried into the GPO.

The *Irish Independent* called for the execution of the leaders of the Rising and was especially harsh on Connolly. The following appeared in its editorials:

*4 May:* 'No terms of denunciation that pen would indict would be too strong to apply to those responsible for the criminal and insane rising of last week.'

*10 May:* it published a photo of Connolly with the caption: 'Still lies in Dublin Castle slowly recovering from his wounds'.

*10 May:* 'If these men are treated with too great leniency they will take it as an indication of weakness on the part of the government and the consequences may not be satisfactory. They may be more truculent than ever, and it is therefore necessary that society should be protected against their activity. Let the worst of the ringleaders be singled out and dealt with as they deserve.'

*12 May:* after Connolly was executed, but before it was known: 'Certain of the leaders remain undealt with, and the part they played was worse than that of some of those who have paid the extreme penalty ... We think in a word that no special leniency should be extended to some of the worst of the leaders whose cases have not yet been disposed of.'

**111 Abbey Street Middle**: The Sunday Independent. The editor was Paddy J. Little. It was in this paper that MacNeil placed his notice 'cancelling' the Rising on Easter Saturday night. MacNeil gave the notice to Cogley, the night editor, at midnight:

*Owing to the very critical position, all orders given to the Irish Volunteers for tomorrow, Easter Sunday, are hereby rescinded, and no parades, marches or other movements of the Irish Volunteers will take place. Each individual Volunteer will obey this order strictly in every particular.*

The editor during the time of the War of Independence was Tim Harrington and the sports sub-editor at the same time was George Gormby. The building also housed offices for the *Evening Herald*. The *Irish Independent's* offices became overcrowded so some of the staff moved to Carlisle House on Westmoreland Street.

**10 Abbey Street Upper**: George Moreland, cabinet makers. Bill Stapleton chose the name 'George Moreland' because he said it sounded 'Protestant and Jewish'. Meeting place for 'The Squad' after they moved from the Antient Concert Rooms. Some of the Squad were craftsmen and could answer callers' queries, but they always told callers that business was so good it would be many months before they could deal with their orders, whereupon 'customers' would take their business to other shops.

**41 Abbey Street Upper and Liffey Street**: Bannon's Pub, where Michael Collins first met Dave Neligan.

**36 Ailesbury Road**: Mrs Mary Ellen Humphrey's home; sister of The O'Rahilly. The Cabinet and Army Council sometimes met here during the War of Independence. Ernie O'Malley stayed here and used it as an office from September to November 1922. O'Malley was captured here on 4 November 1922. At the outset of the raid he went to a hidden room built by Batt O'Connor during the War of Independence. But the Free State troops knew of it, and went right to it. O'Malley fled and was shot several times, but lived and was imprisoned in Mountjoy; sixteen bullets were removed from his body in hospital. Mrs Humphrey's children, Richard (Risteard MacAmblaoibh) and Sheila, were arrested and imprisoned after O'Malley's capture.

**37 Ailesbury Road**: home of Dennis Gwynne, editor of *New Ireland*

**16 Airfield Road, Rathgar**: Julia Donovan's home; grandmother of Fionnuala Donovan. This was one of Michael Collins's two main safe houses in Dublin. On the night of

Bloody Sunday, Collins had dinner here. The famous wedding party photo, with Collins 'hiding' his face, was taken here after the wedding of Elizabeth Clancy and Michael J. O'Brien on 22 November 1920.

**13 Alphonsus Road, Drumcondra**: Áine Ceannt stayed here while Eamonn was in Richmond Barracks.

**Amiens Street**: Amiens Street Railway Station. The terminus for the Drogheda and Dublin Railway, also known as the Great Northern Railway, built between 1844 and 1846. It was renamed Connolly Station in 1966.

**26-30 Amiens Street**: North Star Hotel. M. P. Colivet, Commandant of the Limerick Brigade, met Padraig Pearse here on Spy Wednesday. The meeting took place in the restaurant and they 'disguised' their conversation by pretending to be a buyer (Pearse) and seller (Colivet) of farmers' goods. Colivet asked about the Rising and Pearse confirmed it was on for Sunday. This was to cause problems when the news got back to MacNeill.

**41 Amiens Street**: J. M. Butler, newsagent. He was prosecuted and fined £20 in June 1916 for publishing a statement purporting to be that of Thomas MacDonagh in the dock. Four hundred and seventy copies of the publication were seized.

**55 Amiens Street**: Tom Clarke's first shop; in 1910 the family moved to 77 Amiens Street. This was also the home of Sean Doyle, killed in the Custom House fire.

**77 Amiens Street**: Tom Clarke's second shop: the family lived in a flat above the shop until they moved to Richmond Street.

**77a Amiens Street**: Houlihan's basketmakers shop. The Volunteer Military Council often met here prior to the Rising.

**100-105 Amiens Street:** Parcels Office of General Post Office; Con Collins was a clerk here.

**26-27 Andrew Street and Church Lane**: Jammet's Restaurant was located here for some time (see Nassau Street).

**5 Anglesea Road, Ballsbridge**: last and best known home of the writer Brendan Behan, nephew of Peadar Kearney, author of the Irish national anthem *A Soldier's Song*. As a youth in 1940 Behan was arrested in Liverpool and sentenced to two years in Borstal for carrying explosives for the IRA. On his return to Dublin in 1942 he was involved in a shooting outside Glasnevin Cemetary and sentenced to fourteen years, of which he served four years. Author of the autobiographical *Borstal Boy* and the plays *The Quare Fellow* and *The Hostage*.

**38 Anglesea Road, Ballsbridge**: Sean T. O'Kelly lived here with his family during the period before he was elected President in 1945.

**Arbour Hill**: Arbour Hill Detention Centre; built in 1835 and redesigned in 1845, it was the smallest of Dublin's Victorian prisons. Its chapel has stained-glass windows by Harry Clarke Studios. The bodies of the executed 1916 leaders are buried here in a pit of quicklime: some British soldiers reported that they were buried in the order in which they were executed. C. S. Andrews was a prisoner here, as was Ned Broy (during the War of Independence) and Maire Comerford (during the Civil War). Maire was shot in the leg while escaping from here. She was recaptured and imprisoned in Kilmainham Gaol where she went on hunger strike.

**8, 10, 11-12 and 22 Ardee Street**: Watkins' Brewery; Con Colbert's headquarters, from which the garrison moved to the South Dublin Union during Easter week.

**Ashtown, Co Dublin**: ambush of Viceroy Lord French on 19 December 1919; the Volunteers were Dan Breen, Vinnie Byrne, Paddy Daly (O/C), Sean Hogan, Tom Kehoe,

Tom Kilcoyne, Joe Leonard, Mick McDonnell, Seamus Robinson, Sean Treacy and Martin Savage. This was the latest of several attempts on French. Dan Breen calculated that in all twelve attempts were made. Tomas MacCurtain was involved in one attempt and told Treacy and Robinson that the only good thing about it was he (MacCurtain) had been able to retain a revolver which he hadn't had before. The Volunteers were to hang about near 'Kelly's Inn' (the Halfway House), and to let the first car go by, because their information was that French would be in the second car. In fact, French was in the first car and escaped. The plan went awry, the road was not barricaded, Breen was wounded and Savage was killed.

**14-18 Aston Quay**: McBirney's General Retailers; had a reputation for the best linens. British snipers fired from this location directly across the Liffey on Hopkins and Hopkins, jewellers, on Eden Quay.

**Auburn Street**: home of James Larkin in 1913

**Aungier Street**: *An tÓglach* (The Youth/Volunteer/Soldier), conceived by Michael Collins in 1918 and edited by Piaras Béaslaí, was published from here. The first issue appeared on 15 August 1918. It was a 'secret' internal journal printed in Dublin and distributed to the Volunteers through the IRA. It was not only a 'military journal' but contained much of the Sinn Féin ideology, and had a great influence on the Volunteers and, later, the IRA. Instead of preaching the politics of a party or of any particular leader, it always emphasised that the Volunteer's allegiance was to the Irish nation. The first leading article stated:

*Volunteers are not politicians; they were not created for the purposes of parades, demonstrations, or political activities; they follow no particular leader as such; their allegiance is to the Irish Nation. To their own chosen leaders they render the obedience that all soldiers render to their officers. Their obedience to their officers is not affected by personal considerations. It is the office, not the man, to whom deference is due.*

*The Irish Volunteers have chosen in open Convention those leaders in whom they have confidence to control the public policy of the organisation. It is the duty of those leaders to conform that policy to the national will, by co-operating on the military side with those bodies and institutions which in other departments of the national life are striving to make our Irish Republic a tangible reality.*

**77 Aungier Street**: a union office for the workers of Jacob's Biscuit Factory, locked out in the Lockout of 1913.


**Bachelor's Walk**: On 26 July 1914 at 6.30 pm, following retrieval of the Howth Rifles, three civilians were killed and more than thirty-five were seriously injured when fired on by the King's Own Scottish Borderers ('King's Own Scottish Murderers'). About one hundred of the Borderers under the command of Cpt Cobden had marched back from Howth to the Malahide Road where there was a confrontation with the Volunteers. Negotiations took place between the Volunteers and William Vesey Harrel, the Assistant Commissioner of the DMP, who had originally called in the military. The troops continued towards the city and were met along the way by a further sixty men under the command of Major Coke. They were harassed by civilians along the route and when they turned from Sackville Street onto Bachelor's Walk the command was turned over to a Major Haig.

*Corner of Bachelor's Walk and Lr. Sackville Street.*

A British inquiry found that Harrell decided to illegally seize the arms from the Volunteers, and everything that happened afterwards was illegal. Those killed were James Brennan (18), Mrs Mary Duffy (50, she was the mother of a soldier serving in the British army), and Patrick Quinn (46). Colonel Edgworth-Johnstone, the Chief Commissioner, and Sir Neville Chamberlain, the Inspector General of the DMP were exonerated.

**32 Bachelor's Walk**: second office of the Irish National Aid and Volunteers' Dependents' Fund. Michael Collins went to work as Secretary of the Fund on 19 February 1917, at a salary of £2.10s a week. Originally he worked in the 10 Exchequer Street office. The office was used concurrently for intelligence work by Collins, Tom Cullen, Bill Tobin and Frank Thornton from 1917 to 1921. Another office in the building was used by Collins as a Finance Office. He was arrested here on 2 April 1918 and was taken to the DMP's Brunswick Street Station accompanied by Detectives Smith and Thornton. From there he was taken to the Longford Assizes where he refused to recognise the court. Because it was not Volunteer policy to avail of bail he was then sent to prison in Sligo on 10 April 1918. Ultimately he was freed on bail from Sligo. (See also Ballinamuck, Co Longford, under section headed Michael Collins's Addresses).

**56 Bachelor's Walk** (corner of Lower Sackville Street): Kapp & Peterson's, pipes and tobacco; built on the site of 'Kelly's Fort' after it was demolished during the Rising. The second floor housed the New Ireland Insurance Company, run by Michael Staines who was in the GPO during the Rising.

**Back Lane**: Tailor's Hall, built in 1706; replaced the Jesuit college which had been built on the site in 1627. It was the meeting place of the Dublin Society of United Irishmen (raided 23 May 1794). The so-called 'Back Lane Parliament' met here, the Catholic Committee organised by Theobold Wolfe Tone. Tailor's Hall is the only surviving Guild Hall in Dublin. It is noted for its five long Queen Anne windows and is now the home of An Taisce, the Irish National Trust.

**67 Baggot Street Lower**: home of Thomas Davis, composer of the song *A Nation Once Again*. Davis was born in 1814 and died in 1845. With John Blake Dillon and Charles Gavan Duffy, he founded *The Nation* in 1841, the idea for which was conceived while the three men were walking in the Phoenix Park, and the first issue appeared in October 1842.

**92 Baggot Street Lower**: this house was owned by a Mrs Stack. On Bloody Sunday, Cpt W. F. Newbury, Royal West Surrey Regiment, was killed here by Bill Stapleton and Joe Leonard. He was killed in front of his wife who was eight months pregnant, and she gave birth to a stillborn child two weeks later.

**119 Baggot Street Lower**: on Bloody Sunday, Cpt George T. Baggally, a one-legged barrister and Courts Martial Officer, formerly the Army Judge Advocate, known as a redoubtable prosecutor of the IRA, was killed here. He was in charge of the detail that killed John Lynch, in the Royal Exchange Hotel on 23 September 1920. He had previously lived at 19 Eccles Street. One of 'The Squad' responsible for his death was Seán Lemass, future Taoiseach. Thomas Whelan and Patrick Moran were hanged in Mountjoy Prison on 14 March 1921 for this killing despite both having solid alibis placing them outside Dublin on Bloody Sunday.

**128 Baggot Street Lower**: home of John and Henry Sheares. Members of the United Irishmen, they were beheaded outside Newgate Prison. Their coffins can be seen in the vaults of St Michan's Church in Church Street.

**134 Baggot Street Lower**: Ferguson's Garage. The Fergusons were a branch of a well-known Belfast firm. In June 1922 the garage was raided by a group of Republicans/IRA led by Leo Henderson who were intent on commandeering vehicles (valued at £9,000) on 26 June 1922. The raiders were stopped by Free State troops led by Frank Thornton, on the orders of Michael Collins, and Henderson and his men were taken prisoner. The raid was in line with the so-called 'Belfast Boycott'. The capture of Henderson's group led to the retaliatory taking of General J. J. 'Ginger' O'Connell (suggested by Ernie O'Malley) by the Republicans (Four Courts garrison), which led directly to the shelling of the Four Courts on 28–29 June.

**139 Baggot Street Lower**: Toner's Pub; alleged to be the only one visited by W. B. Yeats (he was taken there by Oliver St John Gogarty).

**16, 18 Baggot Street Upper**: Royal City of Dublin Hospital; commonly called Baggot Street Hospital. Dr Alfred Parsons, Alfred Fannin's brother-in-law, worked here. He was singled out for his great service during the Rising. He was a leading Dublin doctor and included J. M. Synge among his patients. He also gave evidence that Cpt J. C. Bowen-Colthurst, the officer who unlawfully shot Francis Sheehy-Skeffington during the Rising, 'was unbalanced'. George Jameson Johnston was a surgeon and lecturer in clinical surgery here, and was also Professor of Surgery at the Royal College of Surgeons in Ireland. Richard Atkinson Stoney was another famous surgeon who worked here.

**Ballsbridge**: Royal Dublin Society. The first enrolment of An Garda Síochána (The Civic Guard) took place here on 21 February 1922; the first Commandant was Joseph Staines.

**Ballymun Road**: 'Jameson' (John Charles Byrne) was shot dead here on 2 March 1920.

**Beechwood Avenue, Ranelagh**: home of Seamus Moore and his sisters, Bride and Mary, it was used as a safe house and meeting place by the Volunteers, and then by Republicans/IRA during the Civil War. Josephine Ahern, Desmond FitzGerald, Frank Gallagher, Maureen McGavock and Ernie O'Malley stayed here.

**Beechwood Avenue Upper, Ranelagh**: home of James Larkin

**Belgrave Road, Rathmines**: became known as 'Rebel Road' because of all the Fenians, TDs and Republicans living in close proximity to each other here.

**3 Belgrave Road, Rathmines**: home of the Plunkett family before they moved to Kimmage.

*Liberty Hall, Dublin*
*(W. & G. Baird Ltd., Belfast)*

**7 Belgrave Road, Rathmines**: home of Thomas Kelly, Dublin Alderman. He read the document 'forged' by Joseph Plunkett, at the Dublin Corporation meeting (see under Larkfield, Kimmage).

**7 Belgrave Road, Rathmines**: home of Hanna Sheehy-Skeffington. She was born in 1877 in Co Cork and was raised in Co Tipperary. She attended the Royal University, and received a BA in 1899 and an MA in 1902. She and Francis Skeffington were married on 27 June 1903. She lived here after being evicted from 11 (now 21) Grosvenor Place, Rathmines, where she lived with Francis and their son Owen. She was a judge of the Dáil courts and was a member of the first Fianna Fáil Executive in 1926. Rosamund Jacob sometimes lodged here.

**9 Belgrave Road, Rathmines**: home of Dr Kathleen Lynn and Madeleine ffrench Mullen. Educated in Dublin, England and Germany, Lynn qualified as a doctor in 1899. Awarded degrees in surgery and medicine from the Royal University in 1899, having interned at Holles Street Hospital (1897–99), the Rotunda Hospital (1899), the Royal Victoria Eye and Ear Hospital (1899) and also the Richmond Lunatic Asylum. She became a Fellow of the Royal College of Surgeons in Ireland in 1909. She fought in the Rising, was imprisoned and deported, but was released in 1918 to fight the influenza epidemic of that year. Helena Molony often lodged here. (See also under Charlemont Street, St Ultan's Children's Hospital.)

**10 Belgrave Road, Rathmines**: home of Robert and Una Brennan

**Belmont Ave, Donnybrook**: home of Mrs Áine Heron, a judge of the Republican courts.

**7 Belvedere Place**: Home of John Redmond in the early 1900s and later home to William (Bill) O'Brien, a member of the IRB. James Connolly sent his son Roddy here for safety. Nora Connolly and Lily Connolly stayed here when James was in Dublin Castle. O'Brien succeeded James Connolly as head of the ITGWU.

**Benburb Street**: Croppies' Acre; an area of untended grass left uncultivated because buried here are the United Irishmen killed in the eighteenth century; they were called 'croppies' because many of them cut their hair short in imitation of the revolutionary French.

**18 Beresford Place** (at Eden Quay): Liberty Hall. In the early nineteenth century the building had been a chop house. Later in the century it was the site of the Northumberland Commercial and Family Hotel that had been the meeting place for members of the Young Ireland movement. Still later, the Northumberland became the meeting place for members of the Land League. By 1911 the hotel had become almost derelict.

In 1912 it became the headquarters of the Irish Transport and General Workers' Union. A decision to establish the Union was taken at a meeting in Dublin in December 1908. (Larkin had arrived in Ireland in 1907 to begin his organising work.) At that meeting a decision was made to revolt against the English National Union of Dock Labourers which suspended Larkin from his post as organiser because of his concentration on specifically Irish problems. The first members were enrolled, and union cards were issued, on 20 January 1909, as the Irish Transport Workers' Union. The Union's first office was on Townsend Street, but soon it managed to rent a room at 10 Beresford Place. Later it secured affiliation to the Dublin Trades Council and, in May 1910, to the Irish Trade Union Congress. In March 1912 the rented room at 10 Beresford Place, was vacated and the Northumberland Hotel was taken over in its entirety. Also, in early 1912, at the suggestion of William O'Brien, the words 'and General' were formally added to the Union's title, following the lead of James Connolly, who had returned from the United States and begun his syndicalist teaching, especially his 'One Big Union' concept and his socialist ideals. Guinness workers remained outside of the Union because they were well treated by their employer, Lord Iveagh.

On Monday 25 August 1913, at 9.40 am, tramcars all over Dublin stopped in their tracks. It was the first day of Horse Show Week. All the drivers and conductors affixed the Red Hand Union Badge on their clothes and ordered the passengers off because they were on strike. Though the trams were started again, Larkin's action was to shut down the tram system and instigate a general strike. Under the leadership of William Martin Murphy, the owners rushed up scab (strikebreaking) workers for many businesses and the Great Lockout of 1913 was underway.

On 28 August, during a speech, Larkin paused to say: 'Before I go any further, with your permission I am going to burn the Proclamation of the King. People make Kings and people can unmake them.' For this statement he was arrested for seditious libel. On Friday, 29 August, the government arrested P. T. Daly (full-time official of the ITGWU), William O'Brien (Vice-President of the Trades Council, and president of the Tailor's Society), Thomas Lawlor (Tailor's Society), W. P. Partridge (ITGWU organiser and president of the Dublin district of the Amalgamated Society of Engineers, a British union) and Larkin. After they were released on bail, Larkin promised a speech and sneaked into the Imperial Hotel on Sunday, 31 August, in order to deliver it. That speech was proscribed by an order of Magistrate Swifte. Larkin had just begun his speech when the DMP broke into the room and arrested him. This caused a riot. Fighting erupted in Sackville Street, Great Brunswick Street, Abbey Street Lower, Eden Quay and Foley Street. John Byrne and James Nolan were seriously injured during these disturbances and died as a result (see Eden Quay and Foley Street). Larkin was released on 12 September.

DUBLIN RIOTS

THE VOICE OF THE PEOPLE
IS THE VOICE OF GOD.

ARREST
OF
IM LARKIN
N DISGUISE

*Shoulder to Shoulder we'll bravely stand
And with Larkin to lead we'll fight,
A long strong fight for the famed Red Hand
The Emblem of justice and right.*
EVA HAYDEN.

Four hundred Dublin employers decided to lock out all workers who were members of the Union. At a meeting outside Liberty Hall during the Lockout, Larkin proclaimed: 'If Carson has the right to arm his men in the North, then you men have a right to arm to protect yourselves from police attack'. An Irish Citizen Army (ICA) was proposed in October 1913, giving equal rights to men and women. The Starry Plough Banner made its first appearance at that time. In early 1914, Connolly announced the establishment of an Irish Citizen Army 'to protect workers' meetings' and 'to prevent the brutalities of armed thugs occurring in the future'. On 22 March 1914, Larkin presided at a meeting reconstituting the ICA. The new constitution was drawn up primarily by Countess Markievicz, James Connolly, and other militarily-minded members of the ITGWU. It provided for an Army Council, and included explicitly nationalist aims:

*Article One: The first and last principle of the Irish Citizen Army is the avowal that the ownership of Ireland, moral and material, is vested of right in the people of Ireland.*

*Article Two: That its principal objects should be:*

*a) To arm and train all Irishmen capable of bearing arms to enforce and defend its first principle.*

*b) To sink all differences of birth, privilege and creed under the common name of the Irish people.*

*Article Three: The Irish Citizen Army shall stand for the absolute unity of Irish nationhood, and recognition of the rights and liberties of the democracies of all nations.*

*Article Four: That the Citizen Army shall be open to all who are prepared to accept the principles of equal rights and opportunities for the People of Ireland and to work in harmony with organised labour towards that end.*

*Article Five: Every enrolled member must be, if possible, a member of a Trade Union recognised by the Irish Trades Union Congress.*

The Army Council was chaired by Jack White. The vice-chairmen were Larkin, P. T. Daly, Countess Markievicz, William Partridge, Thomas Foran and Francis Sheehy-Skeffington. The secretary was Sean O'Casey and the treasurers were Countess

Markievicz and Richard Brannigan. (The Council at first did not include Connolly who returned to Belfast to take care of the Union's affairs there, returning later in 1914.)

The Dublin Trades Council approved the Army on 6 April 1914. In 1914 James Connolly spoke in commemoration of the workers killed in the 1913 Lockout: 'If you are itching for a rifle, itching to fight, have a country of your own; better to fight for our country than for the robber empire. If you ever shoulder a rifle let it be for Ireland ... Make up your mind to strike before the opportunity goes.'9

On 24 October Larkin left for America and Connolly was in complete charge of the Union and the ICA. After 1914, this building was the headquarters of the Irish Citizen Army, of which Connolly was O/C. Officers included: Lt Michael Kelly, Cpt Richard MacCormack, Cpt John O'Neill, Maj Michael Mallin (second in command), Countess Markievicz, Sgt Joseph Doyle, Sgt Frank Robbins. Robbins was imprisoned after the Rising and upon his return felt that the spirit of the ICA had changed greatly. He wrote: 'There was a new atmosphere, a new outlook entirely from that which had been moulded by Connolly and Mallin. The kernel of the problem was that the majority of the new members, strange as it might seem, did not hold or advocate the social and political views that had motivated those who fought in 1916.'10

The *Irish Worker* was published here and was suppressed in 1914. *The Worker* – which James Connolly also edited was subsequently founded and was suppressed after six issues. On 24 March 1916 the print shop attached to Liberty Hall was raided. Much of the type was taken, so the printers had to 'borrow' type (from W. H. West of Capel Street) to set the *Proclamation*, and it was printed in two parts – the first three paragraphs were set, then the type was broken down and 'reused' to set the final three paragraphs. This was because the printers at Liberty Hall could borrow only about half the type needed for the job.

On 16 April 1916 the Irish Republic Flag, with the Harp but without the Crown, was first raised over the Hall; it was unfurled by Miss Molly Reilly. Massed were the Irish Citizen Army, the ICA Women's Section, the ICA Boy Scouts under Cpt Carpenter, and the Fintan Lawlor Pipe Band. Cpt Poole led a colour guard of sixteen which escorted the Colour Bearer who was also accompanied by three young girl dancers known as the Liberty Trio. From 26 March to 16 April James Connolly's play, *Under Which Flag*, had its first performances at Liberty Hall, with Sean Connolly in the lead role. It was about an Irishman torn between serving Ireland in the IRB and the British Army. On 16 April, in his final lecture on tactics, Connolly warned: 'The odds against us are a thousand to one. But if we should win, hold onto your rifles because the Volunteers may have a different goal. Remember, we're out not only for political liberty, but for economic liberty as well. So hold onto your rifles.'11

On 19 April, Spy Wednesday, Connolly informed Citizen Army officers R. McCormack, Joseph Doyle and Frank Robbins that the Rising was scheduled for Easter Sunday – it would begin at 6.30 pm in Dublin and 7.00 pm in the provinces. On 23 April *The Proclamation of the Irish Republic* was printed in the Liberty Hall print shop. Thomas MacDonagh gave the manuscript to three men to compose the type and print the

9. Foy, Michael and Brian Barton, *The Easter Rising*, 1999, p. 49.
10. Kostick, Conor, *Revolution in Ireland, Popular Militancy 1917 to 1923*, 1996, p. 175.
11. Caulfield, Max, *The Easter Rebellion, Dublin 1916*, 1963, 1995, p. 24.

*Irish Rebellion, May, 1916,*
*Soldiers bivouacking opposite Liberty Hall, the rebel headquarters in Dublin*

sheets: the primary printer, Christopher Brady (in the printing department of the Bank of Ireland), Michael Molloy (a printer at the *Independent* newspaper) and Liam F. O'Brien (who worked at O'Reilly's Printing Works). They finally finished late on Sunday night, after borrowing the type and coping with problems with the press. They printed 2,500 copies. The machine used was a 'Wharfdale Double-Crown' of a very old pattern and in poor condition.

William Oman was the bugler who sounded the 'fall in' for the ICA on Easter Monday, 24 April. Originally the 2nd Battalion of Volunteers was to muster here and march to St Stephen's Green. Frank Thornton and Seamus McGowan commanded the unit guarding the munitions which were transferred to the GPO on Monday afternoon in fifteen commandeered lorries and cabs. Thereafter the Hall was deserted except for Peter Ennis, the caretaker. On 26 April Liberty Hall was fired upon by HMS *Helga* – she fired twenty-four rounds.

On 10 June 1917 a protest meeting was held on behalf of the prisoners still in English jails; it was addressed by Cathal Brugha and Count Plunkett. Inspector Miles of the DMP was hit on the head with a hurley during the protest and later died.

Standing at 195 feet the present-day Liberty Hall is the tallest building in Dublin and rises sixteen stories. Building began in 1961 and finished in 1965. It is the headquarters of the SIPTU trade union.

**Beresford Place**: across from Liberty Hall stands the James Connolly Statue. The sculptor was Eamonn O'Doherty and the work was unveiled by President Mary Robinson in 1996. The flag that forms the background is the Starry Plough, the stars representing socialism and the plough representing labour.

**10-13 Berkeley Road**: St Joseph's Church, noted for its Volunteer Commemorative Masses; celebrates an annual Mass on 22 August for Michael Collins.

**26-50 Bishop Street** (corner of Peter Row, touching Wexford Street): Jacob's Biscuit Factory; the company's full name was W. & R. Jacob Co Ltd. It employed approximately 3,000 at the time of the Great Lockout of 1913. Its main gate was on Bishop Street, near Bride Street. One hundred and fifty Volunteers, including about twelve members of Cumann na mBan, held it during the Rising. The occupying force, commanded by MacDonagh, mustered in St Stephen's Green and left just as the ICA contingent arrived to occupy the area. Fr McCabe, prior of the Carmelite Priory, attempted to dissuade the Volunteers from their course, declaring that the Rising was insane.

The factory was a virtually immune stronghold during the Rising and didn't have to be defended against frontal attack. Forty Volunteers were sent from here to reinforce the Portobello area and twenty more were sent back to St Stephen's Green. The Dublin Institute of Technology now occupies most of the site, the remainder housing the National Archives.

**5 Blackhall Street**: Gaelic League Hall; meeting place of the Gaelic League and of the Columcille Branch of Cumann na mBan. The Volunteers first 'paraded' here on 1 December 1913. The 1st Battalion of the Dublin Brigade (less D Company) mobilised here for the Rising under Commandant Daly, who declared: 'Today at noon, an Irish Republic will be declared, and the Flag of the Republic hoisted. I look to every man to do his duty with courage and discipline. The Irish Volunteers are now the Irish Republican Army.' Only about a third of the Volunteers appeared for the muster on Easter Monday, though some took their positions later. Piaras Béaslaí was second in command.

**Blackrock, Co Dublin**: Glenvar; de Valera's office from May 1921; raided on 22 June 1921 by the Worchestershire Regiment. He was arrested and taken from Dublin Castle to Portobello Barracks, from which he was released after one night.

**Bolton Street**: Messrs Moore and Alexander, wholesale druggists, burned during the Rising

**Booterstown, Co Dublin**: Kevin O'Higgins' home; nephew of Tim Healy. He was shot here on his way to Mass on 10 July 1927. Eoin MacNeill was the first to reach him. His killers were Archie Doyle, Timothy Coughlin and Bill Gannon. It was thought 'in part it was prompted by motives of revenge, in part by an impetus to reactivate the parent body [IRA]. The Civil War was five years away; the country was beginning to enjoy peace. It was time to stir things up again.'[12]

**Booterstown, Co Dublin**: Dave Neligan's home; his DMP Badge was No 46. He left the DMP on 11 May 1920; then at Michael Collins's request he returned to become *The Spy in The Castle*. Joined the British Secret Service in May 1921 and became Agent No 68. Count Sevigne was the head of the Secret Service at the time.

**89 Botanic Road, Glasnevin**: home of Sean (Johnny) Collins when he settled his brother, Michael's, estate. Nancy O'Brien, Michael's cousin, lived here while employed in Dublin Castle. Michael died intestate, leaving an estate of £1,950.9s.11d.

**1 Brendan Road, Donnybrook**: Batt O'Connor's home. O'Connor was a builder and 'built' Brendan Road, naming it after the patron saint of his native Kerry. Michael Collins often stayed here.

12. Coogan, Tim Pat, *Ireland Since the Rising*, 1966, p. 261ff gives a personal account of the men involved.

**6 Brendan Road, Donnybrook**: house owned by the Dáil, frequently used by Michael Collins.

**23 Brendan Road, Donnybrook**: Susan Mason, Michael Collins's secretary, lived here with her aunt. Collins often stayed here.

**Bride Street and Ross Road**: Ceannt and MacDonagh surrendered to Captain Wheeler in this location

**9 Bridge Street Lower**: Limerick Clothing Factory; three hundred Irish Volunteer uniforms were ordered from here in 1914, while awaiting the official ones from Cork.

**19 and 21 Bridge Street Lower**: Doherty's Hotel

**20 Bridge Street Lower**: Brazen Head Pub and Hotel. The rebels of 1798 and 1803 met here to plan.

**Bridgefort Street** (at the corner of Usher's Quay): location of 18-pounder guns used to shell the Four Courts at the start of the Civil War, under the command of Emmet Dalton.

**Brighton Square, Rathgar**: home of Ewart Wilson, cousin of C. S. Andrews. Andrews often stayed here when 'on the run' during the War of Independence and the Civil War.

**4 Brunswick Street North**: North Dublin Union; occupied by Ned Daly's men.

**5-9 Brunswick Street North**: Richmond Hospital. Fifteen dead and 200 wounded were received here during the Rising. A teaching hospital for surgery, Sir Thomas Myles, former President of the Royal College of Surgeons in Ireland, and A. A. McConnell, Ireland's first neurosurgeon, both practised here, as did Sir William Stoker, Sir William Thomson and Sir Conway Dwyer. Oliver St John Gogarty studied here and was a clinical clerk for Sir Thomas Myles.

About a week after the Rising, members of the DMP came looking for Volunteers Patrick Daly and Liam Archer, but the house surgeon, Michael Bourke, informed them that they had been discharged. When the policemen then asked about Eamon Martin, Bourke told them Martin was dying.

**12-13 Burgh Quay**: Tivoli Music Hall; occupied by British soldiers firing on Liberty Hall.

**Bushy Park, Dublin**: home of Sir Frederick Shaw; raided in December 1919 by E Company (Rathfarnham Company) for arms. None were found.

**11 Bushy Park Road, Rathgar**: Mrs Jackson's home; converted to an auxiliary hospital during the Rising.

**12 Bushy Park Road, Rathgar**: the last Dublin home of Erskine Childers.

**Cabra, Dublin**: Sean Harling's home; he witnessed de Valera's signing of the Letters Plenipotentiary and delivered them to the Treaty Representatives.

**Cabra Park, Dublin**: Martin Conlon's home. Bulmer Hobson was held here just before the Rising by Martin Conlon, Michael Lynch, Con O'Donovan and Maurice Collins. Sean T. O'Kelly was sent from the GPO on the night of Easter Monday 1916 to have him released.

**5 Cabra Road**: Michael Foley's home, where Michael Collins first met Ned Broy.

**24 Cabra Road, Phibsborough**: home of Louise Gavan Duffy, member of the Provisional Committee of Cumann na mBan and its Honorary Secretary.

**Camden Street**: Hartigan's Pub; gathering place for those with Republican sentiments during the War of Independence.

**Camden Street**: The Bleeding Horse Pub, founded in 1648; often appeared in the works of Sean O'Casey written during the War of Independence.

**Camden Street Lower**: the area comprising this street together with Wexford Street, Aungier Street and South Great Georges Street was known as 'The Dardanelles' during the War of Independence. Also location of Mrs Padraig (Nora) O'Keefe's restaurant; Michael Collins often lunched here. There was a room above the shop where Collins stayed for a few weeks in 1919 until he moved to 5 Mary Street.

**5 Camden Street Lower**: Corrigan and Sons Mortuary; K Company (3rd Battalion) used the premises to make bombs.

**34 Camden Street Lower**: formerly housed the Irish National Theatre Society. The first meeting of Fianna na hÉireann in Dublin took place here on 16 August 1909: Bulmer Hobson (President), Countess Markievicz (Vice-President), Padraig O'Riain (Secretary), Liam Mellowes (appointed National Organiser). On 21 August there was a report in *An Claidheamh Soluis* noting the meeting and stating that about one hundred boys attended. Sean Heuston was the leader of the Fianna on Dublin's Northside, while Con Colbert was the leader on the Southside. The Volunteers used this premises as a drill hall. It was the fourth meeting place of K Company (3rd Battalion) after the Rising. In 1919 the Dáil met here and it was here that all TDs took the Oath to the Dáil.

**67 Camden Street Lower**: home of Councillor Richard O'Carroll who was shot by Captain J. C. Bowen-Colthurst on Wednesday 26 April, after his capture in an evacuated Volunteer post. O'Carroll died nine days later in Portobello Hospital. He was the General Secretary of the Bricklayers' and Stoneworkers' Union.

**Capel Street**: home of Harry O'Farrell, Captain of K Company (3rd Battalion) following Tom Cullen.

**4 Capel Street**: home of Seán and Noel Lemass. Seán fought for the Republicans/IRA. He was Taoiseach from June 1959 to 1966. Noel was captured in Glencullen but escaped and fled to the Isle of Man during the Civil War. He was suspected of tampering with Michael Collins's mail; he was recaptured on 3 July 1923. Allegedly kidnapped by the CID and murdered, his body was found in the Dublin mountains on 12 October 1923.

**45A Capel Street**: premises of William Henry West, printer; he provided the type for the *Proclamation*. He was prosecuted under The Defence of the Realm Act (DORA) in June 1916 for printing a statement purportedly made by Thomas MacDonagh in the dock; fined £5.

**106 Capel Street**: Dublin Municipal Library; Thomas Gay was the librarian. The premises was used as a 'drop' by Michael Collins and his men. Gay gave information to Harry Boland about the 17–18 May 1918 'German Plot' arrests. Boland passed the information along to Collins, who told the Cabinet. De Valera however advised that they should all remain at home that night and many of the Cabinet members were arrested.

**Castle Street** (8 Bristol Buildings): home of Miss Florence Williams; received the Military Medal from the British for her heroic saving of men inside and outside Dublin Castle during the Rising.

**16 Castle Street**: Dublin Municipal Buildings, where Eamonn Ceannt worked in the City Treasurer's Department.

**11 Cathedral Street**: Dublin United Tramways Company, owned by William Martin Murphy.

**6 Cavendish Row**: home of John Gore, an elderly solicitor and first Hon Treasurer of the Irish Volunteers. Bulmer Hobson said of him: 'He was not noted for his reticence'. Hobson purposefully misled him when Hobson told him that the guns to be landed at

Howth were to be landed into Wexford. Hobson felt that Gore would repeat this to all of his clients 'in confidence'. Whether he did or not, the English ship HMS *Panther*, which had been anchored in Dublin Bay, steamed south to Wexford. On Sunday, while the arms were brought ashore, the *Panther* was immobilised in Wicklow because the crew had been given shore leave.

**Charlemont Street**: James Connolly and family (his wife and three daughters) lived here in a one-roomed flat upon his arrival in Dublin in 1896. He married the former Lillie Reynolds from Co Wicklow. Shortly afterwards, along with seven like-minded socialists, he formed the Irish Socialist Republican Party.

**37 Charlemont Street**: St Ultan's Children's Hospital; founded in 1919 (with £70 and two cots) by Dr Kathleen Lynn and Madeleine ffrench-Mullen. Louie Bennett, Kathleen Clarke, Charlotte Despard, Maud Gonne, Countess Markievicz and Helena Molony all greatly contributed. Louie Bennett fundraised for the hospital on her trips to the United States, as did Kathleen Clarke, who also sat on its board.

**Charles Street West**: during the Rising the Royal Lancers under the command of Colonel Hammond, took the medical mission on Monday afternoon and held it until relieved on Thursday evening. These Lancers had been escorting an ammunition delivery from the North Wall to Phoenix Park. They were attacked by Volunteers in the Four Courts, and the survivors took shelter here. These were *not* the Lancers who had been sent from Marlborough Barracks to investigate the fighting and who trotted down Lower Sackville Street and were attacked in front of the GPO.

**Charleston Road**: Margaret Foley's home. Frank Gallagher (David Hogan) stayed here while on the run after the early summer of 1920.

**Church Road, East Wall**: home of Tommy Dorrins, killed in the Custom House fire.

**Church Street, Howth**: Michael Collins's relations named Butterley lived here in 1914. Collins often stayed here and some say he was here during the landing of the Howth guns.

**Church Street**: Church of St Mary of the Angels; opened in 1868 and completed in 1881; the main altar was designed by James Pearse, father of Padraig and Willie. Later in 1916 Masses were said for those who died for Ireland in the Rising. The inscriptions on the Stations of the Cross are in Irish.

**Church Street** (and North King Street) Reilly's Pub (known as 'Reilly's Fort'); Jack Shouldice commanded a unit here during the Rising.

**Church Street**: home and shop of Alice and Kate Ryan; their niece was May Quigley, to whom Sean Treacy became engaged.

**5 Church Street**: home of Mr Lennon; Brighid Lyons Thornton hid here following the Rising.

**66, 67 Church Street**: these two tenement houses collapsed on 2 September 1913. Seven people were killed, including two children (aged four and five); another eight tenants were seriously injured. These tenants were representative of the workers involved in the Lockout of 1913 and the outcry among workers was immediate. One of those killed, Eugene Salmon, had been laid off by Jacob's Biscuit Factory the day before and died trying (unsuccessfully) to save his four-year-old sister.

**79-80 Church Street**: Monks' Bakery; during the Rising, Commandant Daly oversaw the distribution of bread from here to the local residents who depended upon the bakery for their food.

Kevin Barry was captured here after an ambush on 20 September 1920 in which three British soldiers were killed. He stopped to re-load his .38 caliber Luger (which the IRA always referred to as a 'Parabellum') and hid under a lorry. When it was about to be driven off a bystander innocently shouted 'There's a man under the lorry' and Barry was arrested. The British troops engaged in this incident were from the 2nd Battalion of the Duke of Wellington's Regiment, commanded by Sgt Banks. The unit was on a thrice-weekly scheduled collection of the detachment's bread ration. The Volunteers mustered at the O'Flanagan Sinn Féin Club on Ryder's Row; 2Lt Tommy McGrane, John Joe Carroll, James Douglas, Dave McDonagh and Frank O'Flanagan had entered the bakery through the side entrance at 38 North King Street and were waiting for the British troops. Jim Moran and Paddy Young were to wait at the Brunswick Street corner. Maurice Higgins and Tom Kissane were to wait at the North King Street corner. Kevin Barry, together with 2Lt Bob O'Flanagan and Sean O'Neill were to follow the lorry into Church Street and hold up the troops for their weapons. Harry Murphy, Thomas (Tucker) Reilly and Christy Boy Robinson were to close on the lorry from the Brunswick Street side. Seamus Kavanagh (the O/C), Frank Flood, Tommy O'Brien and Mick Robinson were to close on the lorry from a pub directly opposite. Eugene Fox, John Kenny, John O'Dwyer and Tom Staunton were to cover the withdrawal up Constitution Hill, where an escape lorry was waiting on Coleraine Street with drivers Davy Golden and Jimmy Carrigan.

Barry's .38 Parabellum jammed and he knelt down beside the lorry to clear it. He rose and it jammed again (on the fifth round) and he knelt under the lorry a second time. That's when the rest of the Volunteers withdrew due to the returned fire and he was left isolated, hiding under the lorry. Privates Harold Washington, Thomas Humphries and Marshall Whitehead were killed. Barry was tried for the murder of Marshall Whitehead,

*Fathers Albert and Dominic OSFC, who attended the patriots executed in Kilmainham Gaol.*
*(Cashman, Dublin)*

though Whitehead was killed with .45 caliber bullets. It is thought Barry shot Private Washington, but he was not charged with this killing.

Kevin Barry was the first Volunteer captured in action since 1916 and he was the first person executed during the War of Independence.

**138-142 Church Street**: Capuchin Franciscan Friary and **131-137 Church Street**: Father Mathew Hall, also known as Capuchin Hall. Named after Father Theobold Mathew (1790–1861), who preached against alcohol abuse throughout Ireland and the U S. He was *very* successful in getting the Irish to take the 'pledge'. It is estimated that by 1842 out of a population of just over eight million, some five million had taken the pledge. He was born in Rathclogheen, near Thomastown, Co Tipperary, in the same house used as a hiding place by Dan Breen, Sean Hogan and Sean Treacy on the night of 21 January 1919, after the Soloheadbeg ambush.

The building was used as a hospital in 1916. There is a plaque on the wall commemorating its importance during the Rising. It was the headquarters under Ned Daly of the 1st Battalion before it moved on Friday to the Four Courts. The Friars who attended those executed in Kilmainham Gaol lived here, and they were instrumental in bringing the British and the Battalion O/Cs together at the end of the Rising (Fathers Albert Bibby, Aloysius, Augustine, Columbus, Dominic and Sebastian).

**North Circular Road**: home of James Larkin

**North Circular Road**: Con Collins's home; he was sent to Tralee to help Roger Casement bring guns back to Dublin.

**North Circular Road (**near Jones Road): MacDermott Sinn Féin Club

**North Circular Road, Cowley Place**: Mountjoy Prison ('The Joy'). Sean Treacy was imprisoned here in September 1917, and was one of the prisoners who demanded political status, which led to the hunger strike. The three leaders of the hunger strike were Austin

Stack, Fionan Lynch and Thomas Ashe. Ashe was force-fed here during that strike; a lung was pierced during feeding on 23 September and he was taken to the Mater Hospital where he died on 25 September 1917 of 'heart failure and congestion of the lungs'. Ashe had been arrested on 20 August, just before he was to travel to Skibbereen with Michael Collins. Upon hearing of his arrest, Michael Collins wrote to his sister Hannie: 'Tom Ashe has been arrested so that fixes him'. In Mountjoy, as Ashe was carried away to be force-fed, Fionan Lynch cried out, 'Stick it, Tom'. Ashe replied, 'I'll stick it, Fin'.

At Ashe's funeral in Glasnevin on 30 September, after the IRA fired three volleys over his grave, Michael Collins (in Volunteer uniform) said: 'Nothing additional remains to be said. That volley which we have just heard is the only speech it is proper to make above the grave of a dead Fenian.'

*Thomas Ashe*

Collins arranged Robert Barton's escape on 16 March 1919. Another hunger strike for 'prisoner of war' status began on 5 April 1920 and continued until 15 April 1920. The prisoners had served the following demand on the governor on 1 April: 'The undersigned, acting on behalf of all untried and uncharged prisoners, hereby demand that on or before the morning of April 5th all such prisoners be released or given prisoner-of-war treatment.'[13] Among those on strike were Frank Gallagher and Peter Starkey.

Kevin Barry was hanged in Mountjoy Prison on Monday, 1 Nov 1920. The hangman was John Ellis, brought over from England for the execution. Barry was hanged one day after Terence MacSwiney was buried in Finbarr Cemetery in Cork (he died on 25 October in Brixton Prison). Barry was attended and accompanied onto the scaffold by Canon Waters and Fr MacMahon from Clonliffe College. Acting Judge Myles Keogh signed Barry's death warrant, and it was in this warrant that the details on Barry's torture were outlined.

On the eve of Kevin Barry's execution a large crowd gathered outside Mountjoy. People held lighted candles and recited the Rosary right through the hours of darkness. Barry's mother was in the crowd outside the prison; she was invited inside but refused and remained with the crowd, although in a very distressed state. Those gathered continued to pray that he would be shot as a patriot, rather than hanged, as he had been arrested in uniform.

---

13. Gallagher, Frank, *Days of Fear, A Diary of Hunger Strike*, 1967, p. 88.

Kevin Barry was buried in Mountjoy in a plain, roughly painted coffin at 1.30 pm on 1 November, All Saints Day. The grave was in a small laurel plot near the women's prison. In April 2002, his body was re-interred in the Republican Plot in Glasnevin. There was a huge funeral parade through the streets of Dublin and he was buried with the honours he so richly deserved.

Also hanged in Mountjoy and then buried there during the War of Independence were Thomas Bryan, Edmond Foley, Patrick Maher, Thomas Traynor, Patrick Doyle, Frank Flood, Patrick Moran, Bernard Ryan and Thomas Whelan. Moran and Whelan were hanged on 14 March 1921 for their 'participation' in the Bloody Sunday killings, though both had clear alibi's placing them outside Dublin at the time (however, the Volunteers at the Gresham Hotel on Bloody Sunday were actually under the command of Paddy Moran). John Ellis was employed as the hangman in these cases as well. All have since been re-interred with full honours in their 'home' cemeteries, many in Glasnevin. (Paddy Moran was imprisoned in Kilmainham Gaol when the escape of Simon Donnelly, Ernie O'Malley and Frank Teeling was planned. Moran was one of those Michael Collins wanted to 'break out.' However, he was so sure of acquittal due to his alibi that he absolutely refused to leave, saying that his trying to get away would be interpreted as guilt if he were captured. He paid for his reliance on British justice with his life.)

While imprisoned here in December 1920, Arthur Griffith and Michael Staines met with Archbishop Clune (see also under 5 Merrion Square, Dr Robert Farnan). Women arrested and imprisoned here during the War of Independence included Mary Burke, Eithne Coyle, Moya Llewelyn Davies, Patricia Hoey, Linda Kearns, Aileen Keogh and Eileen McGrane. Seán MacEoin was imprisoned here in March 1921 and thereafter Collins devised several attempts to free him. All failed however and he was finally released when the Truce was signed. The most ambitious of these attempts took place on 14 May when a commandeered armoured car, commanded by Emmett Dalton, and with a 'crew' of Joe Leonard, Pat McCrea, Tom Keogh, Bill Stapleton and Paddy McCaffrey attempted to break MacEoin out. The 'schedule' at Mountjoy had MacEoin in the warden's office at the appointed time on a daily basis, but on that day the schedule was changed and he was in the infirmary.

Among the captured IRA men in the Four Courts were Dick Barnett, Joe McKelvey, Liam Mellowes and Rory O'Connor. They were executed in Mountjoy Prison on 8 December 1922 in reprisal for the shooting of Sean Hales and wounding of Padraic O'Maille on 7 December. This was such an infamous event during the Civil War that it has long been questioned as to who was 'responsible'. It appears Mulcahy took the initiative and O'Higgins and McGrath were the last Cabinet members to give their consent. (Rory O' Connor was best man at O'Higgins' wedding in late 1921.) Terence De Vere White notes: 'O'Higgins was appalled, and argued against it in Cabinet at great length, only agreeing after Eoin MacNeill, whom he greatly respected, acquiesced. Kevin was the second to last to agree, followed by Joseph McGrath, who was utterly opposed and gave in for the sake of unanimity.'[14] Ernest Blythe thought O'Higgins had been 'over-sensitive about

---

14. White, Terence DeVere, *Kevin O'Higgins*, 1948, 1986, p. 131.

*Military Operations, Dublin, June-July, 1922: National Troops Searching Civilian*
*(E. & S. Ltd., Dublin. Photo, Hogan, Dublin)*

the executions'.[15] Tim Pat Coogan has written 'a certain awfulness hung about his name.'[16]

Mary Bourke, Eithne Coyle, Aileen Keogh and Annie M. P. Smithson were imprisoned in Mountjoy during the Civil War and escaped. Maire Comerford was imprisoned here after being arrested for attempting to kidnap W. T. Cosgrave. She was wounded in the leg in an escape attempt here, and was taken to the North Dublin Union from where she escaped. She was re-arrested and imprisoned in Kilmainham, where she went on hunger strike, and was finally released.

**422 North Circular Road**: last Dublin home of Sean O'Casey.

**South Circular Road**: home of Professor Michael Hayes, raided on 10 November 1920; Richard Mulcahy was almost captured in this raid, but escaped. The raid did generate some crucial files for the British, which included almost 200 names and addresses of Volunteers.

**South Circular Road**: Kilmainham Gaol. There had been a prison on this site dating back to the twelfth century; originally it was known as the Dismal House of Little Ease. Over the door is a bronze-relief of five entangled snakes. These were known as the 'Demons of Crime' and were twisted and chained together to represent a warning to all who passed through its gates. The gaol was opened in 1796, altered in 1857, and again in 1863. Henry Joy McCraken was a prisoner here after the 1798 Rebellion, as was Robert Emmet in 1803. The Invincibles were held and executed here in 1882. John J. O'Leary, John Devoy, Jeremiah O'Donovan Rossa, and Charles Stewart Parnell were all imprisoned here.

---

15. Hopkinson, Michael, *Green Against Green: a History of the Irish Civil War*, 1988, p. 191.
16. Coogan, T. P., *Ireland Since the Rising*, 1966, p. 52.

Brigadier J. Young was in charge here and laid down the procedures for the executions after the Rising; the first prisoner to be executed was paraded at 3.30 am to face a firing squad of twelve men. The commander of the firing squad was Major H. Heathcote. All those executed in Dublin were executed in the Stonebreaker's Yard here. The marriage of Grace Gifford and Joseph Plunkett, presided over by Fr McCarthy, took place at 11.30 pm on 3 May. Two soldiers of the Royal Irish Regiment signed the register as witnesses (John Smith and John Lockerby). Fr McCarthy then took Grace to Mr Byrne's home on James's Street after the ceremony.

On 14 February 1921, Simon Donnelly, Ernie O'Malley and Frank Teeling escaped from here. The bolt cutters and weapons had been provided by a sympathetic British soldier. Paddy Moran, Frank Flood, Thomas Bryan, Pat Doyle, Thomas Whelan and Bernard Ryan were also prisoners at the time and did not escape. They were all hanged in Mountjoy. (The Volunteers at the Gresham Hotel on Bloody Sunday were under the command of Paddy Moran. The others pleaded for him to escape, but he said he would not because he would not betray those who placed him in Blackrock at his home or at Mass that morning. He was hanged on 14 March 1921 in Mountjoy Prison for participation in the Bloody Sunday executions at Upper Baggot Street. See also North Circular Road, Mountjoy Prison.)

The gaol was occupied by Republican/IRA troops on 13 April 1922. During the Civil War Maire Comerford, Sheila Humphries, Dr Kathleen Lynn, Maud Gonne MacBride, Dorothy Macardle, Mary MacSwiney, Nora Connolly O'Brien, Lily O'Brennan, Kate O'Callaghan, Áine O'Rahilly, Grace Gifford Plunkett and Nell Ryan (among other women) were held prisoner here. The first executions of the Civil War were on 17 November 1922. Peter Cassidy, James Fisher, John Gaffney and Richard Twohig were all executed here for illegally possessing arms. The gaol was closed in 1924.

**28 South Circular Road**: home of Patrick Dowling, Kevin Barry's uncle, his mother Mary's brother. Barry often stayed here and had been staying there for several nights before the raid on Monks' Bakery. After the raid the home was itself raided and pulled asunder.

**1, 2 Clanwilliam Place**: Clanwilliam House, corner of Clanwilliam Place and Mount Street Lower, home of Miss Wilson, occupied during the Rising by elements of de Valera's Boland Mills Garrison (see also under 25 Northumberland Road). Clanwilliam House was on the city side, east side of the intersection; St Stephen's Parochial Hall, was on the opposite side (the south east side) of the Grand Canal on the east side of the street; 25 Northumberland Road was on the same side of the canal but further towards the south east, towards Kingstown (Dun Laoghaire). There was a total of thirteen men in the three outposts. Patrick J. Doyle was the O/C in the Parochial Hall; he and Joe Clarke, William Christian and P. McGrath held off the Sherwood Foresters from their position as long as they could, then fled to Percy Place where they were captured. George Reynolds was O/C in Clanwilliam House; he was killed as were Richard Murphy and Patrick Doyle (company musketry instructor); Willie Ronan, James Doyle, Thomas Walsh and James Walsh survived. James Doyle (17) had his rifle shot out of his hands. Richard Murphy was killed as he fired from the middle windows, partially reclining on a chair. He was to be married a week later. The Walsh brothers were using Howth Mausers. At one point Patrick Doyle suddenly stopped firing and spoke no more; he was an inveterate talker and when one of the Walshes shook him he fell over dead. A soda siphon was used to dowse a fire and it was shot out of Jim Walsh's hand. The survivors abandoned the burning house only when they had no more ammunition. In this engagement the Sherwood Foresters' casualties were four officers killed, fourteen wounded, and 216 other ranks killed or wounded.

**Clare Street**: one of the offices of Kevin O'Higgins as Minister of Local Government.

**18 Claremont Road, Sandymount**: de Valera's home after his release from prison in 1924.

**Clarence Street South**: home of the Pearse family before they moved to Great Brunswick Street.

**Clarendon Street**: Carmelite Priory and St Teresa's Church and Hall; the first church was built here between 1793 and 1797. On 2 April 1902 *Cáitlín Ní hUallacháin* was first performed here. Yeats had written it for Maud Gonne, and she 'lived' the part.

**28 Claude Road, Drumcondra**: home of Sara and Molly Allgood, two of the most renowned Abbey Theatre actresses of the twentieth century. Both were in Cumann na mBan.

**Clonliffe Road**: Padraig O'Riain's home

**Clonskeagh, Dublin**: Roebuck House; home of Sean MacBride, son of John and Maud Gonne MacBride. MacBride fought for the Republicans/IRA during the Civil War, and became IRA C/S, succeeding Moss Twomey in 1936. He worked as a journalist for the *Irish Press*. In 1946 he founded the political party Clann na Poblachta and became Minister of External Affairs (1948–1951, this was the first coalition government). In 1957 he left politics. He was one of the founders of Amnesty International. He received the Nobel Peace Prize in 1974, the Lenin Prize in 1977, and was awarded the American Medal of Justice by President Carter in 1978, and the Dag Hammarskjold Prize for International Solidarity in 1981. He was the author of the *MacBride Principles*, an anti-discrimination code, which have been adopted by many states in America and are aimed at obliging American companies operating in Northern Ireland to ensure equal employment opportunities for all, including Catholics.

**Clontarf**: Croydon Park. The Park had been taken over by the ITGWU several years before the Rising and was used by Cpt J. R. White for drilling the Irish Citizen Army. After the 1913 Lockout, White offered Countess Markievicz £50 to buy shoes for the workers so they could drill and form an army. There was a house and three acres.

**Clontarf**: Town Hall; frequent meeting place for the Volunteer Military Council prior to the Rising. Michael McGinn, its curator, was a friend of Pearse and was an old IRB man himself.

**Clontarf**: Marino Casino; there was a disused, wide, dry tunnel here in which Michael Collins, Harry Boland, Gearóid O'Sullivan, Tom Barry and others fired and practised with the Thompson Machine Guns Clan na Gael purchased in America for the Volunteers.

**Coleraine Street**: John Beirnes was killed here by South Staffordshire Regimental troops.

**College Green**: Bank of Ireland; former Irish Parliament Building. The Bank took possession on 24 August 1803 following the Act of Union. The Upper Chamber remains as it was when the building housed parliament. Designed by Sir Edward Lovet Pearce in 1728. The reviewing stand for the Volunteers' Parade on St Patrick's Day 1916 was here.

**College Green**: statue of Thomas Davis, composer of *A Nation Once Again*

**College Green**: meeting place of The Contemporary Club

**College Green**: Trinity College Dublin (TCD); founded in 1592 by Queen Elizabeth, it was built on land confiscated from the Priory of All Hallows. The College's complete name

is the College of the Holy and Undivided Trinity. It was not until 1972, upon the death of Archbishop John Charles McQuaid, that it was no longer a 'mortal sin' for a Catholic to attend Trinity without written permission. Brigadier-General Lowe made it his HQ during the Rising. The Provost at that time was J. P. Mahaffey.

**College Green** (towards Grafton Street): Regent House, Trinity College

**College Green**: Thomas Ashe Memorial Hall; James Larkin lay in state here prior to his funeral in January 1947.

**College Green**: G-Division Detective Sergeant John Barton was shot here on 29 November 1919 by Sean Treacy.

**1 College Green:** *Fianna* publishing office

**1 College Green** (College Street): office of John R. Reynolds; the first office used by Kathleen Clarke for the Irish Volunteers' Dependents' Fund; Michael Collins worked here for her. The Fund combined with the Irish National Aid Association and moved to 10 Exchequer Street.

**7 College Green**: The O'Connell Press, printed *The Eye Opener*, a strongly nationalist paper. Thomas Dickson was the editor, and he was shot in the same tragic incident during the Rising as Francis Sheehy-Skeffington and Patrick MacIntyre. C. S. Andrews called *The Eye Opener* 'a scandal sheet which was non-political but directed at exposing the sex life of British officers.'[17] Others noted that *The Eye Opener* was 'rabidly loyalist'.

---

17. Andrews, C. S., *Dublin Made Me*, 1979, 2001, p. 83.

*'The Sinn Féin Revolt in Dublin' – General view of the devastated city*
*(Rotary Photo, E.C.)*

**12-14 College Green**: Star Assurance Buildings; Committee for Compensation for Property Destroyed in the Rising.

**12-14 College Green**: office of solicitor Michael Noyk who often appeared in Republican courts during the War of Independence, and gave advice to the Dáil.

**16 College Green**: office of Walter Hume, Assessor of Property Destroyed in the Rising.

**5b College Street**: police station, near Trinity College; Dave Neligan was posted here in 1918.

**Connaught Street, Phibsborough**: home of Mr and Mrs Seamus Doherty; Volunteers 'on the run' often stayed here. Sean Treacy was a frequent visitor.

**67 Connaught Street, Phibsborough**: home of Michael O'Hanrahan; he lived here with his mother, his brother Harry and two sisters, one of whom was Eily.

**Constitution Hill, Phibsborough**: Broadstone Railway Station, the terminus of the Midland Great Western Railway. This is the most monumental of the five railway termini of Dublin and the only one not controlled during the Rising because it was retaken on Tuesday, 25 April. Sited on a hill, its most dramatic feature was its railway shed with its huge colonnade. Designed by Richard Turner, the shed proved too ambitious for the span and was replaced after it collapsed in the early 1850s.

**The Coombe**: The Coombe Maternity Hospital, founded in 1826, occupied the building used by the Meath Hospital before the Meath moved to Long Lane. The hospital moved to Cork Street in 1967.

The Tenth Sinn Féin Ard Fheis was held here on 25–26 October 1917. About 1,700 delegates attended, including delegates from over 1,000 Sinn Féin Clubs. De Valera was elected President of Sinn Féin and the Irish Volunteers. Vice Presidents: Arthur Griffith and Father O'Flanagan; Secretaries: Darrell Figgis (later Harry Boland) and Austin Stack (he remained Hon Secretary until his death in 1929); Treasurers: Lawrence Ginnell and William Cosgrave; Eoin MacNeill was elected to the twenty-four member Sinn Féin Executive Council (there was controversy when MacNeill was proposed for the Executive – Eamon de Valera, Arthur Griffith and Sean Milroy voted for him but Kathleen Clarke, Helena Molony and Countess Markievicz opposed him – but he received an outstanding majority of votes); the other members of the Executive were: Piaras Béaslaí, Ernest Blythe, Harry Boland, Cathal Brugha, Kathleen Clarke, Michael Collins, Dr Thomas Dillon, Dr Richard Hayes, David Kent, Dairmuid Lynch, Fionan Lynch, Dr Kathleen Lynn, Sean MacEntee, Countess Markievicz, Joseph McDonagh, Joseph McGuinness, Sean Milroy, Sean T. O'Kelly, Count Plunkett, Grace Gifford Plunkett, Fr Matt Ryan, Fr Thomas Wall, J. J. Walsh.

Cathal Brugha proposed the Constitution, and Sean Milroy seconded it on 25 October. The meeting began with Brugha barely consenting to sit in the same room with Griffith, and with Michael Collins and Rory O'Connor walking out and being brought back by de Valera. Clearly, even then there were cracks in the 'Republicanism' and these would widen until the treaty split.

De Valera devised the following formula to open the Ard Fheis: 'Sinn Féin aims at securing the international recognition of Ireland as an independent Irish Republic. Having achieved that status the Irish people may by referendum freely choose their own form of government'. He subsequently closed the Ard Fheis declaring: 'We are not doctrinaire Republicans'.

On 18 April 1918 a national conference was convened in the Mansion House by the Rt Hon Laurence O'Neill, Lord Mayor of Dublin. All sections of 'nationalist' opinion formed the 'National Cabinet': the Irish Parliamentary Party was represented by Joe Devlin and John Dillon, Sinn Féin by de Valera and Griffith, the dissident element of the old Home Rule Party by F. J. Healy and William O'Brien, the Irish Labour Party by Michael J. Egan (Cork), Thomas Johnson (Belfast) and William O'Brien (Dublin), and the Independents by T. M. Healy. The conference was convened primarily as a protest against conscription measures which were passed by parliament on 16 April 1918: 'The attempt to enforce conscription will be unwarrantable aggression which we call upon all true Irishmen to resist by the most effective means at their disposal'.[18] The Catholic hierarchy concurred with this declaration at their annual meeting at Maynooth and declared in a manifesto: 'We consider that conscription forced in this way upon Ireland is an oppressive and inhuman law which the Irish people have a right to resist by every means that are consonant with the law of God'.[19] On 17 May the British authorities decided not to implement conscription in Ireland, but by then the reaction had solidified support for Sinn Féin.

On 7 January 1919 twenty-six Sinn Féin representatives met and made arrangements to convene the First Dáil Éireann. As a result, on Tuesday 21 January 1919 the First Dáil met in the Mansion House. At 3.30 pm, in the Round Room, Count Plunkett called the meeting to order and nominated Cathal Brugha to be Ceann Comhairle (Speaker/Chairperson) for Dáil Éireann. This was seconded by Padraig O'Maille. Twenty-eight TDs attended (*An Poblacht*, 20 January 2000; Holt claims there were twenty-seven, *Protest in Arms*, London: Putnam, 1960, p. 171). Cathal Brugha presided thereafter: 'Deputies, you understand from what is asserted in this Declaration that we are now done with England. Let the world know it and those who are concerned bear it in mind.' Opening prayers were read by Fr Michael O' Flanagan.

The Declaration of Independence was passed. Cathal Brugha read it in Irish, Eamonn Duggan in English, and George Gavan Duffy read it in French (the Provisional Constitution and Declaration of Independence were drafted by Piaras Béaslaí, Con Collins, George Gavan Duffy, Sean T. O'Kelly, James O'Mara and J. J. Walsh). The 'Message to Free Nations' was read by Robert Barton in English and by J. J. O'Kelly in Irish – the answer to the roll call for thirty-four absent members was 'imprisoned by the foreign enemy', and for three absent members 'deported by the foreign enemy'. Answering 'present' were twenty-eight Sinn Féin TDs out of a total of 104 names called, including all other parties. Even Ulster's Carson had received an invitation – in Irish. Some TDs were elected for two constituencies, so there were only sixty-nine persons elected. Two were ill, others had been deported, five were on missions abroad, but the preponderance were in gaol in England (Michael Collins and Harry Boland were in England working on de Valera's escape from prison but were marked present to keep others from asking where they were). Thirty-three per cent of Dáil members were under thirty-five years and another 40% were between 35 and 40. There were only two Protestant members: Ernest Blythe and Robert Barton.

---

18. Kee, Robert, *The Green Flag* (combining three separate volumes entitled *The Most Distressful Country*, *The Bold Fenian Men* and *Ourselves Alone*), 1972, p. 619.

19. Ibid

The officers elected were: President, Eamon de Valera; Vice Presidents, Arthur Griffith and Father O'Flanagan; Secretaries, Austin Stack and Darrell Figgis; Treasurers, W. T. Cosgrave and Laurence Ginnell. The Executive elected was: Harry Boland, Michael Collins, Sean T. O'Kelly, Sean MacEntee, J. J. Walsh and Kathleen Clarke. Clerks appointed were: Risteard O'Fogladha (Chief Clerk), Sean Nunan, Diarmuid O'Hegarty and Patrick Sheehan. The photo taken that day showed twenty-four attendees.

On 1 April 1919 a Private Session of the First Dáil was held. The Ceann Comhairle was Sean T. O'Kelly. Eamon de Valera presided and named the Cabinet as follows:

*Minister of Home Affairs: Arthur Griffith (arrested); succeeded by Austin Stack (arrested); succeeded by Charles Quinlan*

*Minister of Defence: Cathal Brugha; Deputy: William Considine (Richard Mulcahy was Minister from January to April, when he became Assistant Minister under Brugha; he became the Volunteer Chief of Staff)*

*Minister of Fine Arts and of Foreign Affairs: Count George Noble Plunkett; Under-Secretary for Foreign Affairs: Robert Brennan*

*Minister of Labour: Countess Markievicz (first European female minister; when she was appointed, she was in an English prison)*

*Minister of Industries: Eoin MacNeill*

*Minister of Finance: Michael Collins*

*Minister of Education: Michael Hayes*

*Minister of Trade and Commerce: Ernest Blythe*

*Minister of Local Government: W. T. Cosgrave; succeeded by Kevin O'Higgins, assisted by Rory O'Connor*

*Minister of Propaganda: Laurence Ginnell; succeeded by Desmond FitzGerald (arrested in February 1921); succeeded by Erskine Childers*

*Minister of Agriculture: Robert Barton; succeeded by Art O'Connor.*

On 10 April 1919 the Second Public Session of the First Dáil was held. The photo taken on this day is the one most usually seen of the members of the First Dáil. On 17 June 1919 the Third Public Session of the First Dáil was convened. This established the Consular Service and the National Arbitration Courts. The Trustees of the Dáil Loan were appointed as follows: Eamon de Valera, Most Rev Dr Michael Fogarty (Bishop of Killaloe) and James O'Mara. The Fourth Public Session of the First Dáil was held on 19 August 1919. It established the 'Republican Courts'; these were set up under Austin Stack, Minister of Justice, and had civil and criminal jurisdiction. The rules of Court were drawn up by young barristers from the Law Library in Dublin's Four Courts, under the direction of King's Counsel James Creed Meredith, who later became President of the Supreme Court.

On 20 August 1919 in Private Session certain Volunteers took an Oath of Allegiance to the Dáil. The oath, moved by Cathal Brugha and seconded by Terence MacSwiney, was:

*I ____ do solemnly swear (or affirm) that I do not, and shall not, yield a voluntary support to any pretended Government, Authority, or Power inside Ireland hostile or inimical thereto; and I do further swear (or affirm) that to the best of my knowledge and ability I shall support and defend the Irish Republic, which is Dáil Éireann, against all enemies foreign and domestic, and that I will bear true faith and allegiance to the same and that I take this obligation freely without any mental reservation or purpose of evasion. So help me God.*

*Dáil Éireann in session, Mansion House, Dublin, August 1921*
*(E. & S. Ltd. Dublin. Photo: Hogan, Dublin)*

The oath was to be taken by all Dáil Deputies, all Volunteers, all officials and clerks of the Dáil, and 'any other body or individual who, in the opinion of the Dáil, should take the same oath'. It was only in 1921 that Oscar Traynor, O/C of the Dublin Brigade, told his Volunteers that their 'activities would be directed by GHQ, and the Government of the Republic will accept full responsibility for your operations against the enemy and for your future welfare'.

On 10 September 1919 the Dáil was officially suppressed as a 'Dangerous Association'. But on 27 October 1919 the Fifth Public Session of the First Dáil was held in the Oak Room. On October 1919 the Oath of Allegiance was taken by all deputies and officials. On 29 June 1920 the Dáil established Courts[20] of Justice and Equity, appointing James Creed Meredith as President of the Supreme Court, with Arthur Clery and Diarmuid Crowley as the other members of that Court. It appointed Cahir Davitt as a High Court Justice.

The Second Dáil was elected on 19 May 1921 in the Twenty-Six Counties and on 24 May in the Six Counties. This election became known as the 'Partition Election' because it was the first time in which an election in the Six Counties was held at a different time to that for the Twenty-Six Counties. All 'nationalist' parties agreed not to run against Sinn Féin, and the Six Counties were to elect thirteen representatives to Westminster and the Twenty-Six Counties were to send thirty-three. This was also the election in which proportional representation was introduced to Ireland on a national level. (It had been used on 15 January 1920 in urban and borough elections and on 15 June for county council elections.) In the Twenty-Six Counties, no elections were needed. All of the 124 seats filled by the popular election and the four seats allocated to the National

---

20. Ryan, Desmond, *Sean Treacy*, from 'The Active Service Unit', *Dublin Brigade Review*, p. 75.

University were given to men and women pledged to the Irish Republic. The entire elected opposition consisted of the four men returned by TCD unopposed. Churchill remarked that: 'From that moment, the position of Ulster became unassailable'.[21]

On 8 July 1921 a consultation was convened by de Valera preparatory to a truce; it was attended by Lord Mayor Larry O'Neill, General Macready, Lord Middleton (Southern Unionists), Arthur Griffith and Robert Barton. James Craig from Ulster refused to attend. The following day the terms of the truce were agreed upon and settled at a 3.00 pm meeting between Gen Sir Neville Macready, Col J. Brind and A. W. Cope for the British, and R. C. Barton and E. J. Duggan for the IRA. The terms went into effect at noon on 11 July 1921.

The First Session of the Second Dáil was held on 16 August 1921 in the Round Room. There were 130 Republican TDs, 6 Nationalist TDs and 44 Unionist TDs (who absented themselves as usual). All TDs took the oath to the Dáil. On 17 August the Dáil's Foreign Representatives were named as follows: John Chartres (Germany), Harry Boland (USA), Sean T. O'Kelly (Paris), George Gavan Duffy (Rome), Art O'Brien (London), Dr Patrick McCartan (Russia), Eamon Bulfin (Argentina), Frank W. Egan (Chile)

On 26 August the Cabinet and Ministers were elected as follows:

*Minister of Foreign Affairs: Arthur Griffith*
*Minister of Home Affairs: Austin Stack*
*Minister of Defence: Cathal Brugha*
*Minister of Finance: Michael Collins*
*Minister of Local Government: W. T. Cosgrave*
*Minister of Economic Affairs: Robert Barton.*

The following were elected Ministers outside the Cabinet:

*Minister of Fine Arts: Count Plunkett*
*Minister of Propaganda: Desmond FitzGerald*
*Minister of Education: J. J. O'Kelly*
*Minister of Labour: Countess Markievicz*
*Minister of Trade and Commerce: Ernest Blythe*
*Minister of Agriculture: Art O'Connor*
*Minister of Fisheries: Sean Etchingham*
*Minister of Lands: Patrick J. Hogan*
*Minister of Posts and Telegraphs: J. J. Walsh*
*Kevin O'Higgins was elected as a Minister to assist W. T. Cosgrave in Local Government*

On 14 September 1921 the plenipotentiaries were chosen for the treaty negotiations as follows: Robert Barton, Michael Collins, George Gavan Duffy, Eamonn Duggan, Arthur Griffith. On 15 September de Valera proposed that the Army (IRA) 'be put on a regular basis.' The Cabinet, in late November, affirmed: 'The supreme body directing the Army is the Cabinet. The immediate executive representative of the Government is the Minister of Defence who is, therefore, Administrative Head of the Army. The Minister

---

21. Macardle, Dorothy, *The Irish Republic*, 1937, 1965, p. 456.

of Defence is a civilian. All Army appointments are to be sanctioned by the Minister of Defence, who is to have the power of nomination and veto.'

On 30 September 1921 de Valera issued a final 'acceptance' of the Treaty Conference 'Terms':

IRISH REBELLION, MAY 1916

ED. de VALERA
(Commandant of the Ringsend Area).
Sentenced to Death;
Sentence commuted to Penal Servitude for Life.

*We have received your letter of invitation to a Conference in London on October 11th 'with a view to ascertaining how the association of Ireland with the community of nations known as the British Empire may best be reconciled with Irish national aspirations'.*

*Our respective positions have been stated and are understood and we agree that conference, not correspondence, is the most practical and hopeful way to an understanding. We accept the invitation, and our Delegates will meet you in London on the date mentioned 'to explore every possibility of settlement by personal discussion'.*

On 7 October letters were issued to the plenipotentiaries.

*TO ALL WHOM THESE PRESENTS COME, GREETING:*

*In virtue of the authority vested in me by Dáil Éireann, I hereby appoint Arthur Griffith, T.D., Minister of Foreign Affairs, Chairm., Michael Collins, T. D., Minister of Finance, Robert C. Barton, T. D., Minister for Economic Affairs, Edmund J. Duggan, T. D., George Gavan Duffy, T. D. As Envoys Plenipotentiary from the Elected Government of the REPUBLIC OF IRELAND to negotiate and conclude on behalf of Ireland with the representatives of his Britannic Majesty, GEORGE V, a Treaty or Treaties of Settlement, Association, and Accommodation between Ireland and the community of nations known as the British Commonwealth.*

*IN WITNESS WHEREOF I hereunto subscribe my name as President.*

*[signed] Eamon de Valera*

*Done in the City of Dublin this 7th day of October in the year of our Lord 1921 in five identical originals.*

On 6 December 1921 the Treaty was signed in London and two days later the Cabinet met. Those in attendance were Robert Barton, Cathal Brugha, Michael Collins, W. T. Cosgrave, Eamon de Valera, Arthur Griffith, Austin Stack, Erskine Childers and Gavan Duffy. Brugha, de Valera and Stack voted against the Treaty. Barton (reluctantly), Michael Collins, Cosgrave and Griffith voted for it. That evening de Valera issued a 'Proclamation to the Irish People' indicating he could not recommend acceptance of the Treaty.

*Sinn Féin Flag*

On 14 December 1921 the Dáil assembled but there was no 'debate' on the Treaty, just the discussion of the actions of the plenipotentiaries in signing the Treaty without 'permission' from the Cabinet. The next day the Dáil assembled in private session and de Valera proposed his 'External Association'/Document Number Two. It was rejected and he 'withdrew' it asking that it to be held as confidential. On 19 December the debates continued, but the Dáil adjourned on the motion of Michael Collins to reassemble on 3 January 1922. The debates were continued in the Convocation Hall of the National University in Earlsfort Terrace.

On 12 January 1922 the Dáil delegates again assembled in the Oak Room of the Mansion House following the Treaty debates and vote at Earlsfort Terrace. On 14 January officers and ministers of the Provisional Government were elected as follows:

*Arthur Griffith: President*
*Michael Collins: Minister of Finance*
*William Cosgrave: Minister of Local Government*
*Eamonn Duggan: Minister of Home Affairs*
*Kevin O'Higgins: Minister of Economic Affairs*
*Patrick J. Hogan: Minister of Agriculture (replaced Art O'Connor)*
*Joseph McGrath: Minister of Labour (replaced Countess Markievicz)*
*Michael Hayes: Minister of Education (replaced J. J. O'Kelly)*
*Desmond FitzGerald: Minister of Publicity*
*Ernest Blythe: Minister of Trade and Commerce*
*Fionan Lynch and Eoin MacNeill were added to the Provisional Government*
*The Ministers of the Dáil became Ministers of the Provisional Government.*

On 22 January the Belfast Boycott was initiated. On 21 February the Civic Guard, An Garda Síochána, was established. The draft Constitution was ready to be examined by T. H. Healy and George O'Brien by 15 March 1922. The committee which was established to draft the Constitution was chaired by Michael Collins, but Darrell Figgis wrote most of it. The Committee members were: Collins, James Douglas, Darrell Figgis, C. P. France, Hugh Kennedy, James Murnahan, John O'Byrne, James O'Neill, Alfred O'Reilly and Kevin O' Sheil. Figgis was the Deputy Chairman of the Committee (that same year he wrote a book: *The Irish Constitution Explained)*.

On 26 March 1922 the IRA Convention was convened in the Mansion House. Over 230 delegates attended, representing forty-nine brigades of the IRA and claiming to represent approximately 95,000 members of the organisation (about 80% of its membership). The meeting went forward despite the fact that Richard Mulcahy, as Minister of Defence, tried to avoid convening a body that was clearly Anti-Treaty

Only Anti-Treaty men attended the Convention. It was adjourned until 9 April when Liam Lynch was elected chairman. The control of the IRA was turned over to a sixteen-man 'Executive' and Liam Lynch was named Chief of Staff. The Executive also included: Frank Barrett, Liam Deasy, Joseph Griffin (Director of Intelligence), Tom Hales, Michael Kilroy, Tom McGuire, Joe McKelvey (Deputy Chief of Staff), Liam Mellowes (Quartermaster General), Sean Moylan, Joseph O'Connor, Rory O'Connor (Director of Engineering), Peadar O'Donnell, Florrie O'Donoghue (Adjutant General), Seamus O'Donovan (Director of Chemicals), Sean O'Hegarty, Ernie O'Malley (Director of Organisation), Liam Pilkington, Seamus Robinson, Sean Russell (Director of Ammunition) and P. J. Ruttledge. (Twelve members of the Executive were in the Four Courts when it was attacked – Liam Lynch had left the building shortly before the attack and was arrested but then released because Mulcahy hoped he would be an influence for peace.) The Convention demanded that the recruitment for the Civic Guard and the Beggar's Bush Army of the Republic cease immediately. On 9 April this Convention of the IRA narrowly rejected a proposal for a Republican military dictatorship.

On 26 April a Labour Party Conference was held, convened by Dr Byrne, Archbishop of Dublin, Lord Mayor O'Neill and Stephen O'Mara of Limerick. William O'Brien, Tom Johnson and Cathal O'Shannon were among those who attended. The Conference made proposals to all parties for: a return to the Dáil's sovereignty; the unification of the Army; the establishment of a police force under civilian control; a revised electoral register. It proposed a meeting between Arthur Griffith and Michael Collins, de Valera and Cathal Brugha, and the Republican Army Executive but Griffith and Collins refused to attend.

On 4 May 1922 a conference was held between the Free State Army leaders and the IRA. The two factions declared a truce to last while the conference continued, then an open truce was agreed upon. The objective was to try to reunify the Army and avert a civil war. The Free State Army was represented by Michael Collins, Sean MacEoin, Richard Mulcahy, Eoin O'Duffy, Diarmuid O'Hegarty and Gearóid O'Sullivan. The IRA was represented by Liam Lynch, Liam Mellowes, Sean Moylan, Rory O'Connor and Seamus Robinson. The parties presented conflicting reports to the Dáil on 16 May.

On 3 June 1922 the Collins/de Valera Election Manifesto was agreed and on 15 June the Constitution was published. The next day a general election was held. The turnout was just less than 60% and the results were announced on 24 June. The Pro-Treaty party received 239,193 votes and 58 of its members were elected to the Dáil as TDs. The Anti-Treaty party (Cumann na Poblachta) received 133,864 votes and a representation of 36 TDs. Seventeen TDs were elected for the Labour Party, 7 for the Farmers Party, 6 Independents and 4 TDs for Trinity College. Anti-Treatyites won only 5 of 44 seats in Leinster and did poorly in Ulster and in Cork City. Connaught produced a small Anti-Treaty majority and Munster a small Pro-Treaty majority. A total of 466,419 electors voted for the Treaty and 133,864 voted against it. The Anti-Treaty candidates would have done considerably worse had there not been an election panel, pursuant to the Collins-de Valera Pact.

The election was notable for the large anti-Sinn Féin vote. It did not however represent a vote of confidence in the Provisional Government, and still less an expression of resistance to Republican ideals. It represented a popular realisation of the need for stable government, and the acceptance of realistic compromise with regard to Anglo-Irish relations. Settled conditions were more important to the electorate than the endless debate over constitutional authority. The election had an important role in legitimising the Treaty and the status of the Provisional Government. Although it did not prevent the Civil War, it greatly helped to facilitate the establishment of the Free State government during and after the War.

On 18 June 1922 an Extraordinary Convention of the Republican Army was held. Tom Barry suggested there should be an immediate attack on the British. A majority of the executive were in favour of this. Cathal Brugha opposed the suggestion, as did Liam Lynch, Liam Deasy, Frank Barrett and Sean Moylan. The twelve who favoured the action were subsequently in the Four Courts, repudiated the authority of Liam Lynch, and appointed Joe McKelvey Chief of Staff.

On 12 July Michael Collins resigned as Head of State, and thereafter acted as Army O/C. The First Session of the Third Dáil was convened for 9 September 1922. It met in Leinster House in Kildare Street, where it meets to this day. This Dáil was never 'accepted' by the Republicans, and the Second Dáil remains the 'Provisional Government' of Ireland, according to strict Republican doctrine.

**Dawson Street** (at Nassau Street): Morrison's Hotel: Charles Stewart Parnell was arrested here on 13 October 1881.

**2 Dawson Street**: Irish Volunteer HQ prior to the Rising (see 206 Great Brunswick Street). *Irish Volunteer* was printed here, edited by Eoin MacNeill. On 22 May 1914, Padraig Pearse wrote in it: 'We want recruits because we are absolutely determined to take action, the moment action becomes a duty....' P. S. O'Hegarty was a member of the Supreme Council of the IRB from 1908 until he was deported to Wales in August 1914. He wrote: 'The Insurrection of 1916 came because the Supreme Council of the Irish Republican Brotherhood decided that it would come....It was the Supreme Council of the I.R.B. which decided the Insurrection, planned it, organised it, led it and financed it.'[22] The paper was suppressed and subsequently re-issued by a pro-Unionist printer in Belfast. The last issue was dated 22 April 1916. The Fianna also had an office here. Michael O'Hanrahan worked here as a clerk before the Rising. Claire Gregan, who later married him, was Bulmer Hobson's secretary.

---

22. O'Hegarty, P. S., *The Victory of Sinn Féin*, 1924, 1998, p. 2.

In 1914, the General Council of the Volunteers consisted of Eoin Mac Neill (President), Pearse, Plunkett, MacDonagh, Ceannt, McDermott, Hobson and a representative from each county. The Volunteer HQ Staff were:

*Eoin MacNeill: Chief of Staff*
*Bulmer Hobson: Quartermaster General*
*∗Padraig Pearse: Director of Organisation*
*∗Joseph Plunkett: Director of Military Operations*
*∗Eamonn Ceannt: Director of Communications*
*Thomas MacDonagh: Director of Training*
*The O'Rahilly: Director of Arms*
*Sean Fitzgibbon: Director of Recruiting (moderate, ally of MacNeill/Hobson) J. J. O'Connell: Chief of Inspection (had the best military mind in the Volunteers; moderate, ally of MacNeill/Hobson)*
*(∗As late as August 1915, these three were the only members of the HQ staff who knew what was really being planned for the Volunteers.)*
*The Volunteers had to reorganise after the split with Redmond's National Volunteers in September 1914. This formal reorganisation took place at their Convention on 25 October 1914.*

**21 Dawson Street**: home of Ms Eileen MacGrane; she was a lecturer at the National University (now UCD). The house was raided on 31 December 1920; Ned Broy's documents were found here, leading to his arrest, and MacGrane was imprisoned until 1 January 1921. Part-time office for Michael Collins and Ernie O'Malley.

**48 Dawson Street**: Royal Hibernian Hotel; second Dublin home of the Arthur Hamilton Norway family. Tom Barry stayed here in February 1923 when he met with Liam Lynch and tried to convince him to hold a Republican/IRA Executive meeting to determine how to put an end to the Civil War.

**56-58 Dawson Street**: Hodges & Figgis Books, associated with Darrell Figgis. Ms Susan Killeen worked here; she was one of Michael Collins's most valuable couriers and 'The Bookshop' became a veritable post office for messages to Collins.

**DeCourcy Square**: home of Mr and Mrs John O'Mahony. Volunteers from the country often stayed here, and it was frequently raided. Liam Lynch stayed here when he came to Dublin.

**Denzille Lane**: 'National' Republican/IRA munitions factory during the Civil War

**12 D'Olier Street**: office of *Nationality*; Bulmer Hobson was the first editor, then Arthur Griffith and Sean T. O'Kelly (Seamus O'Kelly immediately followed Griffith, but died of a heart attack on 11 November 1918 when there was a riot outside the office in celebration of the Armistice). *Nationality* was suppressed after the Rising and printed in Belfast. John Chartres was a lead writer and contributor from 1917 onward, though not always under his own name. His first submission, on 6 October 1917, was an editorial on the death of Thomas Ashe. At the time he was still working in the Intelligence Section of the British Ministry of Munitions.

**12 D'Olier Street**: second office of *Irish Freedom–Saoirse* run by Sean MacDermott; it was suppressed in late 1914.

**13 D'Olier Street**: Protestant Defence Association of the Church of Ireland; managed by a retired army officer, Captain Robert Wade Thompson, who was also Secretary of the Reformed Priests Protection Society and one of Dublin's High Sheriffs.

*James Connolly, who was executed 9 May, 1916*

**Dolphin's Barn, Dublin**: Connolly was 'kidnapped' on 19 January 1916 and 'held' in a brickworks here until 22 January. An agreement was reached for the ICA and Volunteers to work together towards a Rising at Easter. Connolly agreed to abandon his openly declared intention to strike independently with the ICA. Prior to this, Connolly had been regarded by the Military Council as endangering the ICA's plans and he suspected them as 'would be Wolfe Tones – legally seditious and peacefully revolutionary'. His writings in *The Worker's Republic* week by week had intensified the lack of understanding between the Volunteers and the ICA. The Military Council simply preferred its own plans and timing for the Rising.

There has always been speculation about Connolly's disappearance, and recent authors have concluded that he met agreeably with the Military Council, and was not forcibly kidnapped and detained for the three days. Particularly so since even Mallin realised that the British were not likely to 'take' Connolly and leave the other ICA and Volunteer leaders in place, and the Volunteers really didn't want to kidnap him. Upon his return, he went to Countess Markievicz's home. When asked the next day by Bill O'Brien, he would not tell O'Brien where he had been. To Helena Mooney he refused also ('That would be telling you'), though his final word to her was that he 'had walked 40 miles that day'. To Markievicz he said he had been 'through hell'. The 'latest' theories seem to concur only that Connolly spent those three days in secret consultation, probably with Pearse, Clarke and Plunkett, and that he did so either on his own initiative and/or their invitation, without any element of coercion or military detention being involved.

In any case, from February 1916 onward, the 'War Parties' in the ICA, IRB and the Volunteers were a united bloc. Volunteers Frank Daly and Eamonn Dore were the ones who took him to Dolphin's Barn.

2 **Dolphin's Terrace, Dolphin's Barn/Rialto** (off South Circular Road and Herberton Road): Eamonn and Áine Ceannt's home. Ceannt was quite tall at about six feet and was an excellent musician, playing the uilleann pipes before Pope Pius X in Rome in 1908. His father was a member of the RIC, and Eamonn was said to have been born in the RIC Barracks in Ballymoe. He taught at St Enda's. He was an official in the City Treasurer's Office of Dublin Corporation. In the first week of February 1916, there was a meeting of Ceannt, Clarke, Connolly, MacDermott and Pearse (MacDonagh and Plunkett were absent). These men formed the entire Military Council. Connolly had agreed to abandon his openly declared intention to strike independently with the ICA, and he attended all Military Council meetings thereafter. Of all the members of the Council, Ceannt was closest to Connolly's social views, though Pearse was nearly so.

Irish Rebellion, May, 1916.

*Arrest of Edmund Kent, at 4 a.m. He was subsequently shot.*

*Arrest of Eamonn Ceannt*

**Dominick Street Lower**: St Saviour's Church; opened in 1861 by the Dominican Fathers. James Boland was buried from here.

**13, 14 Dominick Street Lower**: these houses were held by Republican/IRA forces until driven out.

**25 Dominick Street Lower**: St Mary's National School (since demolished); attended by Sean O'Casey.

**4 Dominick Street Upper**: Arthur Griffith's birthplace (since demolished); he became a printer by trade.

**Donnybrook, Dublin**: Montrose House, the ancestral home of the Jamesons of Donnybrook. Guglielmo Marconi was their grandson.

**Donnybrook, Dublin**: Dublin Metropolitan Police Station; Sgt Mannix, an undercover IRA agent, was stationed here. He obtained the names and addresses of all the senior British secret service men sent from England, and he gave them to Frank Thornton. This formed a great deal of the information Michael Collins used for the Squad's raids on Bloody Sunday.

**68 Dorset Street Lower**: birthplace of Peadar Kearney in 1883; well-known poet and writer, he wrote the words to *A Soldier's Song*. His nephew was the writer Brendan Behan. Kearney was a house-painter by trade, but preferred to work as a stage hand at the Abbey Theatre.

**75 Dorset Street Lower**: Keogh Bros Ltd, photographers, who produced several postcards showing ruined buildings and Dublin streetscapes after the 1916 Rising.

**85 Dorset Street Upper**: birthplace of Sean O'Casey in 1880, christened John Casey.

**87 Dorset Street Upper**: office of *Irish Fun*, 'A Magazine for Boys and Girls', edited by Brian O'Higgins.

**Drumcondra**: Archbishop Dr William Walsh's House. His feelings had always been nationalistic, but he thought the Rising 'madness'. Count Plunkett went to inform him of the Rising as Plunkett had been asked to do by the Pope. Walsh was ill and Plunkett was giving the message to his secretary, Fr Curran, when word came of the fighting at the GPO. De Valera stayed in the Gate Lodge here in February and March 1919 prior to leaving for New York.

**Drumcondra**: Police Detective Cpt Patrick Smith's home; known as 'Dog Smith', he was killed here on 30 July 1919. He was the first member of 'G-Division' to be killed.

**Dublin Castle**: Construction began in 1204 under the orders of King John. The entrance used to be on Castle Street, now the main route is on Lord Edward Street. The Statue of 'Justice' is above the old Castle Gate; small holes are drilled in her scales to drain water so they don't become 'unbalanced' in the rain:

*The Statue of Justice*
*Mark well her station*
*Her face to the Castle*
*And her arse to the Nation.*

The Church of the Most Holy Trinity in the Castle is a Catholic Church since 1943; it was the Viceroy's Chapel at the time of the Rising. *Hue and Cry* was the official police paper of Dublin Castle. When the Rising began the Castle was quite empty of British troops, it was a Bank Holiday and many had gone to the Fairyhouse Races. As the Rising continued, the Castle filled up with troops and was not attacked by the rebels. A sniper in the Bermingham Tower was responsible for fifty-three rebel casualties before he was killed on Saturday.

Sir James McMahon was director of the Posts and Telegraphs Office here. In 1918–1919 he hired Nancy O'Brien, Michael Collins's second cousin, to decode messages in his office. Nancy married Johnny Collins (Michael's brother) after Johnny's wife died leaving eight children.

Cpts King and Hardy led the intelligence officers in the Castle at this time. They beat Christopher Carberry and made him drink his own blood. They beat Ernie O'Malley unconscious; he gave them the name Bernard Stewart, and gave no information. They were the ones who interrogated Peadar Clancy, Dick McKee and Conor Clune on Bloody Sunday and murdered them 'trying to escape'. The Castle was formally handed over to Michael Collins and the Free State Forces on 16 January 1922 by Lord Edward Talbot Fitzallen, Lord Lieutenant of Ireland, who said: 'I am glad to see you, Mr Collins.' To which Collins replied 'Like hell ye are!' The British O/C was General Macready. Collins arrived late for his meeting with him. To Macready's comment that he was 'seven minutes late,' Collins replied: 'You've been here seven centuries, what bloody difference does seven minutes make now that you're leaving?'

**Duke Street**: Cummiskey's Pub; after the Civil War, it became a Fianna Fáil/Anti-Treaty meeting place.

**2 Duke Street**: The Bailey Pub; upstairs was the smoking room where Parnell and his followers were wont to meet. A barrister/solicitor favourite for those from the Four Courts and surrounding area; a particular favourite of Oliver St John Gogarty. It was also a meeting place for the IRA during the War of Independence. Arthur Griffith liked this pub and in 1922, when the Ministers of the Free State were virtual prisoners in the

*Looking from Nelson Pillar down North Earl Street*
*(W. & G. Baird, Ltd., Belfast)*

Castle, Griffith had food imported from The Bailey! A very popular pub for writers, including Kavanagh, Behan, Gogarty, Padraic Colum, Brian O'Nolan, and a favourite of James Joyce.

**21 Duke Street**: Davy Byrne's Pub; frequented by Michael Collins and Arthur Griffith, as well as Brendan Behan and Padraic O'Connor later.

**Earl Street**: thirty-two buildings were burned here during the Rising, including:

    **3 North Earl Street**: J. J. Lawlor, Catholic art repository

    **4 North Earl Street**: Meagher's

    **5 North Earl Street**: James Winstanley, boot warehouse

    **6, 7 North Earl Street**: Sir Joseph Downes' Restaurant and Confectionery

    **20-22 North Earl Street**: Boyer's drapery shop

    **23, 24 North Earl Street**: Hickey and Co, drapers

    **25 North Earl Street**: Nagle's Pub

    **26 North Earl Street**: Sheridan's Pub (also a grocery); owned by Mrs Elizabeth Sheridan.

    **27 North Earl Street**: Delaney and Co

    **28 North Earl Street**: H. Rowe and Co

    **29-31 North Earl Street**: Tyler's shoe shop, looted during the Rising

    **North Earl Street** (and 34 Sackville Street): Noblett's sweet shop, also looted

    **North Earl Street** (and 32 Sackville Street): Dunne's hatters, also looted

**1 Earlsfort Place**: second home in Dublin of Douglas Hyde, after he moved here from Upper Mount Street; it was later demolished, but prior to that its address became 65 Adelaide Road.

**Earlsfort Terrace**: during the Rising 3rd Battalion A Company mustered here under Cpt Joseph O'Connor who led his men to Grand Canal Street, Upper Lotts Road, and elsewhere. Thirty-four men of 3rd Battalion C Company mustered here under Cpt Simon Donnelly. Donnelly marched his men to Upper Mount Street, where they met Malone and Reynolds and proceeded on to Boland's Bakery.

**Earlsfort Terrace** (at corner of Hatch Street): University College Dublin (UCD); founded in 1851 as the Catholic University of Ireland on St Stephen's Green. A constituent college of the National University of Ireland. In 1879, the University Education (Ireland) Act provided for the formation of a new university in Ireland, named Royal University. Previously, Queen's College was composed of the Universities in Belfast, Cork and Galway. Following this 1879 Act, Queen's College (Cork and Galway branches) was granted a charter and was renamed Royal University, and Queen's College was dissolved on 3 February 1882. In 1908, UCD was incorporated and, combined with the former Queen's Colleges of Cork and Galway, formed the constituent colleges named the National University of Ireland (NUI). It moved to these premises from St Stephen's Green at that time. The Universities Act of 1997 set down the legislative provisions which must be met for an educational institution or college to be established as a university in Ireland. The seven recognised universities are:

*University of Limerick*
*Trinity College, Dublin*
*University College, Dublin*
*University College, Cork*
*National University of Ireland, Galway*
*National University of Ireland, Maynooth*
*Dublin City University.*

Padraig Pearse attended the Catholic University and took a BA in 1901. Oliver St John Gogarty and James Joyce attended UCD at the same time before moving together into the Martello Tower in Sandycove. Joyce paid the rent (£8 annually) and Gogarty furnished the rooms. Dr Denis Coffey was President of UCD in 1916. Kevin Barry enrolled in the autumn of 1919 to study medicine. He joined a UCD Volunteer contingent that included Frank Flood, Tom Kissane, Mark Robinson. They were all on the Church Street ambush. Flood was hanged on 14 March 1921 for 'high treason'.

The 'Treaty Debates' took place here on 19 December 1921. The Dáil assembled in public and 'Document No. Two' was derided by Griffith and Sean Milroy. Griffith moved that the Treaty be ratified and it was seconded by Sean McKeon. The next day the debate continued; de Valera remarked that 'Something else besides the Treaty came from Downing Street'.[23] On 21 December the Dáil adjourned on the motion of Michael Collins to reassemble on 3 January 1922. The debates resumed on that date and continued for five days in the Convocation Hall of the National University of Ireland. On 4 January de Valera 'resigned,' but it was unclear whether he resigned as President or Prime Minister or both.

On 7 January 1922 the Dáil voted 64–57 to ratify the Treaty. (Strangely, a total of 122 TDs had answered the roll for the day.) It was an afternoon meeting, beginning at 4.00 and voting began at 8.35, continuing until 9.00. Several TDs represented more than one constituency (e.g. Collins and de Valera). However, all such TDs cast only one ballot.

---

23. De Burca, Padraig and John Boyle, *Free State or Republic?*, 1922, 2002, p. 18.

Those who voted for the Treaty were:

*Robert Barton, Piaras Béaslaí, Ernest Blythe, Patrick Brennan, Eamon Bulfin, Seamus Burke, C. M. Byrne, T. Carter, Michael Collins, R. Cornish, Philip B. Cosgrave, W. T. Cosgrave, J. Crowley, L. De Roiste, P. Derham, J. N. Dolan, G. Gavin Duffy, E. J. Duggan, Desmond Fitzgerald, Paul Galligan, Arthur Griffith, Sean Hales, Dr Hayes, Michael Hayes, Sean Hayes, William Hayes, P. J. Hogan, Peadar Hughes, Andrew Lavin, Frank Lawless, Sean Leddy, Finian Lynch, Joseph Lynch, Joseph MacBride, Alex McCabe, Patrick McCartan, Daniel McCarthy, Sean McGarry, J. P. McGinley, P. J. McGoldrick, Joseph McGrath, Joseph McGuinness, Justin McKenna, Sean McKeon, Sean Milroy, Richard Mulcahy, James Murphy, G. Nicolls, Thomas O'Donnell, Eoin O'Duffy, J. O'Dwyer, Kevin O'Higgins, P. O'Keefe, Padraig O'Maille, D. O'Rourke, Gearóid O'Sullivan, Lorcan Robbins, William Sears, Michael Staines, Joseph Sweeney, J. J. Walsh, Peter Ward, J. B. Whelehan, Vincent White.*

Those who voted against the Treaty were:

*E. Aylward, Harry Boland, Cathal Brugha, Donal Buckley, Frank Carty, Erskine Childers, Kathleen Clarke, M. P. Colivet, Con Collins, Daniel Corkery, Dr Crowley, Brian Cusack, Eamon Dee, Thomas Derrig, Eamon de Valera, James Devins, Seamus Doyle, Ada English, Sean Etchingham, Frank Fahy, Dr Ferran, James Fitzgerald Jr, Thomas Hunter, David Kent, James Lennon, Joseph MacDonagh, Sean MacEntee, Mary MacSwiney, Sean MacSwiney, Countess Markievicz, Thomas McGuire, Liam Mellowes, P. J. Moloney, Sean Moylan, Charles Murphy, Sean Nolan, P. J. Count O'Byrne, P. S. O'Cahill, Kate O'Callaghan, D. O'Ceallachain, Art O'Connor, T. O'Donoghue, Samuel O'Flaherty, Brian O'Higgins, J. J. O'Kelly ('Sceilg'), Sean T. O'Kelly, Sean O'Mahoney, Margaret Pearse, Count Plunkett, Seamus Robinson, E. Roche, P. J. Rutledge, James Ryan, Philip Shanahan, Austin Stack, W. F. Stockley.*

There were six women TDs. All voted against the Treaty. Four* of the six had lost male relatives in the Rising or the War of Independence: Kathleen (Tomas) Clarke*, Dr Ada English, Mary (Terence) MacSwiney*, Countess Markievicz, Kate (Michael) O'Callaghan* (ex Lord Mayor of Limerick), Margaret (Padraig and Willie) Pearse.
The HQ staff of the IRA was split on the issue. Those against the Treaty were:

*Cathal Brugha: Minister of Defence*
*Austin Stack: formerly Deputy Chief of Staff*
*Liam Mellowes: Director of Purchases*
*Rory O'Connor: Director of Engineering*
*Sean Russell: Director of Munitions*
*Seamus O'Donovan: Director of Chemicals*
*Oscar Traynor: O/C of the Dublin Brigade.*

Those for the Treaty were:

*Richard Mulcahy: Chief of Staff*
*J. J. O'Connell: Assistant Chief of Staff*
*Eoin O'Duffy: Deputy Chief of Staff*

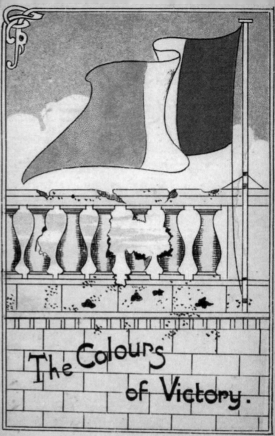

*Selection of commemorative postcards*

*Michael Collins: Director of Intelligence*
*Diarmuid O'Hegarty: Director of Organisation*
*Piaras Béaslaí: Director of Publicity.*

On 9 January de Valera resigned and put himself forward for re-election as President; he was defeated for President on 10 January (60 to 58 votes); Griffith was elected; de Valera did not vote. De Valera's expressed view was that 'The Republic must exist until the people disestablish it'.[24] He also said 'I hope that nobody will talk of fratricidal strife. That is all nonsense. We have a nation that knows how to conduct itself.'[25] On 12 January the Dáil delegates again assembled in the Oak Room of the Mansion House.

**3 Earlsfort Terrace**: home of W. F. Bailey; John Dillon and Sir Matthew Nathan often met here before the Rising.

**17 Earlsfort Terrace**: Oliver St John Gogarty's first home when he married and qualified as a doctor.

24. De Burca, Padraig and John Boyle, *Free State or Republic?*, 1922, 2002, p. 78.
25. Ibid

*Cathal Brugha*

**28 Earlsfort Terrace**: Cpt John Fitzgerald was killed here on Bloody Sunday. He had previously been kidnapped and the IRA attempted to kill him in Co Clare, but he escaped with a dislocated arm and had been sent to Dublin for treatment. The 'Squad' asked for 'LTC Fitzpatrick'. Could it have been mistaken identity?

**132 East Wall Road**: Lawlor's Candles

**Eccles Street**: Lily O'Donnell's Private Nursing Home; often used by the Volunteers and IRA to care for wounded.

**15-17 Eccles Street**: St Mary's College for Girls run by the Dominican order; Louise Gavan Duffy had a job here.

**32-38 Eccles Street** (and Berkeley Road): Mater Misericordiae Hospital. Dan Breen was taken here to recover from the wounds he suffered in the raid on Professor Carolan's home on 11 October 1920. Cathal Brugha died here on 7 July 1922, at age forty-eight. It was a 'First Friday' and he received Communion from Fr Young, a hospital chaplain. The last rites were administered by Fr Francis Ryan. He lay in the chapel here on 8 and 9 July, then the body was taken to St Joseph's Church on Berkeley Road on the evening of 9 July. There was a High Requiem Mass at 10.00 am on the following day and the body was then taken to Glasnevin. He died faithful to the Republic, and to him the Republic and Ireland were inseparable. Of him, Michael Collins said: 'I would forgive him anything. Because of his sincerity, I would forgive him anything. When many of us are forgotten, Cathal Brugha will be remembered.'

**70 Eccles Street**: home of Helena Molony, 'owner' of *The Worker's Republic* on behalf of James Connolly and Countess Markievicz; this was the successor to *The Worker*, which had been suppressed after six issues and which was, itself, the successor to *The Irish Worker* which had been suppressed in December 1914, and finally stopped in February 1915. In September 1914, Connolly wrote: 'A resurrection! Aye, out of the grave of the first Irishman murdered for protesting against Ireland's participation in this thrice-accursed war there will arise a new Spirit of Irish Revolution. We defy you! Do your worst!'

Sean O'Casey was Secretary of the ICA and wrote the 'ICA Notes' in *The Worker* and *The Irish Worker*. He attacked the Volunteers week by week. He demanded that Countess Markievicz sever her ties with the Volunteers; she was vindicated by one vote of the ICA. When his hostility was overruled he resigned and, following his departure, the ICA and the Volunteers started to work together.

**Eden Quay**: a thirty-three year old labourer, James Nolan, was injured in riots during the Lockout on Saturday 30 August 1913; he died in Jervis St Hospital on Sunday morning.

**Eden Quay**: fourteen buildings were burned here during the Rising, including:

**Eden Quay** (and Lower Sackville Street): Hopkins and Hopkins, jewellers and silversmiths; now Irish National Building Society.

1, 2 **Eden Quay**: Barry, O'Moore and Co, accountants and auditors

3 **Eden Quay**: Gerald Mooney, wine and spirit merchant

4 **Eden Quay**: The London and North-Western Railway Co

5 **Eden Quay**: GR Mesias, military tailor

8 **Eden Quay**: The Globe Parcel Express

9 **Eden Quay**: J. Henry Smith, ironmongers

10 **Eden Quay**: Joseph M'Greevy, wine and spirit merchant

11 **Eden Quay**: Douglas Hotel and Restaurant

13 **Eden Quay**: The Mission to Seamen Institute

14 **Eden Quay**: Moore's Pub

*Harry Boland*

**Elm Park**: St Vincent's Hospital (located in St Stephen's Green during the War of Independence and the Civil War); the hospital was established in Stephen's Green in 1834 and was relocated to its present site in Elm Park in 1970. Harry Boland died in St Vincent's and Michael Collins was 'laid out' in the Mortuary Chapel before being removed to the Pro-Cathedral for burial. Oliver St John Gogarty and Desmond FitzGerald supervised the embalming. Gogarty sent Sean Kavanagh for sculptor Albert Power to fashion Michael Collins's death mask. Dr Richard Tobin was a surgeon in St Vincent's at the time.

**Ely Place**: surgeon Sir Thornley Stoker's home. The house was originally built circa 1770 by the Marquis of Ely; it is said to have the best Georgian stucco of any house in Dublin.

4 **Ely Place**: birthplace of John Philpott Curran in 1750; later the home of George Moore

15 **Ely Place**: home of Oliver St John Gogarty (now demolished); the house was a Queen Anne house 'modernised' by Sir Thomas Dean, architect of the National Library and Museum. After the Treaty was signed, Michael Collins often came here. Senator Gogarty was kidnapped from here on 12 January 1922 by the Republicans/IRA but escaped by diving into the Liffey.

**Emerald Square, Dolphin's Barn** (off Cork Street): the 4th Battalion of the Volunteers mustered here under Eamonn Ceannt.

33 **Emorville Road** (South Circular Road): first Dublin home of George Russell (AE)

6 **Essex Street West**: home of Henry B. Knowles, killed during the Rising

**Eustace Street**: Gearóid O'Sullivan's GHQ Office

**Exchange Street Lower**: Catholic Church of Saints Michael and John; the sound of the Angelus Bell ringing over the river Liffey was heard by the Irish Citizen Army as they marched up Dame Street to seize City Hall.

**Exchequer Street**: one of Kevin O'Higgins' offices as Minister of Local Government

10 **Exchequer Street**: Irish National Aid Association, first under the direction of George

Gavan Duffy and Alderman Corrigan, combined with Kathleen Clarke's Irish Volunteers' Dependents' Fund to form the Irish National Aid and Volunteers' Dependents' Fund; this was the first 'real' office: Kathleen Clarke, President; Áine Ceannt, Vice President; Maire Nic Shiubhlaigh, Treasurer; E. MacRaghaill, Secretary. Michael Collins worked here after the Rising, starting on 19 February 1917 at a salary of £2. 10s a week. The football match arranged at Croke Park on Bloody Sunday was held as a benefit for this Fund; about £500 was raised.

**Fairview Strand**: Gilbey's Wine Branch Depot; on the north-west side of the Tolka Bridge. Harry Boland fought here during the Rising with the Volunteers commanded by Frank Henderson, before going with them to the GPO.

**Fairview Strand**: Lambe's Pub; on the north-east side of Tolka Bridge. There was a small garrison here under the command of Sean Russell, before going to the GPO with the rest of Henderson's men.

**Findlater Place**: Findlater Building; directly across from Thomas's Lane which ran parallel to Lower Sackville Street and behind 'the Block'. The shot that killed Cathal Brugha was fired from this building according to John Pinkman.

**5 Findlater Place**: office of *Irish Freedom-Saoirse*; 'official' publication of the IRB. The first 'Republican' newspaper was *Northern Star*, published on 4 January 1792 by the Belfast Society of United Irishmen; the proprietor was John Rabb; its offices were raided in January 1793, again on 16 September 1796, and it finally closed on 19 May 1797. It was followed by *The Press* on 28 September 1797.

The establishment of this paper, *Irish Freedom-Saoirse*, is generally credited to Tom Clarke. As soon as he returned to Ireland he recognised the need for a newspaper, but it took him some time to raise the funds. By 1910 he succeeded in getting sufficient funds to make a start. The original committee of IRB men at the time was: Dr Pat McCartan, John Daly, Bulmer Hobson, Sean MacDermott, Ernest Blythe, Denis McCullough and Clarke. The paper was originally published as a monthly under the cover of the Dublin Wolfe Tone Clubs Committee. Sean MacDermott (MacDiarmada) was manager. Dr Pat McCartan was first editor, then MacDermott. Started in October 1910, its first issue appeared on 15 November 1910; Bulmer Hobson and P. S. O'Hegarty did most of the writing. Contributors included: Piaras Béaslaí, Ernest Blythe, Roger Casement, Fred Cogley, Pat Devlin, Joe W. Good, P. S. O'Hegarty, Bulmer Hobson, Terence MacSwiney, Padraig Pearse and Sean O'Casey. The true purpose of its IRB sponsors was made clear in its first issue:

*We believe in and would work for the independence of Ireland ... and we use the term with no reservation, stated or implied; we stand for the complete and total separation of Ireland from England and the establishment of an Irish Republic.... Freedom can take but one form amongst us – a Republic.*

In an early issue, P. S. O'Hegarty concluded an article thus: 'Concessions be damned, England, we want our country!' In December 1910, O'Hegarty wrote: 'History has a fashion of repeating itself, and we welcome with a shout this revival of public arming in Ulster. One hundred and thirty years ago it began also in Ulster, but it did not end there, it only ended where the four seas of Ireland stopped it.'

**Finglas Road**: Glasnevin Cemetery; officially opened in 1832, it is the largest cemetery in Ireland, opened after a series of events prompted Daniel O'Connell to establish a burial place for the Catholic nation of Ireland (the O'Connell Tower in the cemetery rises to a height of 164 feet). The land was consecrated by Monsignor Yore in September 1831 and its first internee, Michael Carey, was buried in February 1832. All graves were dug by hand until 1972 when the first machine was used. Among others, the following are buried in Glasnevin, many in 'The Republican Plot':

*William Phillip Allen (Manchester Martyr)*
*Thomas Ashe*
*Kevin Barry*
*Piaras Béaslaí*
*Brendan Behan*
*Harry Boland*
*Cathal Brugha (Charles William St John Burgess)*
*Roger Casement*
*Erskine Childers*
*Molly Childers*
*Peadar Clancy*
*J. J. Coade*
*Michael Collins*
*Kitty Kiernan Cronin*
*James Daley (Connaught Ranger Mutiny)*
*Eamon de Valera (Sinead)*
*Anne Devlin  (Robert Emmett's housekeeper)*
*John Devoy*
*Thomas Dickson*
*Charles Gavan Duffy*
*Arthur Griffith*
*Grace Gifford (Plunkett)*
*Peadar Kearney*
*Jim Larkin*
*Michael Larkin (Manchester Martyr)*

*Maud Gonne MacBride*
*Sean MacBride*
*Michael Malone*
*Countess Constance Gore Booth Markievicz*
*Dick McKee*
*Terence Bellew McManus (First Fenian Funeral)*
*Michael O'Brien (Manchester Martyr)*
*Daniel O'Connell – 'My soul to heaven, my heart to Rome, my body to Ireland'*
*Batt O'Connor*
*Elizabeth More O'Farrell*
*Brian O'Higgins (Anna)*
*Kevin O'Higgins*
*Gearóid O'Sullivan*
*Muriel Gifford MacDonagh*
*The O'Rahilly (Michael Joseph)*
*Charles Stewart Parnell*
*John (Seán) A. Pinkman*
*Jeremiah O'Donovan Rossa*
*Francis Sheehy-Skeffington*
*James Stephens*
*Oscar Traynor*
*Thomas Traynor*
*Monument to Hunger Strikers 1917, 1981*

On 1 August 1915 Jeremiah O'Donovan Rossa was buried after a great Fenian funeral here. Padraig Pearse gave the graveside oration and William Oman of the Irish Citizen Army played the Last Post.

**Fitzwilliam Place**: Dr Brighid Lyons Thornton's home: *Ireland's Unfinished Revolution; Curious Journey.* She was commissioned in the Medical Services of the National Army in 1922, thus earning the distinction of being the only woman to serve in the army at the time.

**42 Fitzwilliam Place**: home of James Stephens, author of *The Inrrection in Dublin* (1916). He was Registrar of the National Gallery in 1916.

**43 Fitzwilliam Place**: home of James O'Mara; often used by de Valera for meeting with British emissaries prior to the Truce.

**20 Fitzwilliam Square**: home of Dr R. Travers Smith, visiting physician to Richmond Hospital, where he treated casualties of 1916 Rising.

*Kevin Barry*

**29 Fitzwilliam Square**: City of Dublin Branch of the Red Cross.

**32 Fitzwilliam Square**: home of Miss Meade; converted to a field hospital during the Rising.

**35 Fitzwilliam Square**: home of Miss Fletcher; converted to a field hospital during the Rising.

**64 Fitzwilliam Square**: Tommy O'Shaughnessy's home; he was the Dublin City Recorder (judge); often escorted by Dave Neligan.

**69 Fitzwilliam Square**: home of A. A. McConnell, Ireland's first neurosurgeon, and surgeon at the Richmond Hospital, where he treated casualties of 1916 Rising.

**15 Fitzwilliam Street Upper**: the 1890s home of John Redmond.

**26 Fitzwilliam Street Upper**: first Dublin home of the Plunkett family, before they moved to 3 Belgrave Road in Rathmines. This was the address Joseph Mary Plunkett listed on his engagement announcement.

**31 Fitzwilliam Street Upper**: house owned by Mrs MacGarry; used to 'shelter' a Dáil Department during the War of Independence; it was raided on 13 April 1921.

**5 Fitzwilliam Terrace, Upper Rathmines** (Darthy Road): Áine Ceannt stayed here while Eamonn was in Richmond Barracks.

**8 Fleet Street**: home of Kevin Barry; he was born here on 20 January 1902, fourth of a family of two boys and five girls; Kathleen, Mick, Monty, Kevin, Sheila, Elgin and Peggy. Kathleen (known as Kathy) was a courier for the Republicans/IRA during the Civil War. (See also under North Circular Road, Mountjoy Prison and Church Street Upper.)

**13 Fleet Street**: Wood Printing Works; *New Ireland* office, editor David Gwynne, then Patrick J. (Paddy) Little. Later Little was de Valera's Minister for Posts and Telegraphs. Prior to the Rising, *New Ireland* was the 'official' organ of the Redmondite Volunteers, under Little. Staff: Austin Clarke, Mario Esposito, Frank Gallagher, Kathleen Goodfellow, Fred Higgins, Peadar Kearney, Stephen MacKenna, Seamus McManus, Andrew Malone, Jack Morrow, Liam O'Briain, Padraic O'Conaire, Rory O'Connor, Michael Scott, Liam Slattery, Jack B. Yeats.

*New Ireland* first published the 'Castle Document' just prior to the Rising. According to Little's account, Rory O'Connor first produced the Document at a meeting at Dr Seamus O'Kelly's house in Rathgar. The Document was read by Alderman Thomas Kelly at a Dublin Corporation meeting on 19 April, and he indicated he had received it from Little (see under Larkfield, Kimmage, 'The Castle Document').

**Foley Street** (Montgomery Street –'Monto'): noted for prostitutes; re-named for Elizabeth Montgomery who married Lord Gardiner.

**Foley Street**: on 30 August 1913 there was serious fighting here when a large police raid destroyed several worker's homes and left John Nolan (on Eden Quay) and John Byrne so badly injured that they both died. Nolan died in Jervis Street Hospital and, after being treated there, Byrne died a few days following discharge. Although 'The Great Lockout' began on 26 August when William Martin Murphy locked out workers from his businesses, this event really sparked the general Lockout. Most of those arrested during the riots were from an area bounded by Foley Street, Corporation Street, Gloucester Street and Buckingham Street. (See also under Beresford Place, Liberty Hall.)

**Foley Street**: Phil Shanahan's Pub; Shanahan was originally from Tipperary and his pub was 'home' to Volunteers from 'the country'. He often advanced them money and gave shelter. This was a haunt of Dan Breen, Sean Hogan, Seamus Robinson, Sean Treacy and others while in Dublin. Dick McKee and Peadar Clancy were here before their capture on the night before Bloody Sunday; they left the pub and went to a 'safe house' on Lower Gloucester Street where they were captured.

**20 Fontenoy Street**: Sean Heuston's mother's home; Sean lived here before the Rising.

**1 Foster Place**: Wm. Montgomery & Son, assessors for property destroyed in the Rising.

**2 Fownes Street**: Lawlor's money exchange which sold guns and ammunition; prior to the Rising, Volunteers 'thronged' Lawlor's buying bandoliers, canteens, belts, haversacks, swords, bayonets, and all sorts of 'military' material.

**17 Fownes Street**: Arthur Griffith's first office of the *United Irishmen* (1899–1906) and then *Sinn Féin* (1906–1914) newspapers. Griffith often wrote under the pseudonym of 'Cugaun' ('dove') from the language of the Kaffirs whom he oversaw when he worked in a mine in South Africa.

**21 Fownes Street**: home of Patrick MacIntyre; he was thirty-eight when he was killed and is buried in Mount Jerome Cemetery. Editor of *The Searchlight* which was noted as a 'nationalist newspaper that was rabidly anti-German'.

**Francis Street**: Church of St Nicholas of Myra; built on the site of the original Franciscan Church built in 1235, the present Church was built between 1829 and 1845. There is stained glass from the Harry Clarke Studios dating from 1928 and statuary by John Smith. The Legion of Mary was founded here by Frank Duff on 7 September 1921

**100 Francis Street**: Myra House. The Legion of Mary, worldwide lay apostolic organisation, has its headquarters here.

**Frankfort Avenue, Rathgar**: St Mary's – home of Count and Countess Markievicz, a wedding present to her from her mother.

**16 Frankfort Avenue, Rathgar**: home of Susan Mitchell

**Frederick Street North**: home of Martin Walton; a close friend of Michael Collins, he became the Republic's largest music publisher with several outlets around Dublin.

**Frederick Street North**: American Rifles Hall; Volunteers used to drill here after the Rising.

**Frederick Street North**: Jim Larkin was attacked here on Thursday, 21 August 1913 by an unemployed clerk, Peter Sheridan. It was just before the Lockout and Larkin and Sheridan were summoned to appear in court on 23 August. Sheridan was a former Socialist, briefly succeeding Connolly as secretary of the Irish Socialist Republican Party, but had consistently opposed Larkin's efforts to affiliate the ITGWU with the ITUC. When Larkin won a seat on the Dublin City Council, Sheridan mounted a successful legal challenge to his election. Sheridan later joined the Irish National Workers' Union, and as it too was opposed to Larkin, Sheridan felt it was his membership that resulted in his firing. Larkin asked for leniency for Sheridan and he was 'bound over to keep the peace'.

*Michael Collins*

**14 Frederick Street North**: Countess Markievicz's Dáil Department of Labour office. RIC Constable Jeremiah Mee went to work for her here after he left the RIC in Listowel.

**15 Frederick Street North**: home of Maire Tuohy, member of the Provisional Committee of Cumann na mBan.

**18 Frederick Street North**: Keating Branch of the Gaelic League. Prior to the Rising, Michael Collins was active here. Cathal Brugha was Branch President and members included Con Collins, Richard Mulcahy, Diarmuid O'Hegarty, Gearóid O'Sullivan and Rory O'Connor. At 8.00 pm on Easter Sunday night, Pearse arrived here with dispatches which couriers were to take throughout the country: 'We start operations at noon today, Monday. Carry out your instructions.'

**28 Frederick Street North**: office of Stephen Bollard, editor of *The Hibernian*.

**33 Frederick Street North**: Studio of Joshua Clarke, father of Harry Clarke (1889–1931). Harry Clarke was acclaimed as a stained glass artist of genius. He worked and studied with another stained glass artist, A.E. Child. He designed the windows for the 'Stations of the Cross' in St Patrick's Cathedral on Lough Derg in 1928, as well as the windows in the chapel in Arbor Hill Prison. He died in 1931 of tuberculosis at the age of forty-two.

**18 Frederick Street South**: office of the Volunteer Training Corps Fund for the Relief of Dependants: T.F. Moloney (Chairman).

**Fumbally Lane**: the 2nd Battalion of Volunteers assembled under Thomas MacDonagh and occupied Barmacks' Malthouse here; Peadar Kearney was in the group.


**17 Gardiner Place**: home of James Larkin

**Gardiner Row**: Linda Kearns' home; she was born in Sligo. Michael Collins used it for meetings. She was in the ambulance that took the wounded Cathal Brugha to the Mater Hospital and applied compression to his femoral artery.

**Gardiner Row**: Fleming's Hotel; Sean Mahoney's home. Tom Clarke stayed with him on Holy Saturday night, thinking he might be captured otherwise. Next day, he, Tom O'Connor and Sean McGarry returned to the Clarke's home on Richmond Avenue.

In November 1916, Cathal Brugha organised a meeting here attended by about fifty Volunteers. He presided, though still on crutches. This was the start of the 'reorganisation' of the Volunteers.

**4 Gardiner Row**: Plaza Hotel; used as a Volunteer HQ by 1920.

**6 Gardiner Row**: HQ of the Dublin Brigade of Volunteers during the War of Independence. In 1919, the HQ Staff of the Volunteers comprised:

*Chief of Staff: Richard Mulcahy*
*Adjutant General: Gearóid O'Sullivan*
*Quartermaster General: Sean McMahon*
*Director of Intelligence: Michael Collins*

Others included:

*Piaras Béaslaí, Seamus Donovan, Liam Mellowes, J. J. (Ginger) O'Connell, Rory O'Connor, Diarmuid O'Hegarty, Eamonn Price, Sean Russell, Michael Staines.*

On 21 May 1921 a meeting was held here to finalise the plans to burn the Custom House. In attendance were: Michael Collins, Sean Dowling, Richard Mulcahy, Ginger O'Connell and Oscar Traynor.

**Gardiner Street**: home of Dr John Ryan; a friend to the Volunteers, and later the IRA, he often treated them and 'patched them up' without notifying the police.

**14 Gardiner Street Lower**: home of Sean O'Reilly. Killed in action at City Hall, Dublin, 24 April, 1916. Buried, family plot, St Paul's, Glasnevin.

**17 Gardiner Street Lower** (and Talbot Street): Moran's Hotel. Cumann na mBan, during Civil War hostilities in Dublin, used the basement as a large kitchen and several smaller rooms as an auxiliary hospital.

**35 Gardiner Street Lower**: Typographical Union Hall, HQ of Dublin Printer's Union. Most of Dublin's printers were members of the IRB and their premises were centers of Dublin Brigade activities. Michael Collins often attended meetings here. Dick McKee had his office as O/C of the Dublin Brigade here. On 20 November 1920 Michael Collins met Cathal Brugha, Peadar Clancy, Paddy Daly, Dick McKee, Dick Mulcahy and Sean Russell here to finalise plans for Bloody Sunday. Then Michael Collins went to the bar at the Gaity Theatre with Dave Neligan and others. 'The Squad' used this as a meeting place; most members of 'The Squad' got their orders here for Bloody Sunday.

**Gardiner Street Upper**: St Francis Xavier's Jesuit Church; the foundation stone was laid in 1829, the year of Catholic Emancipation.

**41 Gardiner Street Upper**: home of Joe McGuinness: 'Put him IN to get him OUT'. On 9 May 1918 he was elected for South Longford, winning by thirty-seven votes. He was in Lewes Gaol in England at the time of the election.

**Glasnevin**: Bon Secours Hospital. Sister Angela, from the hospital, smuggled food and comforts to Mountjoy prisoners during the Civil War.

**Glasnevin**: Cuilleannach, Lindsay Road, home of Maureen MacDonagh O'Mahoney, member of the Provisional Committee of Cumann na mBan and Hon Treasurer.

**Gloucester Place**: Hynes' Pub. James (Shanker) Ryan, the one who betrayed Peadar Clancy and Dick McKee, was killed here on 5 February 1921. Ryan was the 'fancy man' of Becky Cooper, one of Dublin's most well known madams. The squad that killed him was led by Bill Stapleton, and included Paddy Kennedy and Eddie Byrne.

**Gloucester Street (now Sean MacDermott Street)**: Tara Hall Printer's Union; HQ of C Company, 2nd Battalion, Dublin Brigade, under the command of Dick McKee from 1917; Joe Good was a member of C Company.

**15 Gloucester Street Upper (now Sean MacDermott Street)**: Painter's Hall; HQ of C Company, 3rd Battalion, Dublin Brigade.

**35 Gloucester Street Lower (now Sean MacDermott Street)**: Tom MacPartlin's home; on upper floor of Builder's and Carpenter's Union H.Q. It was here that the National

Executive agreed upon the General Strike of 13 April 1920, notice of which was sent out from offices at 32 Abbey Street Lower.

**36 Gloucester Street Lower**: Sean Fitzpatrick's home, used as a safe house. McKee and Clancy were here when captured on the night of 20–21 November 1920. They were taken to Dublin Castle and were tortured and killed by a squad led by Cpts King and Hardy. Fitzpatrick was arrested with McKee and Clancy.

**Grafton Street**: on 24 June 1921 Leonard Appleford and George Warnes were shot here by the Tans.

**Grafton Street**: Kidd's Buffet (commonly known as 'Kidd's Back'); hangout for Castle 'touts' and Tom Cullen, Frank Thornton, and Frank Saurin; at the back of what was the Berni Inn in Nassau Street.

**Grafton Street**: office of Rt Hon Lord John Graham Hope de la Poer Beresford, The Baron Decies, Censor-in-Chief during the War of Independence.

**Grafton Street** (Trinity College Dublin): Ponsonby and Gibbs, booksellers; Irish Volunteer companies bought the *English Infantry Manual, 1911* here, price one shilling.

**1 Grafton Street**: home of the Provost of Trinity College. During the Rising Trinity's Provost was Dr J. P. Mahaffey, who memorably wrote on one occasion: 'In Ireland the inevitable never happens, the unexpected always'. An 'Irish Convention' sat in Trinity from 25 July 1917 to 5 April 1918 (there were some sessions in Cork and Belfast); Horace Plunkett was its Chairman. Its ninety-five members included mayors and chairmen of public bodies, together with almost every prominent Irishman outside politics, but its weakness was on the political side; Sinn Féin had five seats, but declined to take part; William O'Brien's All for Ireland Party declined. It reaffirmed the measure of disagreement between the North and South.

**14 Grafton Street**: Trinity College Officers' Training Corps Commemorative Fund: Secretary, Lewis Beatty.

**22a Grafton Street**: D. A. Stoker, jewellers. Stoker was in the GPO buying stamps when it was overrun in the Rising. Grace Gifford bought her wedding ring here.

**41 Grafton Street**: Fannin's surgical and medical supply. In 1916, this was a major company with a virtual monopoly on supply to all Dublin's hospitals; now named Fannin Healthcare, and no longer on Grafton Street.

**79 Grafton Street**: Bewley's Oriental Café; during the early twentieth century (as now) a popular meeting place for all. In the nineteenth century it was Samuel Whyte's School. The stained-glass windows are by Harry Clarke.

**94-95 Grafton Street**: Edmund Johnson, jewellers; made the Liam McCarthy Cup, presented to the GAA in 1921, made from a 2.5 kilo single sheet of solid silver, with only one seam, which was panelled into four sections before adding a celtic design to each, with the four handles soldered last. The whole process took four months. The original was replaced by a replica in 1988.

**96 Grafton Street** (and corner of Wicklow Street): Weir and Sons, jewellers. Michael Collins bought Kitty Kiernan's 'unofficial' engagement present, a watch, here.

**Grafton Street** (and Suffolk Street): Jeanne Rynhart statue of Molly Malone, erected to mark the Dublin Millennium 1988

**13 Granby Row**: Granby Pub; used as interior for Vaughan's Hotel in the film *Michael Collins*.

**Grand Canal Street**: Sir Patrick Dun's Hospital. Sir Arthur Ball was a surgeon here in 1916.

The official records indicate that 73 military and 69 civilians were treated here during the Rising; 10 of the military and 11 of the civilians were either dead on arrival or died thereafter. Almost all of the casualties happened in the fighting around the Mount St Bridge.

In June 1927 Countess Markievicz was admitted here to a ward filled with the poor. She had appendicitis and was operated on by Sir William Taylor. An infection set in following the operation and she developed peritonitis. She was very run down as a result of her many activities on behalf of the poor of Dublin and in support of Republicanism, and her health suffered badly. She was also heartsick, could not accept the oath and could not enter the Dáil. At first she appeared to be getting better, but passed away on 15 July 1927.

*Countess Markievicz*

**Grand Canal Street**: Boland's Bakery. This was an important strategic stronghold because it covered the railway line out of the Westland Row terminus. De Valera's HQ was actually in a small dispensary next door. He knew every inch of the territory, and did not reduce his area of responsibility even though MacNeill's order had greatly reduced the men who came to fight. He has been depicted as one who scorned danger almost to recklessness. He had the great confidence of all his men that he was a leader who was capable of the unexpected stroke that would extricate them from danger. On Thursday afternoon, shelling from a 1-pounder gun taken from HMS *Helga* began. (Following the Irish takeover of power after the Treaty, the *Helga* served in the Fisheries Protection Service as the *Murchu*.) De Valera ordered Cpt Michael Cullen to lead a party to raise a flag on the top of a tall disused distillery tower and this attracted the shelling. (In fact the first shell missed the tower and landed in the water near the *Helga*. Thinking she was under fire, the *Helga* fired back! That was soon sorted out.) The tower was hit, rupturing the water tank and almost drowning the defenders, but the British had been fooled and this saved Boland's.

De Valera had not slept during the early days of the Rising, and for two days prior to it. He was exhausted by Thursday/Friday: 'I can't trust the men – they'll leave their posts if I fall asleep, if I don't watch them'. When Lt Fitzgerald assured his O/C he'd sit by him, de Valera relented and fell asleep immediately. Soon he awoke screaming 'Set fire to the railway!'[26] Late on Friday, de Valera ordered the bakery to be evacuated, but there was

26. Coogan, T. P., *1916, The Easter Rising*, 2001, p. 118.

*Edward O\Daly*

no place for the Volunteers to go so they re-occupied it and remained in their positions until their surrender on Saturday.

**Grangegorman Road Upper**: Richmond Barracks (now Richmond Female Penitentiary). The courts marshal following the Rising were held here (Connolly's was held in Dublin Castle because of his injuries). They were directed by Brigadier General Charles Blackadder and three other associates. The brigadier said of Padraig Pearse: 'I have just done one of the hardest tasks I have ever had to do. I have had to condemn one of the finest characters I have ever come across. There must be something very wrong in the state of things, that makes a man like that a rebel.'[27] The Prosecutor was William Wylie. Although he fought against the rebels, he was strongly opposed to the speed and secrecy of the trials. He was rebuffed in his proposal to allow the defendants defence counsel, and only after MacDonagh's execution were they allowed to call witnesses. Alderman Laurence O'Neill, Lord Mayor of Dublin, refused to act as Crown Prosecutor, but acted as Counsel for the Defence. They all faced the same basic charge that was handed to them only moments before the trial. It alleged that they 'did an act, to wit did take part in an armed rebellion and in the waging of war against His Majesty the King, such an act being of such a nature as to be calculated to be prejudicial to the defence of the realm, being done with the intention and purpose of assisting the enemy'. In some cases there was an additional charge that they 'did attempt to cause disaffection among the civil population of His Majesty'.[28] All the defendants, except Willie Pearse, pleaded not guilty. Daly attempted to plead guilty to just one part of the charge ('did take part in an armed rebellion') but he was told this was not permitted. Ned Daly was prisoner No. 21, Willie Pearse No. 27 and Sean MacDermott was prisoner No. 91; James Connolly was designated prisoner No. 90 even though he was never actually a resident prisoner here.

**Grantham Street**: Morris's sweet shop; frequented by students from the Synge Street Christian Brothers' School.

**13 Grantham Street**: home of Mrs Malone, mother of Michael Malone (Northumberland Road), Brighid and Áine. Dan Breen was taken here to convalesce after the Ashtown raid of 19 December 1919. Breen married Brighid.

**Grattan Street**: de Valera surrendered the Boland's Volunteers here.

27. Foy, Michael and Brian Barton, *The Easter Rising*, 1999, p. 231.
28. Ibid

**Great Britain Street (now Parnell Street)**: The Rotunda Hospital; its official name is The Dublin Lying-in Hospital. It was founded in 1745, and moved to its present location in 1748. The hospital was totally dependent on charity and for this reason the buildings and environs were created with an eye to fundraising. The 'social' rooms of the Rotunda existed to provide entertainment. The 'Round Room' is now the Ambassador Cinema, the former 'Supper Rooms' are the Gate Theatre, and the 'Pillar Room' is used for concerts. The Roller Rink was in the basement.

On Tuesday, 28 November 1905, Arthur founded Sinn Féin at a meeting here in the Round Room. The First Convention of the National Council of Sinn Féin proposed a Council of 300, comprised of

*Arthur Griffith*

abstentionist MPs and local officials, to assume the powers of a *de facto* government. The name 'Sinn Féin' was suggested by Maire de Bhuitleir (Mary Ellen Butler/Mrs O'Nuallain, cousin of Edward Carson) at a meeting with Griffith in his earlier offices in Fownes Street. She was a language enthusiast and had used the name in her small news sheet, published in Oldcastle, Co Meath, in 1902–1903; it came from the early motto of the Gaelic League: 'Sinn Féin, sinn féin amháin' – Ourselves, ourselves alone.

On 25 November 1913 Eoin MacNeill and Laurence Kettle (son of A. J. Kettle, aide to Charles Stewart Parnell) held the first meeting to enrol the Irish Volunteers. They intended the meeting to be held at the Mansion House but the then Lord Mayor, Lorcan Sherlock, refused to rent the Dawson Street premises to them. Sherlock later went on the Executive as one of Redmond's 'forced' nominees (see 206 Great Brunswick Street). The band that started off the night was the St James's Brass and Reed Band. The doors were opened shortly after 8 pm and the meeting was chaired by Sean T. O'Kelly. Over 4,000 people signed up that night. Padraig Pearse was one of the principal speakers. Others were Sean MacDermott, James McMahon, Michael Judge and Councillor Richard Carroll. Batt O'Connor and Bulmer Hobson addressed the crowd outside. The IRB pressed many nationalists to join the Volunteers, but the organisation had not backed the ITGWU in The Great Lockout. Kettle was a well-known opponent of the Union. When he spoke, fights broke out between Union protestors but the disturbances were soon drowned out by the song *God Save Ireland*. This marked the start of the disagreements between Union members and other Volunteers and led to Connolly's reluctance to join with the Volunteers (see Appendix III for Manifesto of the Irish Volunteers; see Kildare Street for First Provisional Committee of the Irish Volunteers).

become Larkin's tools'.[31] He first made his threat here, often repeated during the Lockout: 'The company's shareholders will have three meals a day, whether the strike succeeds or not, but I don't know if the men who go out can count on this'.[32] Department of Intelligence Office; this was the first HQ of 'The Squad'; Michael Collins infrequently came here.

**144 Great Brunswick Street (now Pearse Street)**: St Andrew's Club; HQ of the Volunteers/IRA in 1921. It was surrounded by Auxies on 14 March 1921 when it was thought the Dáil was meeting here; a firefight ensued and there were casualties on both sides. The building is now part of Dublin City Library & Archive.

**178 Great Brunswick Street (now Pearse Street)**: Harrison's, monumental sculptors; James Pearse joined this company as a journeyman.

**180 Great Brunswick Street (now Pearse Street)** : 'Red Hand' division of the Ancient Order of Hibernians.

**206 Great Brunswick Street (now Pearse Street)**: HQ of the Irish Volunteers at the time of the Rising (see 2 Dawson Street; Kildare Street). On 12 June 1914 Redmond issued his ultimatum demanding that his nominees be accepted onto the Provisional Committee, and on 16 June the Provisional Committee met here and the resolution was carried by a vote of 18 to 9. Among those who voted for the resolution were Hobson, MacNeill, Plunkett (IRB), Casement and Moore; those voting against included Pearse, Ceannt, Colbert, MacDermott, Béaslaí, Liam Mellowes and Eamonn Martin (all from the IRB), and Michael Judge (AOH) and Sean Fitzgibbon (unaffiliated). MacDonagh was not present and did not vote. This vote effectively ended Hobson's influence in the IRB.

**Great Charles Street**: home of T. M. Healy before he became the first Governor-General of the Irish Free State.

**Great Denmark Street**: Ossary Hotel: Sean Kavanagh, Michael Collins's agent in Kildare, stayed here the night before Bloody Sunday after he was told to vacate Vaughan's Hotel.

**1-2 Great Denmark Street**: Barry's Hotel. The Tipperary football team stayed here before Bloody Sunday; still a popular residence of visiting football and hurling teams. HQ of K Company, 2nd Battalion during the War of Independence. On 13–14 December 1920 a meeting of GHQ was held here to finalise plans to import arms from Italy; Cathal Brugha, Michael Collins, Liam Mellowes, Joe Vize, Liam Deasy and Florrie O'Donoghue attended. Michael Leahy, second-in-command of Cork No 1 Brigade left Dublin on 2 January 1921 to go to Italy, but he soon returned to Dublin after the project failed. This was also the first HQ of the Dublin Brigade of Republicans/IRA during the Civil War until 19 June 1922 when Oscar Traynor moved HQ to 'The Block', and particularly the Hammam and Gresham hotels.

**6 Great Denmark Street**: Belvedere College; Dublin day-school run by the Jesuits. Attended by Kevin Barry when he joined the Volunteers in October 1917.

**2 North Great George's Street**: the family town house of John Dillon; spoke out in parliament condemning the 1916 executions – 'Larne begat Dublin'. He was defeated by de Valera for the East Mayo seat in December 1918.

---

31. Yeates, Padraig, *Lockout – Dublin 1913*, 2000, p. 7.
32. Ibid

**10 North Great George's Street**: here Mariana Peroliz 'owned' *The Spark* for James Connolly and Countess Markievicz. Of the advanced nationalist weeklies in the early part of the war, *The Spark* was the most specifically Catholic in tone.

**Great Strand Street**: Christian Brothers' School; Arthur Griffith attended here.

**Green Lanes**: Patsy O'Toole's home; the arms dump for E Company, 4th Battalion (Rathfarnham Battalion).

**Gregg Lane**: renamed Cathal Brugha Street

**11 Grosvenor Place, Rathmines**: home of Francis and Hanna Sheehy-Skeffington and their son, Owen; situated just on the other side of Portobello Bridge over the Grand Canal from Portobello Barracks. Francis was the first lay Registrar of Trinity College; he resigned after a dispute over allowing academic status to women. He was thirty-seven when he was 'executed' during the Rising. He is buried in Glasnevin Cemetery. Just after his death, Hanna and Owen were evicted and moved to 43 Moyne Road, Rathmines.

**Haddington Road**: St Mary's Catholic Church. British snipers climbed to the belfry here, overlooking the whole of 25 Northumberland Road and the Clanwilliam House area.

**Haddington Road**: home of the British Provost Marshal; raided by members of K Company, 3rd Battalion, disguised as DMP, under the command of Tom Cullen, for its collection of weapons.

**60 Haddington Road**: home of Ben Dwyer and other IRA members in 1920

**Haddon Road, Clontarf**: the house known as 'Craigmillar' was the home of John P Twohig; Michael Collins often visited here. Twohig was said to be his uncle.

**3 Halston Street**: James O'Keeffe, printers; war bulletins were printed here in 1916.

**Harbour Road, Howth** (1 Island View House): home of Mrs Quick. From 1914 to 1917, Nancy O'Brien, Susan Killeen and Dolly Brennan, among others, had lodgings here. Michael Collins often visited here.

**4 Harcourt Street**: Edward Carson's birthplace; his family moved to 25 Harcourt Street, 'the more fashionable end'.

**6 Harcourt Street**: home of John Cardinal Newman (1801–1890). Known as St Mary's University House, it was the residence for students of the Catholic University in St Stephen's Green. Currently HQ of Connradh na Gaeilge (The Gaelic League). In 1910 Arthur Griffith acquired permanent rooms here and thereafter it was the headquarters of Sinn Féin and Inghnidhe na hÉireann branch of Cumann na mBan. The Volunteers used it as a drill hall before and after the Rising. It was the first meeting place of K Company, 3rd Battalion of Volunteers, after the Rising: Cpt Tom Cullen, Adj Larry Nugent, Instructor Sean McClusky.
Sinn Féin Headquarters: on 25 October 1917 at the re-organised Sinn Féin convention held here Eoin MacNeill was proposed for the Executive. Among those who voted for him were Eamon de Valera, Arthur Griffith and Sean Milroy. Kathleen Clarke, Helena Molony and Countess Markievicz voted against him. He received an outstanding majority of votes. About 1,200 Cummain from throughout the country were represented. A constitution was adopted, the preamble to which (the wording suggested by de Valera) declared: 'Sinn Féin aims at securing the international recognition of Ireland as an independent Irish Republic. Having achieved that status, the Irish people may by referendum freely choose their own form of Government.'

Redmond led a raid on the O'Connor's home on 17 January and assured Mrs O'Connor he 'wouldn't bother her again'. Michael Collins made sure of it.

James McNamara was one of Redmond's 'confidants'. He was involved with 'Jameson' (John Charles Byrne) in an attempt to capture Michael Collins. Redmond foolishly ridiculed G-Division detectives, pointing out that he had made contact with a man who had met Collins, only a fortnight after arriving from London. Collins's agent at G-Division Neligan informed Collins through Broy, and Redmond was killed a few days later. 'Jameson' was killed on 2 March 1920.

Lady Gregory stayed here when she was at the Abbey Theatre.

**76 Harcourt Street**: Dáil Office from June 1919; raided in November 1919. Michael Collins escaped through the skylight to the Standard Hotel. The house was purchased for the Dáil by Michael Collins. It was used to house the Dáil Loan. Officially signed receipts in green, gold and black were issued in lieu of bonds; they were printed by Colm O'Lochlainn. There were constituency organisers for each province, paid £30 per week each: Leinster, E. Flemming; Ulster, E. Donnelly; Munster, P. C. O'Mahoney; Connaught: P. Ryan. By September 1920, the following had been subscribed: Leinster: £87,444; Ulster: £41,297; Munster: £171,177; Connaught: £57,797; England and France, £11,647; Cumann na mBan: £801. The final Loan total, subscribed by over 135,000 Irish people, was £378,858 in Ireland alone. $5,123,640 was raised separately in the US. The British attempted to confiscate the funds and on 1 March a secret commission was established which summoned bank managers to appear and identify the funds held in their institutions. Sean Hayes, Frank Lawless, Michael Lynch, Dick McKee, Fintan Murphy, Dan O'Donovan, Diarmuid O'Hegarty, Sean O'Mahoney, and Patrick Sheehan were arrested and spent two months in jail. When Collins heard of it, he had the signatory of the summons, Allen Bell, shot.

Batt O'Connor made hidden closets to hide people and documents here. It currently houses the corporate services division of the Department of Foreign Affairs.

**Harcourt Street** (and 103-104 St Stephen's Green): Russell Hotel; occupied by the British during the Rising. Margaret Skinnider, a teacher of mathematics, was wounded on Wednesday of Easter Week when she was in a party sent to set fire to the Russell Hotel. She was carried back to the College of Surgeons by Bill Partridge. She later wrote *Doing My Bit for Ireland*. Auxies stayed here after the Truce until rounded up by Dave Neligan. At that time it was owned by Count Sevigne's mother-in-law.

**Harcourt Street Station**: terminus (in use from its construction in 1859 until 1959) of the Dublin and South Eastern Railway. Taken early in the Rising by a detachment of the ICA under Cpt R. McCormack, it was almost immediately evacuated by the Volunteers because it was indefensible.

**Hardwicke Street**: Hardwicke Street Theatre; founded in 1914 by Edward Martyn, Thomas MacDonagh and Joseph Plunkett, it was intended to produce foreign and Irish plays ignored or rejected by the Abbey Theatre.

**Hardwicke Street**: Fianna HQ; Sean Heuston was in charge of training and organisation.

**Hardwicke Street**: St George's Church (Church of Ireland); the only church whose steeple can be seen from O'Connell Bridge. Opened in 1814, it is acknowledged as the masterpiece of Francis Johnston, architect of the GPO and the Chapel Royal in Dublin Castle.

**27 Hardwicke Street**: Mrs Kissane's home; Sean MacDermott lived here until he moved to the Munster Hotel the week before the Rising, then on Holy Saturday he moved to the

*The ruins of Henry Street, looking towards Nelson's Pillar*

Fleming Hotel on Gardiner Street to stay with Tom Clarke at Sean Mahoney's home. Used as a 'safe house' by the Volunteers/IRA.

**12 Harrington Street**: home of Thomas Dickson; killed with Francis Sheehy-Skeffington, he is buried in Glasnevin.

**7-8 Harry Street**: Mooney's Pub; a frequent haunt of Kevin O'Higgins when he was a student.

**Hatch Street**: a detachment of the ICA under Frank Robbins was to defend this area and build barricades all around St Stephen's Green.

**20 Lower Hatch Street**: home of Dr Ella Webb

**43 Lower Hatch Street**: a home of Eoin MacNeill

**Henrietta Street**: on Constitution Hill, King's Inns; seized by Volunteers and arms taken on 1 June 1920. One of the Volunteers was Kevin Barry.

**Henry Place**: Volunteers escaping from the GPO rushed through here to get from Moore Street to Moore Lane.

**Henry Street**: an area with many retail outlets in 1916; fifty-three buildings were burned

**9-15 Henry Street**: Arnott's department store; during the Rising, the Volunteers under Frank Henderson bored through the walls of Henry Street buildings from the GPO to here. The IRA/Republicans had a machine gun on the roof during the Civil War.

**18-20 Henry Street**: Bewley's; this was actually the company's Dublin HQ and offices. F. R. Ridgeway was the managing director at the time of the Rising.

**21 Henry Street**: the home of Jenny and Charles Wyse-Power. Charles had been a member of the IRB and Volunteers, but was told he would be more valuable as a lawyer, free from these associations, so he did not take part in the Rising. The Proclamation was agreed upon here and it was signed by six: Clarke, Pearse, Connolly, MacDonagh, MacDermott and Ceannt. Joseph Plunkett signed on Easter Sunday morning. Jenny was a member of

*Interior of the Coliseum Theatre after bombardment*

the Provisional Committee of Cumann na mBan and its Hon Treasurer. Her daughter, Dr Nancy Wyse-Power, was an emissary to Germany during the War of Independence and was a close associate of John Chartres. She was later appointed to the Free State Department of Industry and Commerce. She was a strong advocate for women's rights.

**21 Henry Street**: Irish Farm Produce Co; Collins often used space here as an office.

**24 Henry Street** (just opposite Moore Street): Coliseum Variety Theatre with 3,000 seats; ironically, it opened on Easter Monday 1915. Burned during the Rising, it was never rebuilt. Two British soldiers, Sgt Henry and Pvt Doyle, let go in advance of The O'Rahilly's escape, hid in the basement and were not discovered until Wednesday, 3 May, unaware the Rising had ended.

**27 Henry Street**: McDowell's, jewellers; next to the GPO entrance

**32 Henry Street**: Arch Bar

**40 Henry Street**: Bailey Brothers, tailors; moved from Sackville Street

**42 Henry Street**: John Murphy, spirit merchant

**43 Henry Street**: P. J. Dick Pub

**45 Henry Street**: Austin Stack's first Ministry of Home Affairs office under the name of Murray & Quirke, solicitors

**47 Henry Street**: William's Stores, looted during the Rising

**50 Henry Street**: H. Leedom and Company

**51 Henry Street**: Hayes, Conyningham & Robinson, chemists here during the Rising

**14 Herbert Park, Ballsbridge**: home of Fr Michael O'Flanagan, a member of the organising committee of the Volunteers

**16 Herbert Park, Ballsbridge**: home of Eoin and Agnes MacNeill; he was Professor of Early and Medieval History at UCD and Chief of Staff of the Irish Volunteers and she was on the Provisional Committee of Cumann na mBan. By April 1916 they were living in

Rathfarnham; their home there was known as Woodtown Park. Some people reported that when the Rising went ahead, despite his notice calling it off, he wanted to fight, and on Monday he said: 'I will go home for my Volunteer uniform, and go out and fight! My friends and comrades are fighting and dying, and I must join them'. Others were not so complimentary: 'MacNeill could not make up his mind whether to fight in his uniform or in civilian clothes, and he racked himself so much with speculations on these points that the Rising was over before he made up his mind.'[33] One of Clarke's last comments to Kathleen was that MacNeill's role in the cancellation should never be forgotten or forgiven. MacNeill was arrested on 26–27 November 1920 and imprisoned in Mountjoy. He was originally from Antrim.

**17 Herbert Park**, **Ballsbridge**: home of F. H. Browning

**18 Herbert Park**, **Ballsbridge**: home of Mr and Mrs Arthur Mitchell

**32 Herbert Park**, **Ballsbridge**: home of Alfred and Violet Fannin; it remained in the family until their son Eustace died in 1985, and is now an ambassadorial residence.

**40 Herbert Park**, **Ballsbridge**: The O'Rahilly's home; Michael Joseph O'Rahilly. His wife was Nancie Marie Bonne O'Rahilly, originally from Philadelphia; she was on the Provisional Committee of Cumann na mBan. He was Eoin MacNeill's publisher.

On 2 March 1919 a meeting was held here about the establishment of Republican Courts in the Pembroke and South City areas; Áine Heron and Áine Ceannt were among those chosen to sit as judges. Early in 1921 a meeting was held here to finalise plans for the taking of the Custom House. (De Valera's first choice was to capture Barracks Bush Barracks, but Oscar Traynor determined that was impractical.) Pieras Beaslai, Cathal Brugha, Michael Collins, de Valera, Sean MacMahon, Liam Mellows, Richard Mulcahy, J.J. 'Ginger' O'Connell, Eoin O'Duffy, Diarmud O'Hergarty, Gearoid O'Sullivan, Sean Russell, Austin Stack, and Oscar Traynor attended.

**9 Herbert Place**: Edward Carson's first home as an adult

**Herberton Bridge, Dolphin's Barn** (across the Grand Canal, connects Herberton Road on the north side with Sundrive Road on the south side)

**71 Heytesbury Street**: home of Delaney family; meeting place for Republicans/IRA during the Civil War. Sean Treacy was a great friend and called here often, including the morning of the day he was killed. Miss Delaney was engaged to Seamus Robinson.

**High Street**: Christ Church Cathedral; founded in 1038 by Sitric, the Norse King of Dublin. A stone Church was erected by St Laurence O'Toole in 1172. When he died in France, his heart was returned to Ireland and is preserved in the Chapel of St Laud behind the high altar. The Society of Bell Ringers was established here in 1670. The tenor bell is B-Flat.

**4 High Street**: home of Freddie Ryan. A member of the St Stephen's Green garrison, he was killed (aged seventeen) trying to set the Russell Hotel on fire.

**14-16 High Street**: St Audoen's Catholic Church, built in 1845 adjacent to the site of the original St Audoen's, one of Dublin's oldest churches, built by the Normans in 1190, and repository of the 'Lucky Stone', an early Christian gravestone reputed to have mystical qualities. That church replaced one built and dedicated to St Columcille. In the early 1900s the parish priest was Canon Kavanagh. A group of Volunteers attended Mass in St Audoen's on 17 March 1916.

33. Ryan, Desmond, *The Rising: The Complete Story of Easter Week.* 1949, 1957, p. 119.

**26 Highfield Road**, **Rathgar**: home of Agnes O'Farrelly, member of the Provisional Committee of Cumann na mBan

**7 Hoey's Court**: birthplace of Jonathan Swift

**Holles Street**: National Maternity Hospital, opened to all during the Rising; known simply as Holles Street Hospital; opened in 1884.

**Hume Street** (and Ely Place): Nora Connolly O'Brien had an office here during the Civil War. She replaced Margaret Skinnider as assistant to Austin Stack; she was captured here in November 1922 and was imprisoned at Mountjoy.

**7 Hume Street**: home of Fanny and Anna Parnell; they founded the Ladies' Land League in 1879. They were condemned by Archbishop McCabe and their brother, Charles Stewart Parnell, for 'outraging feminine modesty'. Many thought their League was a front for Fenian activity.

**157 Inchicore Road**: home of the Holland family; the father and his sons Robert (IRB), Dan (IRB), Frank (IRB) and Walter were all members of the Volunteers. Robert and his company set out to equip themselves by buying rifles from British soldiers.

**Infirmary Road** (Montpelier Gardens): King George V Hospital; Sean Treacy's body was taken here and identified by Nora O'Keefe and Mollie Gleason.

**9 Iona Road, Glasnevin**: home of J. J. Farrell, former Lord Mayor of Dublin

**Howth**: arms were landed here on 26 July 1914. The event was planned by Roger Casement, Erskine Childers, Dermot Coffey, Darrell Figgis, Alice Stopford Green, Bulmer Hobson, Sean MacDermott, Eoin MacNeill, Conor O'Brien, The O'Rahilly and Mary Spring-Rice. The O'Rahilly directed Figgis and Childers to the firm in Hamburg where they purchased the arms. They purchased 1,500 rifles and 45,000 rounds of ammunition. The *Asgard* landed 900 rifles and 26,000 rounds of ammunition; on board were Childers, his wife Molly, Mary Spring Rice, a British army officer named Gordon Shepherd and two Donegal fishermen, Patrick McGinley and Charles Duggan. George Fitz Hardinge Berkeley made the largest single financial contribution to the project. The rifles were Mausers, Gewehr 98s, .31 caliber with a 5 shot magazine, and were captured from the Russians by German forces. About 800 Volunteers mustered and marched out to Howth on that day in July 1914. Sean Heuston was in charge of the transport, meaning the Fianna trek-cart. In spite of all the British efforts, the cart brought its entire cargo back to Dublin (see also Bachelor's Walk).

**Howth**: Wentworth Cottage, home of Mary M. Colum, member of the Provisional Committee of Cumann na mBan and Hon Secretary. She was a teacher at St Ita's school for girls, a sister school to Pearse's St. Enda's school for boys.

**Inchicore**: Islandbridge Barracks. Partially demolished, it is now Peadar Clancy Barracks and Keogh Square.

**Inns Quay:** see King's Inns Quay

**James's Street**: South Dublin Union Workhouse, held by Commandant Ceannt. Formerly known as Queen Anne's Mansions, the building was begun in 1702.
The Volunteers occupied buildings here from Easter Monday until Sir Francis Vane took command of a column of British troops under Col Oates on Thursday. After that night Ceannt and the Volunteers were surrounded, but in comparative peace, until they surrendered on Sunday. Ceannt had fewer than sixty Volunteers; he surrendered forty-two

*Joseph Plunkett (son of Count Plunkett),
Commandant-General Irish Republican Army,
executed on May 4th, 1916.*

*Mrs. Joseph Plunkett (Miss Grace Gifford), who
married Joseph Plunkett in Kilmainham Prison a few
hours before his execution. Photo by Keogh Bros.)*

– Cathal Brugha was missing! There were several open fields surrounding the buildings, stretching southwards from the HQ to the Grand Canal: the Master's Fields, McCaffrey Estate and the Orchard Fields. Nurse Margaretta Keogh, a nurse in the Union Hospital, was killed here, the first woman to die in the Rising. She was killed at Number 2 Hospital Building. Cathal Brugha single-handedly saved the Volunteers by his courage here. For two hours he held the British at a courtyard, defending the Nurse's Home unaided. Alone he forced the British to retreat. He was propped against a wall singing 'God Save Ireland' when Ceannt and the Volunteers came to get him. He had been wounded 25 times and survived: '5 dangerous bullet wounds, 9 serious and 11 slight'. He never fully recovered the full use of his legs. He was taken to the Union Hospital on Friday morning by a Carmelite nun and a Red Cross official, then to the hospital in Dublin Castle. He was ultimately released by the British because they did not think he could be of any future danger because he was hurt so badly. Afterward, it was said 'when he walked, one could hear the bullets rattlin'.

**James's Street**: St James's Catholic Church. Fr Eugene McCarthy ministered here. He married Grace Gifford and Joseph Plunkett and also gave the Last Rites to James Connolly. On their wedding certificate, Plunkett was listed as a bachelor with an occupation of 'gentleman' and Grace was listed as a spinster with an occupation of artist. The two British soldiers who were 'witnesses' were John Smith and John Lockerby ('Sgt 3rd Battalion, The Royal Iniskillen Regiment'). At the Presbytery here, Fr McCarthy and Grace Gifford Plunkett were 'assaulted' by British troops after her wedding.

*Exterior Kilmainham Jail, Dublin*

**53 James's Street**: home of Mr Byrne, bell ringer at St James's. Grace Gifford Plunkett rested here after her wedding and was awakened at 2 am and taken to Kilmainham to see Joseph Plunkett for ten minutes before he was executed. Then Fr McCarthy escorted her to lodgings on Thomas Street for the remainder of the night.

**174 James's Street**: birthplace and early home of Phil and William Cosgrave. Phil became Quartermaster of the Dublin Battalion during the War of Independence, and was later Governor of Mountjoy Prison; William succeeded Arthur Griffith as President of the Irish Free State.

**14-20 Jervis Street**: Jervis Street Hospital; Sean Hales and Padraig O'Maille were taken here after being shot on 7 December 1922. Hales was dead on arrival but O'Maille survived.

**Jones Road**: Croke Park. The grounds were originally acquired by the GAA in 1913 and were named after Archbishop Thomas Croke of Cashel, patron of the Association. On 19 November 1917 the Third Convention of The Irish Volunteers was held here: President, Eamon de Valera; Chief of Staff, Cathal Brugha; Director of Organisation, Michael Collins; Director of Communications, Diarmuid Lynch. In March 1918 he was deported to the US, because he was an American citizen. He had 'intercepted' a load of pigs to be sent to England for the army, had them butchered in Dublin, and sent the proceeds to their owners –but they never reached England for the troops, so the British deported him. He wanted to marry prior to deportation to help with his bride's citizenship, but the British wouldn't authorise it, so he was married in secret in Dundalk Gaol, and his bride accompanied him and his supporters to Amiens Street Station.

The General Secretary of the GAA at the time was Sean McGarry. On 21 November 1920 Tipperary played Dublin in Gaelic Football here. The crowd was estimated to be 15,000. The Tans attacked the grounds at 3.45 pm. Jack Shouldice was on the committee and was in charge of the gate and collections that day. Others on the committee with whom

Shouldice discussed the possibility of cancelling the game were Alderman Nowlan, Luke O'Toole, Andy Harty and Dan McCarthy. They decided to go forward with the game. Tipperary player Mick Hogan was killed and is commemorated now by the 'Hogan Stand'. Thomas Ryan was killed as he held Hogan and whispered the Act of Contrition in his ear. Ryan was from Wexford, and soon Dublin's children were singing:

*Croke Park, Bloody Sunday*
*As the dying goalman lay on the ground*
*And as the British bullets went flying round*
*Brave Thomas Ryan from Wexford fair*
*Knelt by his side in dying prayer*
*And as he aided the dying man*
*Was brutally shot by a Black and Tan.*
*God grant that both their souls*
*Find rest in Heaven among the blessed.*

Father Crotty gave Hogan and Ryan the Last Rites. Jane Boyle (26), James Burke, Daniel Carroll, Michael Feery, Thomas Hogan, James Matthews, Patrick O'Dowd, Jerry O'Leary (10), Willie Robinson (11), John Scott (14), Joseph Traynor, and James Teehan were also killed. Sixty-two were injured by the Black and Tans and a further twelve were injured in the stampede out of the grounds. The referee was Mick Sammon from Kildare. The 'Nally Stand' is named after Pat Nally from Bally, Co Mayo, an IRB and early GAA man.

**Jones Road**: home of Paddy and Stephen O'Reilly, both of whom were killed in the Custom House fire.

**53 Kenilworth Square**: de Valera's presidential office after Blackrock was raided

**Kevin Street**: a major DMP barracks and training depot. Once the palace of the Archbishop of Dublin. Collins's spy Dave Neligan was first posted here. It was an 'A' Division post and was in the same yard as a detachment of mounted police. In 1917 it had Inspector Carey, Sergeant Hurley and Constable Birmingham on its staff.

**Kildare Street**: on 24 August 1918 a British recruiting rally address was delivered here by Col Arthur Lynch MP, formerly of the Irish Brigade in the Boer War. He was asked during his speech: 'Why not stop in Ireland and share our dangers?'. His reply, 'Stop in Ireland and Share Your Cowardice', infuriated the Irish.

**1-3 Kildare Street**: Kildare Street Club (fronted the grounds of TCD and extended into Kildare Street); used as a major position by the Republicans/IRA in the Civil War.

**Kildare Street**: National Library of Ireland

**Kildare Street**: Leinster House, where the Dáil now meets, and did so after 1922. Lord Edward FitzGerald was born here in 1763. He did not like the house: 'It does not inspire the brightest ideas'. The First Session of the Third Dáil was held here on 9 September 1922. The Republicans/IRA never recognised this Dáil. To this day, the IRA hold that the Second Dáil was never 'disestablished', is still in existence, and is the basis for their Republican claims, because it was the successor in interest to the 'Republic' established by the Proclamation of 1916. Only the elderly Laurence Ginnell attended as a Republican and he was rapidly ejected for his repeated enquiries as to its constitutionality. Because of the Republican abstention, the only source of criticism came from the Labour Party, especially Thomas Johnson and Cathal O'Shannon.

This Dáil ratified the Constitution of the Irish Free State on 18 September. The document was drafted in the Shelbourne Hotel in the 'Constitution Room', which can now be seen by tourists. The committee appointed to draft the Constitution was chaired by Michael Collins, but Darrell Figgis, the vice-chairman, was responsible for most of its drafting. William Cosgrave was elected President of the Dáil and Minister of Finance. Other Cabinet members included: Ernest Blythe, Minister of Local Government; Desmond Fitz Gerald, Publicity Director and Minister of External Affairs; Patrick Hogan, Minister of Agriculture; Eoin MacNeill, Ceann Comhairle (Speaker) of the Dáil until 9 September, Minister without Portfolio from January to August 1922 and Minister of Education from August to the following September; Joe McGrath, Minister of Industry and Commerce and Economic Affairs (Labour); Richard Mulcahy, Minister of Defence; Kevin O'Higgins, Vice-President of the Executive Council and Minister of Home Affairs; J. J. Walsh, Postmaster General; Eamonn J. Duggan, Minister without Portfolio; Finian Lynch, Minister without Portfolio.

The Senate was established here and originally had 36 Catholic members and 24 Non-Catholic members.

On 27 September 1922 the Public Safety Bill was passed; it set up military courts which were given powers, including that of execution, for various offences. This ushered in a harsher period of the Civil War. Ernest Blythe pointed out that the reluctance to take life had weakened their cause; Mulcahy was convinced that compromise was impossible. The Labour TDs were the only dissenters, pointing out the dangers of a military dictatorship. In early October and amnesty for surrendering IRA was agreed. On 5 December T. M. Healy was appointed Governor General. On 7 December Sean Hales was killed outside the Dáil and Padraic O'Maille, Ceann Comhairle of the Dáil, was wounded. Republicans/IRA of the Dublin No 1 Brigade attacked them in reprisal for the passage of the Public Safety Bill. This was the only time the reprisal orders of Liam Lynch, which were to kill any TD who voted for the Bill, were executed. Dick Barnett, Joe McKelvey, Liam Mellowes and Rory O'Connor were executed in Mountjoy Prison on 8 December 1922 as a reprisal for the shooting. This is such an infamous event in the Civil War that it has long been questioned as to who was 'responsible'. It appears Mulcahy took the initiative, and O'Higgins and McGrath were the last Cabinet Members to give their consent.

In the general election on 27 August 1923 Cumann na nGaedhael won 63 seats (415,000 votes for the former Pro-Treatyites); Sinn Féin (abstentionists) won 44 seats (286,000 for 'Republicans'); Independents won 16 seats; the Farmers won 15 seats; Labour won 14 seats; Independent Labour won 1 seat.

**Kildare Street**: National Museum of Ireland

**41 Kildare Street**: first HQ of the Irish Volunteers; moved to 2 Dawson Street from here, then to 206 Great Brunswick Street. The First Provisional Committee of the Irish Volunteers operated here. (The formal executive was established after the Volunteer Convention of 1914.) The affiliations noted below are those at the time of the inception of the Volunteers (November 1913, not as they became later; for example note P. H. Pearse and his membership of the IRB). Those not formally affiliated with any party at that time are blank: Piaras Béaslaí (IRB); Roger Casement; Eamonn Ceannt (IRB); Con Colbert (IRB); James Deakin; Sean Fitzgibbon; Liam Gogan; John Gore (United Irish League, Irish Parliamentary Party); Bulmer Hobson (IRB); Michael Judge (Ancient Order

*Irish Rebellion May 1916. Soldiers holding a Dublin Street.*
*(Note : the photo was staged – see knapsack in front of barricade).*

of Hibernians); Laurence Kettle (United Irish League, Irish Parliamentary Party); T. M. Kettle (United Irish League, Irish Parliamentary Party); James Lenehan (Ancient Order of Hibernians); Michael Lonergan (IRB); Tomas MacDonagh; Eoin MacNeill; Sean McDermott (IRB); Peadar Macken (IRB); Eamon Martin (IRB); Liam Mellowes (IRB); Col Maurice Moore (United Irish League, Irish Parliamentary Party); Seamus O'Connor (IRB); Colm O'Lochlainn; The O'Rahilly; Peter O'Reilly (Ancient Order of Hibernians); Padraig O'Riain (IRB); Robert Page (IRB); P. H. Pearse (IRB); Joseph Plunkett; George Walsh (Ancient Order of Hibernians); Peadar White.

**Kilmainham**: Royal Hospital, HQ of the British Military in Ireland at the time of the Rising

**Kimmage, Dublin**: Larkfield; Count Plunkett's home. The 4th Battalion, Dublin Brigade trained and billeted here before the Rising. Nearly all the men in the 'Kimmage Garrison' were born in, or came from England. Michael Collins and Joe Good were here prior to the Rising. There was a mill on the property where Volunteers manufactured most of the pikes, buckshot and bayonets used in the Rising. On 13 April 1916 there was a small hand press here on which was printed 'The Castle Document'. This document alleged that the Castle authorities proposed to arrest many important and well-known public figures, and to raid their residences and those of several other persons, including the residence of the Archbishop of Dublin, William Walsh:

*The following precautionary measures have been sanctioned by the Irish Office on the recommendation of the General Officer Commanding the Forces in Ireland. All preparations will be made to put these measures in force immediately on receipt of an order issued from the Chief Secretary's Office, Dublin Castle, and signed by the Under Secretary and the General Officer Commanding the Forces in Ireland.*

*First, the following persons are to be placed under arrest: All members of the Sinn Féin National*

*Kilmainham Jail, place of execution*

*Council; the Central Executive Irish Sinn Féin Volunteers; General Council Irish Sinn Féin Volunteers; County Board Irish Sinn Féin Volunteers; Executive Committee National Volunteers; Coisde Gnotha Committee Gaelic League. See list (a) three and four and Supplementary List (a) two ....*

*...Dublin Metropolitan Police and Royal Irish Constabulary Forces in Dublin City will be confined to barracks under the direction of Competent Military Authority. An order will be issued to inhabitants of the city to remain in their houses until such time as Competent Military Authority may direct or otherwise permit; pickets chosen from units of Territorial Forces will be placed at all points marked on maps three and four. Accompanying mounted patrols will continuously visit all points and report every hour.*

*The following premises will be occupied by adequate forces and all necessary measures used without reference to headquarters: First, premises known as Liberty Hall, Beresford Place; number six Harcourt Street, Sinn Féin Building; number two Dawson Street, Headquarters Volunteers; number twelve D'Olier Street, Nationality Office; number twenty-five Rutland Square, Gaelic League Office; number forty-one Rutland Square, Foresters' Hall; Sinn Féin Volunteer premises in city; all National Volunteer premises in city; Trade Council premises, Capel Street; Surrey House, Leinster Road, Rathmines.*

*The following premises will be isolated and all communication to or from prevented: Premises known as Archbishop's House, Drumcondra; Mansion House, Dawson St; number forty Herbert Park; Larkfield, Kimmage Road; Woodtown Park, Ballyboden; Saint Enda's College, Hermitage, Rathfarnham; and in addition premises in List five (d). See Maps three and four.*[34]

---

34. Ryan, Desmond, *The Rising: The Complete Story of Easter Week.* 1949, 1957, p. 65.

The general consensus today is that after Joseph Plunkett 'forged' the document, he sent Rory O'Connor with it from Miss Quinn's Private Nursing Home in Mountjoy Square to Kimmage. O'Connor took it to George Plunkett and Colm O'Lochlainn to print it. However, its provenance has never been proven. Thomas MacDonagh's son, Donagh, claims that there really was a secret order from a file in Dublin Castle directing that 'immediately on receipt of an Order from the Chief Secretary's Office, Dublin Castle, and signed by the Under Secretary and the General Officer Commanding the Forces in Ireland' all the leaders of the different separatist organisations should be arrested. This document was branded as bogus by the British authorities then and now, but Grace Gifford stated she was present while Plunkett decoded part of it. In addition, Eugene Smyth, a telegraphist at the time in Dublin Castle, gave P. J. Little a signed and witnessed statement that he recognised the document as genuine and abstracted from the Castle files. In Kilmainham, on the night before he was executed, Sean McDermott swore to Mgr Patrick Browne that the Document was genuine. The document had several 'errors' which Joseph Plunkett was unlikely to have made. It was read by Alderman Tom Kelly at the Dublin Corporation meeting on 19 April. Kelly was highly regarded by all parties, and thus the document was taken very seriously.

**King Street South**: Gaiety Theatre; the manager in 1916 was Charles Hyland whose son, C. Hanchette Hyland (29), was killed while looking out the back door of 3 Percy Place: near Northumberland Road. The Carl Rosa Opera Company often played here. The D'Oyly Carte Opera Company opened on 24 April 1916.

On Saturday night, 20 November 1920, Michael Collins went to the bar here for a further meeting after the 'final' Bloody Sunday meeting had been held. He often met people in this bar: 'It had a respectable air of legal and loyal comfort, no one would expect a Republican to pollute its atmosphere'.

**King Street North** (see below King Street North Nos 27, 168, 170, 172, 174, 177): atrocities were committed here by the South Staffordshire Regiment (South Staffs), under the command of Lt Col Henry Taylor, on Saturday, 29 April 1916. Taylor refused to attend the inquest that followed the Rising. The South Staffs lost 5 officers wounded and 42 men killed, mostly in this street. Gen Lowe's orders included the following: 'No hesitation should be shown in dealing with these rebels. They must not be made prisoners.' Sir Edward Troup, the Investigating Law Officer of the Home Office told Prime Minister Herbert Asquith in regard to one of these incidents that he found: 'The source of the mischief was the military order to take no prisoners. This in itself may have been justifiable, but it should have been made clear that it did not mean that an unarmed rebel might be shot after he had been taken prisoner ... I have no doubt that if the evidence were published, he [Sgt Flood, see No 177 King Street North below] should be tried for murder.' In his advice to Asquith, he admitted that if the events had occurred in England, 'the right course would be to refer the cases to the DPP (Director of Public Prosecutions)'.[35] The verdict of the coroner, Dr Louis A. Byrne, held: 'We find the said Patrick Bealen [see No 177 below] died from shock and haemorrhage, resulting from bullet wounds inflicted by a soldier, or soldiers, in whose custody he was, an unarmed and inoffensive prisoner. We consider that the explanation given by the military authorities

---

35. Coogan, T. P., *1916, The Easter Rising*, 2001, p. 148.

is very unsatisfactory, and we believe that if the military authorities had any inclination they could produce the officer in charge.'[36] On 18 May, General Sir John Maxwell issued the following statement: 'Possibly unfortunate incidents, which we should regret now, may have occurred .... it is even possible that under the horrors of this particular attack some of them "saw red". That is the inevitable consequence of a rebellion of this kind. It was allowed to come into being among these people, and could not be suppressed by velvet-glove methods where our troops were so desperately opposed and attacked.'[37] He added in a letter to the Daily Mail: 'A revolt of this kind could not be suppressed with velvet glove methods'.

**27 King Street North**: it was here that a large rebel barricade was first thrown across a street.

**27 King Street North**: Louth Dairy, kept by Mrs Lawless. It was here that Peadar Lawless (21), James McCartney (American citizen, 36), James Finnegan Jr (40) and Patrick Hoey (25) were murdered by the South Staffs.

**38 King Street North**: private entrance of Monks' bakery; three Volunteers entered by this entrance to take over the office in the raid in which Kevin Barry was captured (see Church Street Upper).

**168 King Street North**: Mrs Hickey, shopkeeper, was in her shop when men were taken to from here to 170 North King Street and murdered. Kate Kelly, who did housework for the Hickeys, was a most colourful and damning witness at the inquest.

**170 King Street North**: Peter Connolly (39, lived at 164 North King Street, he was a member of Redmond's Volunteers, but did not participate in the Rising), Thomas (38, the father) and Christopher Hickey (16, the son) were murdered here by South Staffs. They were removed from Hickey's victualler shop at 168 North King Street.

**172 King Street North**: Michael Hughes (36) (Mick and Sally Hughes owned this house), and John Walsh (56) were murdered here by South Staffs.

**174 King Street North**: Michael Noonan (34), who owned a newsagency and tobacconist shop here, and George Ennis (51) were murdered here by South Staffs. Anne Fennel was a resident here and a witness.

**177 King Street North**: a 'licensed house' owned by Mrs Mary O'Rourke. Patrick Bealen (30) and James Healy (44, labourer at Jameson's Distillery) were murdered here by South Staffs Sgt Flood and Cpl Bullock who were spirited away to England prior to the 'line-up' of the South Staffs for ID purposes.

**King's Inns Quay** (between Richmond and Whitworth Bridges): the Four Courts; these were: Exchequer (presided over by the Chief Baron of the Exchequer); Chancellory (presided over by the Lord Chancellor); King's Bench (presided over by a Chief Justice); Common Pleas (presided over by a Chief Justice).

The garrison that occupied the Four Courts during the Rising was led by Joseph McGuinness. It entered through the Chancellory gate. Much of the garrison was composed of the 'football teams' that had tried to blow up the Magazine Fort in Phoenix Park. Fianna members of the garrison included: Paddy Daly, Gerry Holohan, Patrick Holohan, L. Marie and Barney Mellows.

---

36. *Irish Times*, 1 January 2001.
37. Caulfield, Max, *The Easter Rebellion, Dublin 1916*, 1963, 1995, p. 293.

*The Fout Courts, Dublin July 1922,*
*(Lumix Series No.1)*

Others there included Eamonn Martin and Denis O'Callaghan.

On 13 April 1922 the buildings were occupied by Republican/IRA troops, led by Rory O'Connor, although Joe McKelvey was Chief of Staff. Liam Mellowes, Sean Moylan and Ernie O'Malley were there too. Upon taking their positions, they issued this proclamation:

*Fellow citizens of the Irish Republic. The fateful hour has come. At the direction of the hereditary enemy our rightful cause is being treacherously assailed by recreant Irishmen. Gallant soldiers of the Irish Republic stand rigorously firm in its defence. The sacred spirits of the Illustrious Dead are with us in this great struggle. 'Death Before Dishonour'. We especially appeal to our former comrades of the Irish Republic to return to that allegiance and thus guard the Nation's honour.*

De Valera quickly described the members of the Four Courts garrison as the 'best and bravest of our nation' and joined the Republicans/IRA as an unranked soldier.

At 3.40 on the morning of 28 June 1922, the occupying force was given an ultimatum to surrender; firing commenced twenty minutes later. Joe Considine, Sean Cusack and Thomas Wall were killed in the Four Courts bombardment. One hundred prisoners were taken to Mountjoy Prison, among them Rory O'Connor, Liam Mellowes, Joe McKelvey and Dick Barrett. These four were executed in Mountjoy Prison on 8 December 1922 in reprisal for the shooting dead of Sean Hales on 7 December (see North Circular Road, Mountjoy Prison; Kildare Street, Leinster House). Ernie O'Malley was among a group of escapees on the way to Mountjoy.

**32 King's Inns Street**: home of Mrs O'Toole, probably a friend of a soldier to whom Tom Clarke gave a letter for Kathleen while he was in Kilmainham Gaol.

**10 Langrishe Place**: HQ of Irish National Foresters

**Larchfield Road, Inchicore** (3 St Michaels): home of Timothy Donovan; Michael Collins often visited here, and Donovan was said to be an uncle of Collins.

**26 Lauderdale Terrace:** home of Tom Cullen before the Rising

**29 Lawson Terrace, Sandycove Road**: birthplace of Roger Casement in 1864

**Leeson Park**: Litton Hall; auxiliary hospital during the Rising

**Leeson Street**: MacGilligan's home; Volunteers and Republicans/IRA often stayed here; Ernie O'Malley stayed here and often used the house for meetings during the War of Independence and the Civil War.

**Leeson Street**: Ken and Kay Brady's home; Ernie O'Malley often used the house for meetings, as well, during the War of Independence and The Civil War.

**35 Leeson Street Lower**: Irish Jesuit Headquarters; the archives contain original material of the Jesuit Generalate dating back to 1540; office of *Studies*, the Irish Jesuit Quarterly Review.

**89-90 Leeson Street Lower**: Catholic University School, run by the Marist Community; Father Watters was the President, and he was killed at Clanwilliam House fighting on Northumberland Road during the Rising.

**96 Leeson Street Lower**: St. Vincent's Private Hospital, run by the Sisters of Mercy; Arthur Griffith was admitted here by Oliver St John Gogarty and died on 12 August 1922.

**38 Leeson Street Upper**: home of The O'Rahilly and his family between 1909 and 1912

**97 Leeson Street Upper**: Arthur Griffith's home (he was born in 1872)

**25 Leinster Road, Rathmines**: Susan Mitchell moved here late in 1917 and lived here until December 1920.

**49b Leinster Road, Rathmines**: Surrey House; Countess Markievicz's home. She moved into the house in 1912. Jim Larkin hid here after he was arrested on 28 August 1913 and before he addressed the crowd from the Imperial Hotel on Sackville Street on 31 September. Prior to the Rising it was a great meeting and gathering place for nationalists. James Connolly and his family lived here between 1913 and 1916. It was Connolly's place and Markievicz's office for *The Spark* and *The Worker's Republic* (see also 70 Eccles Street) which were printed here. In the 22 January 1916 issue of *The Worker's Republic* the following appeared under the heading 'What is Our Programme?':

*Mark well, then, our programme. While the war lasts and Ireland is still a subject nation we shall continue to urge her to fight for her freedom. We shall continue, in season and out of season, to teach that 'the far-flung battle line' of England is weakest at the point closest to its heart; that Ireland is in a position of tactical advantage; that a defeat of England in India, Egypt, the Balkans, or Flanders would not be so dangerous to the British Empire as any conflict of armed forces in Ireland; that the time for Ireland's battle is NOW, the place for Ireland's battle is HERE; that a strong man may deal lusty blows with his fists against a host of surrounding foes, and conquer, but will succumb if a child sticks a pin in his heart....We are neither rash nor cowardly. We know our opportunity when we see it, and we know when it is gone.*

This was published the day after Connolly's return from his 'kidnapping' but was undoubtedly written before it.

**1-2 Leinster Street**: Finn's Hotel

**26 Lennox Street**: Harry Boland's family moved here in 1907.

**Liffey Street**: O'Neill's Pub; James Connolly was slightly wounded in his arm on returning from observing positions here on Thursday morning of the Rising.

**30 Liffey Street Upper**: *The Gaelic Press* was printed here as well as all kinds of publications and posters.

**Lincoln Place** (near Trinity College): seven civilians were shot in the back here on Bloody Sunday; two died.

**Lincoln Place**: office of *The Irish Homestead*, founded by Horace Plunkett in 1894 as the official publication of his Irish Agricultural Organisation Society. Harry Norman succeeded him as editor, followed by George Russell (AE) in 1905. Susan Mitchell began work here as a sub-editor in 1899. It moved to Merrion Square in 1908.

**Lincoln Place**: United Arts Club; founded in 1907 by Count Casimir Markievicz, Countess Markievicz and Ellen Duncan. The Club circle included William Butler Yeats, Jack Yeats, Frank Cruise O'Brien, Thomas Bodkin, Susan Mitchell, Dermot O'Brien, Lennox Robinson, and Katherine Tynan Hinkson. Most were Unionists who opposed the Home Rule Bill. It moved to St Stephen's Green after the Rising.

**Linenhall Street**: Linen Hall; opened in 1873 and closed in 1928.

**Linenhall Street**: Trueform Shoe Shop; fires were started here by looters during the Rising and the building was burned down.

**6-8 Lisburn Street**: Linenhall Barracks; held by forty members of the British Army Pay Corps, it was taken by Volunteers late on Wednesday of the Rising who set it alight and, though they subsequently tried to control the fire, it burned until Friday.

**4 Little Britain Street**: Arthur Griffith's family moved here from his birthplace at 4 Dominick Street.

**27 Little Britain Street**: James Moore was killed at his front door here by soldiers of the South Staffs during the Rising. The inquiry by Sir Edward Troup found: 'He was probably a perfectly innocent Person' (see North King Street).

**Lombard Street**: Peter Lanigan's Timber Yard. On St Patrick's Day 1858, James Stephens established the Irish Revolutionary Brotherhood here, but the name was soon changed to the Irish Republican Brotherhood (see Appendix 3).

**23 Longwood Avenue**: a home of Francis Sheehy-Skeffington

**29 Longwood Avenue**: home of James Grace

**40 Longwood Avenue**: home of Michael Hayes, Minister of Education in the First Dáil; he became the first Ceann Comhairle of the post-treaty Dáil and, later, a Senator. He was Professor of Irish at UCD.

**Lord Edward Street**: British 'Irish' Department of Labour; John Chartres transferred here in 1920.

**South Lotts Road, Ringsend**: home of James Connolly and his family on his return to Ireland from the US in 1910. He moved to Belfast before returning to Dublin in 1913, when he lived at the home of Countess Markievicz on Leinster Road, Rathmines.


**Malahide Road**: O'Brien Institute; a school maintained by the Christian Brothers for the education of orphans or children of families in dire straits, attended by Gerald Boland.

**24 Manor Place**: home of John Joseph Byrne; fought under Sean Heuston at the Mendicity Institution during the Rising. He worked as a messenger for the Great Southern & Western Railway. He was sentenced to three years penal servitude.

**3 Marino Crescent, Clontarf**: home of Frank Shouldice

**15 Marino Crescent, Clontarf**: Birthplace of Abraham (Bram) Stoker in November 1847, author of *Dracula*; it was written after he left Dublin. The Boland family moved here about 1910. Volunteers from the country, including Sean Treacy, often stayed here.

**Marlborough Road, Donnybrook**: home of the Pearse family in 1904.

**Marlborough Street** (at corner of Findlater Place): St Thomas' Church of Ireland; destroyed in 1922 during Civil War

**Marlborough Street** (at corner of Cathedral Street): Pro-Cathedral (St Mary's); Dublin's Catholic Cathedral, begun in 1815 and opened in 1825. The portico is a copy of the Temple of Theseus in Athens. The three statues on it are Mary the Mother of God in the center, with the two diocesan patrons, St Kevin and St Laurence O'Toole, on either side. During the Rising there was a British sharpshooter in the bell tower. Fr O'Doherty, a priest here, was shot dead when he went to talk to the rebels, fully vested and with a cross in his hand. Sean Treacy was laid out here before being removed to Soloheadbeg for burial. Michael Collins sometimes served Mass here during the War of Independence years. Clancy, McKee, Griffith and Collins were buried from here.

**Marlborough Street**: Rabbiatti's Bar; British intelligence officers' hangout. One day, Cullen and Thornton, who drank here in order to pick up information, were asked how they learned the Irish brogue 'we've been here for the last twelve months and can't get it'.

**29 Marlborough Street**: Central Model School; George Bernard Shaw attended here. Brighid Lyons (Thornton) was medical officer here during Civil War fighting in July 1922.

**14-21 Marrowbone Lane**: Guinness buildings; James (Seamus) Murphy's HQ; he put hats and jackets on brush handles and put them in windows to 'increase' the size of his 'garrison'.

**43-45 Marrowbone Lane**: Marrowbone Lane Distillery, known as Jameson's Distillery

**8 Mary Street**: Thomas Fallon & Co; sold Volunteer uniforms, headdress, badges, etc. Haversacks cost 10d or 1s 6d; great coats were 25s; green Cronje hats (named after the Boer leader Gen Cronje) were 1s 8d; infantry swords in brown leather scabbards were five guineas.

**45 Mary Street**: The Volta Electric Cinema; Dublin's first real cinema, opened and managed in 1909 by James Joyce. It did not prosper and was sold to a group of Englishmen and re-named The Lyceum.

**46 Mary Street**: Samuel Boyd and Co, paints and chemicals

**47 Mary Street**: Todd, Burns & Co, tailors; Harry Boland worked here before the Rising.

**Maunder's Terrace, Ranelagh**: birthplace of Victor Herbert; he made a musical arrangement of *A Soldier's Song* in New York and had the royalties forwarded to Peadar Kearney in Dublin.

**78 Meath Street**: James (Jim) Larkin, fancy baker; no relation to the labour leader, although in 1913 he advertised himself as 'The Worker's Baker'.

**Mecklenburgh Street (later Tyrone Street and now Waterford Street)**: noted for its prostitutes; Joyce used it as a model for the 'Nighttown' episode in *Ulysses*.

**7 Mecklenburgh Street**: home of James Gandon when he designed The Custom House

**101 Mecklenburgh Street**: home of Paddy Heeney, Peadar's Kearney's childhood friend who collaborated with him in writing the music to *A Soldier's Song*.

**Mercer Street**: was named after Mary Mercer who founded the hospital for the poor in 1734. The hospital was built on the site of the ancient St Stephen's Church and the even older leper hospital. Sixteen dead and 278 injured non-combatants and four dead and five wounded soldiers were treated in Mercer's Hospital during the Rising.

Within the image: *Irish Rebellion _ May 1916.*
*A group of Officers with the captured rebel flag.*

*Irish Rebellion, May 1916.*
*A group of Officers with the captured rebel flag, top of O'Connell Street*

**Merrion Avenue**: 'South Hill'; first Dublin home of Arthur Hamilton Norway and his family; he was the Secretary of the GPO in 1916; his wife and son, Neville, were in Dublin at the time (another son, Fred, had died during the First World War near Armentieres). The family later moved to the Royal Hibernian Hotel on Dawson Street.

**Merrion Road**: Pembroke Town Hall, Ballsbridge; C. P. O'Neill was the Chairman of the Pembroke Urban Council during the Rising; J. C. Manly was Town Clerk. The Town Hall was appropriated by the 177th Infantry Brigade (The Lincolnshire Regiment) of the 59th (North Midland) Division after the Rising.

**1 Merrion Square**: home of Dr William Wilde; it was the boyhood home of his son, the playwright and wit Oscar Fingal O'Flahertie Wills Wilde.

**5 Merrion Square**: home of Dr Robert Farnan, a prominent gynaecologist. De Valera stayed here on 26 March 1919 – his first night home from England after his escape from Lincoln Gaol on 4 February 1919 – and in December 1920 on his return from the US. Collins met Archbishop Joseph Clune of Perth, Western Australia, here on 7 December 1920, at Lloyd George's behest, to discuss peace feelers. Archbishop Clune, born in Ruan, Co Clare, was first asked to mediate on behalf of his native land by the Hon Lord Morris, T. P. O'Connor MP and Joe Devlin MP at a luncheon in London on 30 November. That night there were severe Black and Tan reprisals at Lahinch, Co Clare, with several people killed and many homes burned. Prime Minister Lloyd George condemned all reprisals, and asked the Archbishop to go to Dublin, interview the Sinn Féin leaders, arrange a temporary truce, and prepare an atmosphere for negotiations. (These negotiations were opposed by Gen MacReady, but favoured by most of the British government.) However, Lloyd George could not guarantee the safety of the Archbishop, and would not consent to a safe conduct for the Sinn Féin leaders to meet the Archbishop. In order to remain incognito, the Archbishop travelled to Ireland on the mailboat as

'Rev Dr Walsh'. On arrival in Dublin on 6 December, he first stayed at All Hallows College, Drumcondra. On 7 December, accompanied by Dr Michael Fogarty, Bishop of Killaloe, Archbishop Clune was driven here to meet Collins. (Farnan was attending the wives of two Auxies at the time, and to this he attributed the fact that his house was never raided or searched.) Collins was 'on the run' but Arthur Griffith was in Mountjoy Prison at this time, and on 8 December, Dr Fogarty and Archbishop Clune met with A. W. Cope, the Assistant Under Secretary for Ireland, at Mountjoy, and then with Griffith. Griffith enthusiastically welcomed a truce. Then they met with Eoin MacNeill who was not so enthusiastic, but accepted it. Then the idea was presented to Michael Staines. Cope was told to present a draft of a truce to Dublin Castle, but this received a hostile reception by Sir Hamar Greenwood and the British Military. Archbishop Clune returned to London and met Lloyd George on 10 December, had another meeting with him on 11 December, and returned to Dublin that night. Dublin Castle agreed to meet with the Dáil, but Collins and Richard Mulcahy could not attend. Moreover, the IRA would have to surrender all its arms, and the Dáil could not meet publicly. Archbishop Clune returned to London on 18 December, and though meetings continued until 28 December, the negotiations were at an end. Archbishop Clune was an uncle of Conor Clune, who had just been tortured and killed on Bloody Sunday.

**33 Merrion Square**: home of Sir Thomas Myles; former President of the Royal College of Surgeons in Ireland. He was a lifelong nationalist, and had taken part in the running of guns to Ireland, picking up 600 guns from Conor O'Brien's *Kelpie*, which had delivered them from Germany to the Welsh coast, and sailed them in his vessel, *Chotah*, to Kilcoole. He was helped by James Creed Meredith, who became President of the Supreme Court. He disapproved of the Rising, which he considered rash.

**39 Merrion Square**: home of Dr Robert Woods; Oliver St John Gogarty replaced him as the ENT specialist at the Richmond Hospital; Woods went to nearby Sir Patrick Dun's.

**40 Merrion Square**: War Hospital Shipping Department, converted to an auxiliary hospital during the 1916 Rising.

**58 Merrion Square**: Daniel O'Connell's home (it was No 30 in his time)

**80 Merrion Square**: Edward Carson's home as he advanced as a solicitor; he moved here from Herbert Place. He was the first Irish QC to 'take silk' in England. He studied law at TCD and became assistant to the Chief Secretary of Ireland, Alfred Balfour, who appointed him Ireland's Solicitor General in 1892. He became an MP for Dublin University, was the prosecutor in the famous Oscar Wilde trial, and later was leader of the unionist movement in Ulster.

**82 Merrion Square**: home of William Butler Yeats

**84 Merrion Square**: became known as Plunkett House; Sir Horace Plunkett owned the building and had his office here as well. It was the second office of *The Irish Homestead*, in 1908. George Russell (AE) was editor and Susan Mitchell was his assistant. Also the office of *The Irish Statesman*, founded by Plunkett in June 1919. The first editor was Warre B. Wells, who wrote *A History of the Irish Rebellion of 1916* with N. Marlowe (1916). *The Irish Statesman* was the organ of the Irish Dominion League, dedicated to dominion status, with an independent government, avoiding partition. Writers included George Birmingham, Erskine Childers, Stephen Gwynne, Susan Mitchell, Cruise O'Brien, George O'Brien, George Russell (AE), and George Bernard Shaw. In 1923 it was revived and George Russell (AE) became the editor.

**24 Upper Merrion Street**: birthplace of Arthur Wellesley, Duke of Wellington; he disclaimed his Irish heritage and remarked: 'Just because one is born in a stable, one doesn't have to be a horse'. O'Connell's riposte: 'One doesn't have to be an ass, either'.

**Merrion View Avenue**: home of Eamon de Valera after his time in Blackrock College

**77 Mespil Road**: Mrs Julia O'Donovan's dairy, The Pembroke Creamery; she was the aunt of Gearóid O' Sullivan. Michael Collins often used her home here and in Rathgar as shelters, particularly for those coming from Cork. Collins also used her accounts to 'hide' Dáil Loan funds.

**Military Road, Ballybrack**: Rose Lawn; home of Michael Davitt, founder of The Land League. He lost his right arm in a cotton mill when he was eleven. He wrote the following: 'As long as I have tongue to speak, or head to plan, or hand to dare for Ireland, Irish landlordism and English misgovernment in Ireland shall find me a sleepless and incessant opponent.'

**Milltown**: Mount Saint Mary's; the Marist Catholic University School was established here in 1867.

**11 Molesworth Street**: *The Irish Bulletin*; Desmond FitzGerald was the editor, succeeded by Erskine Childers. Piaras Béaslaí, a Dublin journalist, acted as liaison with the Volunteer HQ. An 'underground newspaper', it was the biggest newspaper bane to the British. The office, disguised as an Insurance Society, shared the building with the 'Church of Ireland Widows and Orphans Society'. Its journalists included Robert Brennan, Erskine Childers, Desmond FitzGerald, Frank Gallagher (Gallagher wrote *Four Glorious Years* under the pseudonym of David Hogan). Anna Fitzsimmons (Miss Fitz) Kelly was the secretary, and the staff included Seamus Heaney, Seamus Hynes (messenger), Kathleen McGilligan, Kathleen McKenna, Honor Murphy, Sheila Murphy, Michael Nunan. It was published daily (except on Sundays and Bank Holidays) from 11 November 1919 until the Truce.

On 19 June 1920, it reported the words of Lt Col Brice Ferguson Smyth DSO, King's Own Scottish Borderers, Divisional Commander for Munster, who addressed RIC members at their barracks in Listowel:

*Well, Men, I have something to tell you. Something I am sure you would not want your wives to hear. Sinn Féin has had all the sport up to the present, and we are going to have the sport now. The police have done splendid work, considering the odds against them. The police are not in sufficient strength to do anything but hold their barracks. This is not enough, for as long as we remain on the defensive, so long will Sinn Féin have the whip hand. We must take the offensive and beat Sinn Féin with its own tactics. Martial law, applying to all Ireland, is coming into operation shortly, and our scheme of amalgamation must be complete by June 21st. If a police barracks is burned or if the barracks already occupied is not suitable, then the best house in the locality is to be commandeered, the occupants thrown into the gutter. Let them die there, the more the better. Police and military will patrol the country at least five nights a week. They are not to confine themselves to the main roads, but make across the country, lie in ambush and, when civilians are seen approaching, shout 'Hands up!' Should the order not be immediately obeyed, shoot and shoot with effect. If the persons approaching carry their hands in their pockets, or are in any way suspicious looking, shoot them down. You may make mistakes occasionally and innocent persons may be shot, but that cannot be helped, and you are bound to get the right parties sometime. The more you shoot, the better I will like you, and I assure you that no policeman will get into trouble for shooting any man. In the past, policemen have got into trouble for giving evidence at coroners' inquests. As a matter of fact coroners' inquests are to be made illegal so that in future no policeman will be asked to give evidence at inquests. We want your assistance in carrying out this scheme and wiping out Sinn Féin. Are you men prepared to cooperate?*

A member of his audience, Constable Jeremiah Mee, replied: 'By your accent, I take it you are an Englishman, and in your ignorance you forget you are addressing Irishmen. These, too, are English [taking off his cap, belt, and arms]. Take them, too.'[38] (J.A. Gaughan (ed.) *Memoirs of Constable J. Mee.*) Mee later worked in the Ministry of Labour for Countess Markievicz.[39]

In its 21 June 1920 issue it published lists of RIC men who had resigned. On 17 July 1920 it reported that Col Smyth was killed in the Cork City and County Club. On 10 September 1920 it published its most memorable issue, in which it traced the story of the Dáil stationery stolen from 76 Harcourt Street in November 1919, through the letters to slain Dáil members, and traced/outlined the English knowledge and action in their deaths.

On 26–27 March 1921 (Holy Saturday night) it was raided by C Company of the Auxies. On Tuesday, 29 March, Issue No 56, Volume IV, was published from Maureen Power's front room in Harold's Cross; on the following day there were two issues – one dated No 56, Volume IV, was an 'official' forgery put out by Dublin Castle; the forgery collapsed after a month – it was often quoted by the 'real' *Bulletin*.

**17-18 Molesworth Street**: Masonic Lodge. Daniel O'Connell's regalia are preserved here. Also known as the Freemason's Hall; during the Rising, it was occupied by the Volunteers and surrounded by the British. The British withdrew and the Volunteers abandoned the Hall. There was Masonic influence on both sides.

**25-26 Molesworth Street**: Buswell's Hotel; Casement, Childers and Hobson met here at the end of June 1913 to plan the Howth landing of guns. In April and May 1914 MacNeill (representing the Volunteers) often met here with representatives of Redmond's Irish Parliamentary Party, although the parliamentarians were furious when they discovered that MacNeill had no authority from the Provisional authority to negotiate with them.

**39-40 Molesworth Street**: Molesworth Hall; in 1914 Francis Sheehy-Skeffington wrote and produced a feminist play here, *The Prodigal Daughter*, the benefits to go to the Women's Franchise League.

**Montgomery Street** (now Foley Street): 'Monto'; noted for prostitutes. Named for Elizabeth Montgomery who married Lord Gardiner. Once known as 'World's End Lane'.

**Montpelier Gardens** (Infirmary Road): King George V Hospital. Sean Treacy's body was taken here and identified by Nora O'Keefe and Mollie Gleason.

**Moore Lane** (corner of Henry Place): Cogan's Greengrocer; Volunteers from the GPO went through this shop to get to Hanlon's Fish Shop, which was their last Rising HQ.

**6-8 Moore Lane:** The Flag Pub. Robert Dillon, owner, and his wife and child were killed by the British while running under a flag of truce when fleeing the fire. Upon seeing this, Padraig Pearse determined to surrender rather than have more civilian casualties. Dillon had carried on the business of The Flag for thirty-five years.

---

38. Macardle, Dorothy, *The Irish Republic*, 1937, 1965, p. 360.
39. Marreco, Anne, *The Rebel Countess, The Life and Times of Constance Markievicz*, 1967, p. 250.

*1916 – A type of armoured car used during the revolt.*

**Moore Street**: an area with many food sellers in 1916; eleven buildings were burned here during the Rising.

**Moore Street** (at the corner of Henry Place): McKane family home; escapees from the GPO left at 8 am on Friday 28 April, went into Henry Street, through Moore Street and Henry Place and into Moore Lane. They spent Friday night there. When breaking in, one of the Volunteers shot at the door, but the bullet went through the door, wounding Thomas McKane and killing his daughter, Brigid.

**15 Moore Street**: the home of the Gormans; Elizabeth O'Farrell went out their door at about 12.45 pm on Saturday, in order to find the British commander, Gen Lowe. She first met Col Hodgkin who told her to go back, then said 'I suppose this will have to be reported'. He reported to Col Portal who said 'Take that Red Cross off her, she is a spy'. Gen Lowe treated her in a more gentlemanly fashion.

**16 Moore Street** (corner of Henry Place): the rebel forces fled the GPO on O'Connell Street for Moore Street on April 28th, 1916, and spread themselves throughout the terrace. The following day the leaders congregated in No 16, from where Padraig Pearse eventually approached British forces to declare the surrender. A recent report recommending its preservation notes that the interior of No 16 is 'largely complete' in its 18th-century form.

**Morehampton Road**: house owned by Batt O'Connor; Mrs Andrew Woods lived here; Michael Collins often stayed here.

**117 Morehampton Road**: House owned by Thomas Herbert Smith. On Bloody Sunday, Cpt Donald. L. McClean of the Rifle Brigade, was killed (Chief Intelligence Officer). John Caldow, McClean's brother in law and a former soldier with the Royal Scots Fusiliers was wounded; T. H. Smith, the owner of the house, who was a friend of McClean, but not in intelligence or the Army, also was killed. Vinnie Byrne and Sean Doyle were among the Volunteers according to *An Poblacht* (20 November 1997).

**33 Morehampton Terrace, Donnybrook**: first home of Eamon and Sinead de Valera (nee Jenny Flanagan) 1910–1916.

**Mount Street**: Sinn Féin HQ after 6 Harcourt Street was raided on 20 November 1918.

**Mount Street Bridge (over Grand Canal)**: Some of the heaviest fighting during the Rising took place here on Wednesday 26 April 1916.

**Mount Street Crescent**: St Stephen's Church, also known as the 'Pepper Canister' (Church of Ireland).

**15 Mount Street Lower**: home of Countess Markievicz just prior to the Rising.

**22 Mount Street Lower**: on Bloody Sunday, Lt. H. R. Angliss (known as 'Patrick McMahon') was killed by Tom Keogh. Angliss was one of the men recalled from Russia to organise the intelligence group in Dublin. Lt. Peel escaped by piling all the furniture against the door. Two Auxies were killed outside, Frank Garner and Cecil Morris. These Auxies were sent on foot to Beggar's Bush Barracks, but were intercepted by IRA lookouts and killed. They were the first Auxies killed in Ireland and were shot by Tom Keogh on his escape. Upon arriving, Keogh had made a date with the servant maid who opened the door, and when he was escaping he told the others 'I've got to keep that date'. A military motor-cyclist saw the fight and drove to Beggar's Bush Barracks. Brig Gen Crozier was inspecting the Auxies and drove to the scene. Crozier returned to Beggar's Bush Barracks with the first accurate reports. Jim Slattery, Billy McClean, and Jim Dempsey were in the Volunteer team, as was Frank Teeling who was shot by Auxies and taken to hospital. Michael Collins soon arranged his escape from Kilmainham Gaol with Simon Donnelly and Ernie O'Malley.

**101 Mount Street Lower**: *Honesty*, edited by Miss Mary Walker

**22 Mount Street Upper**: home of Mr and Mrs Larry Nugent; he was a Volunteer Adjutant. Prior to moving to Molesworth Street *The Irish Bulletin* was housed here. Early in 1920, the Nugents agreed to give the Dáil Propaganda Department a flat on the upper floor of their home.

**38 Mount Street Upper**: on Bloody Sunday Lt Peter Ashmunt Ames, Grenadier Guards, and Lt (Brevet Cpt) George Bennett, Royal Artillery, were killed here. Ames was the son of Mrs Eleanor Ames of Morristown, NJ. Bennett had been in intelligence in WWI, and was asked to rejoin to work in Ireland. Vinnie Byrne was in charge of the detail, which walked here after Mass and included Tom Ennis, Tom Duffy, Sean Doyle, Herbie Conroy, and Frank Saurin. Katherine Farrell was the maid who let the IRA into the house.

**69 Mount Street Upper**: first Dublin home of Douglas Hyde and his wife, Lucy Kurtz

**Mount Brown**: Roe's Distillery; Thomas McCarthy's HQ. McCarthy and his entire garrison mysteriously disappeared on Tuesday morning, weakening the entire South Dublin Union area's defences.

**1 Mountjoy Square**: Alderman Walter Coles' home; the Dáil met here in 1919 and 1920. Michael Collins sometimes stayed here.

**1 Mountjoy Square**: home of T. M. Healy before he became the first Governor-General of the Irish Free State.

**27-28 Mountjoy Square**: Joseph Plunkett left Miss Quinn's Private Nursing Home here on Good Friday or Holy Saturday, having had surgery on his neck three weeks prior to the Rising.

**Mountjoy Street**: Sean McGarry's home; he had been in charge of the security party on the pier at Howth. He was editor of the *Literary Souvenir* for the O'Donovan Rossa Funeral.

Rossa died in America on 29 June 1915, and the funeral was held in Glasnevin Cemetery on 1 August. Kathleen McDonnell wrote that it was 'a chance for the Irish to prove that a dead patriot is at once a challenge to British tyranny and an inspiration to his own people'. McGarry approached Connolly to write an article, and Connolly replied: 'When are you fellows going to stop blathering about *dead* Fenians? Why don't you get a few *live* ones for a change? Rossa was prepared to fight England *at peace*. You fellows won't fight her *at war!* Between the Molly Maguires and the Molly Coddles we'll [the ICA] be landed in the soup!' Later Clarke talked to Connolly, and Connolly wrote an article in which he managed to turn a dead Fenian into a live incitement to revolution: 'The Irish Citizen Army pledges its members to fight for a Republican freedom for Ireland'. It was at this funeral that Pearse made perhaps his most famous speech:

*They think that they have pacified Ireland. They think that they have pacified half of us and intimidated the other half. They think that they have foreseen everything, think that they have provided against everything; but the fools, the fools, the fools! – they have left us our Fenian dead, and while Ireland holds these graves, Ireland unfree shall never be at peace* (see Appendix III).

McGarry accidentally shot Tom Clarke in the elbow on 30 January 1916; the wound never completely healed. Collins stayed here on the night the Volunteer Cabinet was arrested, after McGarry had been taken in the 'German Plot' (17–18 May 1918); in all seventy-three were arrested. McGarry escaped from Lincoln Gaol with de Valera and Sean Milroy (Milroy was the prisoner who drew the cartoon Christmas Card of a man with a key – the key was the shape of the one Michael Collins and Harry Boland made to open the doors for the escape). McGarry's home was burned by Republicans/IRA on 10 December 1922, and his seven year old son died later from burns received. His electrical fittings shop was bombed the following month. He was to become an Irish Free State TD.

**19 Mountjoy Street**: Susan Killeen lived here with the family of her uncle Patrick.

**30 Mountjoy Street** (across from Aras na nGael): home of Madeline 'Dilly' Dicker, a 'girl-friend' of Michael Collins before Kitty Kiernan. She lived here with her Father, Edwin. Dilly was an ardent nationalist, and a member of Sinn Féin and Cumann na mBan. She undertook many risky tasks for Collins.

**44 Mountjoy Street**: Munster Private Hotel, also known as Aras na nGael, owned by Miss Myra T. McCarthy. She was a staunch Republican from Kerry. Michael Collins lived here in 1917, as did Fionan Lynch (who was arrested with Austin Stack and Thomas Ashe for violations of the DORA). Even after Collins went 'on the run,' he still left his laundry here and picked it up on Saturdays.

**28 Mount Pleasant Avenue Upper**: home of J. J. Coade; shot by Bowen-Colthurst in Portobello Barracks, he is buried in Glasnevin.

**21 Mountshannon Road**: home of Mrs Mellows

**43 Moyne Road, Rathmines**: home of Hanna Sheehy-Skeffington and her son Owen after they were evicted from Grosvenor Place following the killing of Francis. They then moved to Belgrave Road.

**34 Munster Street, Phibsborough:** de Valera's family home at the time of the Rising

**11 Nassau Street**: home of Grace Gifford Plunkett for many years after the Civil War.

**32 Nassau Street**: British Department of Munitions Office, opened in 1917; it was opened to coordinate Ireland's WWI efforts; John Chartres was said to have been connected with this office.

**45 Nassau Street**: Frank Gallagher, Cigar Importer; later the site of the Berni Inn; at the back of this was Kidd's Buffet, known as 'Kidd's Back'; very important meeting place for English touts. Cullen, Thornton, Tobin and Saurin met their 'contacts' here and passed themselves off as friends of the English officers in order to get information.

**46 Nassau Street**: Jammet's Restaurant (David Hogan wrote of 'Kidd's, which has since become Jammet's'); for some time located at Andrew Street and Church Lane; a French restaurant, the finest in Dublin prior to and after the Rising. Sean MacDermott took his closest friends here for a 'last meal' just prior the Rising. Often used by Michael Collins and Harry Boland, it was raided on 10 January 1921. Harry Boland ate here with former Collins's secretary Ms Anna Fitzsimmons (later Mrs Kelly) on 30 July 1922, and told her 'not to worry'. He was shot on 31 July at the Grand Hotel, Skerries, and died on 2 August in St Vincent's Hospital.

**1-5 Northumberland Road**: St Stephen's Parochial Hall, opposite Clanwilliam House on Clanwilliam Street; the hall was also opposite 25 Northumberland Road. Patrick Doyle (leader), Joe Clarke, William Christian and P. McGrath held off the Sherwood Foresters from here as long as they could, then fled to Percy Place where they were captured. St Stephen's Parish School was across the road. Denis O'Donoghue and a couple of men occupied the school building.

**25 Northumberland Road** (corner of Haddington Road, see 1, 2 Clanwilliam Place): Clanwilliam House was on the city side, east side of the intersection; St Stephen's Parochial Hall was on the opposite side (the south east side) of the Grand Canal on the east side of the street; 25 Northumberland Road was on the same side of the Canal, but further toward the south east, toward Kingstown (Dun Laoghaire). There was a total of thirteen men in the three outposts. They opened fire on the 1st Dublin Battalion Associated Volunteer Corps, the Georgius Rex ('Gorgeous Wrecks', 'George Royals', 'Methusiliers'), wounding seven and killing five – F. H. Browning, Reginald Clery, John Gibbs, Thomas Harborne and James Nolan. G. Hosford was shot by a sniper while in Beggar's Bush Barracks, and died later. One column of the GRs was led by F. H. Browning, who later died. He was a graduate of TCD, was an outstanding cricketer, was president of the Irish Rugby Union and played for his University as well as for Wanderers, and founded the Irish Rugby Volunteer Corps. Known as 'Chicken' Browning, he was one of the best cricketers Ireland ever produced. The other column of GRs was larger and was under the command of Major G. A. Harris of TCD OTC Barracks, and, though coming under some fire, managed to reach the Barracks with only one casualty.

The Sherwood Foresters were the 7th and 8th Battalions, part of the 178th Infantry Brigade. The Sherwood officers Col Oates and Col Maconchy were ordered to go straight to Beggar's Bush Barracks and through the Mount Street Bridge area, even though they had been warned of the casualties to the Georgius Rex reserves. Cpt F. C. Dietrichsen, marching into Dublin with his troops, saw his children on the street watching the troops arrive. His wife had sent them to Ireland without his knowledge for safekeeping from Zeppelin raids in England. He greeted and hugged them, and was later killed at Mount Street Bridge. He was buried in Mount Jerome Cemetery.

Brigid Grace warned the men in 25 Northumberland Road of the advance of the Sherwoods, though she was unable to get food through the blocked door. Lt Michael

Malone (at the top of the house) was killed (he had been de Valera's ADC); James Grace (in the basement) survived but was captured (he had a revolver and four bullets left when he hid in the garden.); two youths, Paddy Byrne and Michael Rowe, were sent home by Malone because he didn't think anyone would survive. He had them leave their weapons and ammunition.

St Stephen's Parochial Hall was the most exposed of the three positions. Holden Stoddart, Superintendent of the St John's Ambulance Brigade, was killed as he accompanied a stretcher party to a wounded soldier here. Three bodies were buried in the grounds of the Parochial Hall, and one body was buried at 25 Northumberland Road; these bodies were not removed until 12 May 1916.

**29, 31, 33 Northumberland Road**: used as field hospitals by the Sherwood Foresters during the fighting at the bridge.

**North Strand**: Creighton House, home of James Larkin

**North Strand Road** (see also Poplar Row): Wicklow Chemical Manure Company

**Nutley Lane**: at the corner of Simmonscourt Road – Elm Park Golf Club. Allen Bell was taken off a tram opposite here and shot on 27 March 1920. ('Come on, Mr Bell, your time has come'). Earlier that month he had signed an order requiring banks to disclose all details of clients' accounts. He had been working with Sir John Taylor, the Under-Secretary and had recently seized £20,000 from accounts in the Munster and Leinster Bank believed to belong to Sinn Féin depositors. He had previously been the English 'spymaster' handling 'Jameson' (John C. Byrne).

**21 Oakley Road, Ranelagh**: Cullenswood House. This was the first site of St Enda's School. It was originally conceived as St Lorcan's School, but took the name St Enda's from the patron saint of the Aran Islands; founded by Padraig Pearse and Thomas MacDonagh, and opened on 8 September 1909. When St Enda's moved to another site on Oakley Road, this site became St Ita's School, where Louise Gavan Duffy was one of the teachers. Kitty, Helen and Maud Kiernan attended St Ita's from 1910 until the school closed in 1912. Mrs Pearse re-opened St Enda's here after the Rising while The Hermitage was occupied by British troops, then moved back to the other Oakley Road site.

**29 Oakley Road, Ranelagh**: The Grace House, Thomas MacDonagh's home. He moved here in 1910 in order to be closer to St Enda's. Muriel Gifford (sister of Grace Gifford Plunkett) married Thomas MacDonagh on 3 January 1912. Grace Gifford Plunkett stayed here at the time of the Rising.

**44 Oakley Road, Ranelagh**: in April 1917 a 'Conference of Women Delegates' met here to petition Sinn Féin for representation and demanded equality of status for women. The petition was for six members to represent women on the Sinn Féin Executive: Áine Ceannt, Kathleen Clarke, Alice Ginnell, Dr Kathleen Lynn, Helena Molony and Jennie Wyse-Power.

**30 O'Connell Villas, Fairview**: home of M. W. O'Reilly, Quartermaster of the Irish Volunteers prior to the Rising, he became O/C at Frongoch.

**25 O'Donohoe Street, Inchicore**: final home of Peadar Kearney; he died here in 1942.

**8 Ontario Terrace, Canal Road, Charlemont Bridge**: home of John Mitchell before he was transported to Van Dieman's Land.

**Ormond Quay**: office of *The Republic*; the editor was Darrell Figgis. It was suppressed in September 1919, following publication of an advertisement for the Dáil Loan. Figgis

**22-28 Peter Street**: Adelaide Hospital; it amalgamated in recent years with several other Dublin hospitals and moved to Tallaght. Kathleen Lynn trained here as a doctor.

**Phibsborough Road**: home of Mrs Toomey; Dan Breen was first taken here after the attack on Gen French on 19 December 1919. His wounds were treated by Dr J. M. Ryan. Breen then went to Mrs Malone's house on Grantham Street.

**Phibsborough Road (rere 61 Connaught Street)**: Dalymount Park, home of the Bohemians Soccer Club. Bohemians GAA team also played here. Also known as 'The Pisser's Field' because it was here that farmers travelling home from the nearby Cattle Market relieved themselves.

**Philipsburgh Avenue, Fairview** (Fr Mathew Park): the 2nd Battalion companies paraded here during Easter Week, 1916. Fr Walter McDonnell, a Fairview Curate, came into the Park on Monday and heard Confessions and blessed the Volunteers.

**Philipsburgh Avenue, Fairview**: National School; Irish classes were taught here by Thomas O'Neill Russell and attended by Frank Henderson.

**Phoenix Park**: the Magazine Fort was attacked here by members of Fianna Éireann after their 'soccer' game. They were led by Paddy Daly and Gerry Holohan. Tim Roche commandeered a horse-drawn jaunting car as an 'escape vehicle'.

**54 Pimlico Street, The Liberties**: home of James Connolly's family on his first stay in Dublin.

**Poddle River Tunnel**: just west of the Ha'penny Bridge on the south side of the Liffey.

**Poplar Row** (and North Strand Road): Wicklow Chemical Manure Company. A force of ICA, originally under the command of a man named Craven, held this early in the Rising. Vincent Poole was second in command. Frank Henderson took charge of this force and in it were Harry Boland and Harry Colley.

**35 Portland Row**: Cleansing Department of Dublin Corporation

**Portland Street North**: Mrs O'Riordan's boarding house. John Pinkman stayed here after he came to Dublin in 1922.

**Prince's Street North**: fifteen buildings were burned here during the Rising.

**4-8 Prince's Street North**: in 1916, this was the office of *The Freeman's Journal*. Prior to the Rising, the *Journal* was John Redmond's paper and a fierce opponent of the Irish Volunteers.

*The seven signatories of the Irish Proclamation (from left):*
*Padraig Pearse, James Connolly, Thomas Clarke, Thomas MacDonagh,*
*Sean MacDermott, Joseph Plunkett and Eamonn Ceannt.*
*All seven signatories of the Proclamation were executed.*

**4-8 Prince's Street North**: La Scala Theatre; in 1926 de Valera founded the Fianna Fáil party here.

**29 Prince's Street North**: Capitol Cinema Theatre; destroyed in the Rising

**Railway Street**: part of the 'Monto' area

**Raheny**: Belcamp Park; Countess Markievicz leased this as a training centre for Fianna Éireann.

**Raheny**: St Anne's; home of Arthur Edward Guinness III, Lord Ardilaun, great-grandson of the founder of the brewery. In 1877 he bought St Stephen's Green and re-opened it to the public.

**7 Ranelagh Road**: Cpt Noble, a British intelligence agent, had rooms here. On Bloody Sunday, Volunteers led by Joe Dolan and Dan McDonnell were assigned to kill him, but he wasn't home. Also in the Volunteer team were C. S. (Todd) Andrews, Francis X. Coghlan, Hubert Earle, and James Kenny.

**19 Ranelagh Road**: the Ryan family home; Jim, Mary (Min) and Phyllis lived here before the Rising.

**16 Rathdown Road**: the Belton family home. Sean Hurley found Michael Collins a room here on his return from London in January 1916.

**Rathfarnham, Co Dublin**: 'The Hermitage', St Enda's (Scoil Éanna) founded by Padraig Pearse was situated here from 1910 until it was occupied by the British army after the Rising. Named for St Enda, who abandoned the heroic life of a warrior to teach a devoted band of scholars in the remote seclusion of the Aran Islands. Formerly known as 'The Hermitage' it was an eighteenth century house, set on fifty acres of woods and parklands, enhanced by a lake and river near its boundary. The motto of the school was: 'Truth on our lips, strength in our hands, and purity in our hearts'. The school was known for liberal teaching methods and unyielding nationalism. Among its teachers (full or part time, or guest lecturers) were Tomás MacDomhnaill (music), Michael Smithwick (mathematics), Dr Patrick Doody (classics), Owen Lloyd (music), John Henry, W. B. Yeats, Douglas Hyde, Padraic Colum, Standish O'Grady, Edward Martyn, and Alice Stopford Green. Among its students were James Larkin's sons Jim, Denis and Fintan, three sons and a nephew of Eoin MacNeill, two sons of Peter McGinley, a son of

Irish Rebellion May 1916.
Ruined Sackville Street Dublin barricaded with Motor Cars

men here prior to the Rising. Doyle led sixteen men in the occupation of Davy's. Michael Kelly led another section of sixteen to a position on the railway bridge crossing of the Grand Canal in support of the Davy's men, and this section was to cover the Davy's retreat.

**Richmond Street South** (and Charlemont Mall, overlooking Portobello Bridge): Portobello Hospital; across from Davy's Pub

**Richmond Street North**: Christian Brothers School: 'A veritable Revolutionary Seminary'; it was said the students sold little flags on which were the words 'Tá ár lá a'teacht' ('Our day is coming'); attended by Eamonn Ceannt, Oliver St John Gogarty and Tom Kettle.

**Ross Road** (and Bride Street): Ceannt and MacDonagh surrendered to Cpt Wheeler here.

**15 Russell Place, North Circular Road**: Sean MacDermott's home; in 1916 Dublin Castle recorded his address as 500 North Circular Road.

**14 Russell Street**: childhood home of Brendan Behan

**Rutland Square (now Parnell Square)**: The first of Dublin's Georgian squares, its four sides were originally known as Charlemont Row, Cavendish Row, Palace Row, and Great Britain Street. The central park was named after the 4th Duke of Rutland, who was Lord Lieutenant of Ireland, 1784–87. Now named for Home Rule leader Charles Stewart Parnell.

**Rutland Square (now Parnell Square)**: Garden of Remembrance; it was in this location that the prisoners were held overnight in the open on 29 April 1916.

**Rutland Square, 8 Cavendish Row**: grocery shop of Robert MacKenzie; he was killed on 27 April 1916 as he was sitting in his shop. He had survived the sinking of the Lusitania in 1915.

**3 Rutland Square**: Edward Fannin's home; a doctor with the Royal Medical Corps

**4 Rutland Square**: old HQ of the Irish Volunteers

**5 Rutland Square**: Oliver St John Gogarty was born here in 1878.

**10 Rutland Square**: the Orange Hall here was seized by Republicans/IRA in March 1922

and converted to a dormitory, while they used the Fowler Memorial Hall, to the rear of the building, as a Centre of Direction for the seizure of private property.

**11 Rutland Square**: Kevin O'Higgins' Office as Minister of Local Government . Also in this building were the offices of Dublin County Council which were raided on 25 November 1920. The British were looking for some specific evidence in the county council offices and though they 'lined up' O'Higgins and his staff, they ignored their offices!

**17 Rutland Square**: Abbey Presbyterian Church, known as Findlater's Church.

**20 Rutland Square**: Banba Hall, a progressive trade union centre.

**25 Rutland Square**: Grocer's Hall/Gaelic League Building (Coisde Gnotha Branch). This was the usual parade hall of C Company, 2nd Battalion, prior to the Rising. It was also the Central Branch of Cumann na mBan (the original branch). The time-lag between the formation of the Irish Volunteers and the formation of its counterpart, Cumann na mBan, was due to disagreement on whether the women would be part of the Volunteers, or whether they would be content to perform tasks like fundraising when requested by the men. Many envisioned women's role to be totally subordinate to the needs of the Volunteers. Cumann na mBan was initiated in April 1914 with Agnes O'Farrelly as its first President: Mary Colum was one of its first organisers. There were forty-three affiliated branches before the Rising. Its officers at the time of the Rising were: Kathleen Clarke, President; Sorcha McMahon, Secretary; Members: Áine Ceannt, Louise Gavan Duffy, Niamh Plunkett, Jenny Wyse-Power. Cumann na mBan played a larger role in the Civil War than in the Rising. It held its own convention on the Treaty on 5 February 1922, and voted 419 to 63 against the Treaty. Countess Markievicz was elected President at the time. Pro-Treaty members were asked to resign, and they formed their own group, called Cumann na Saoirse (Society of Freedom), which was not militarily active during the Civil War. P. S. O'Hegarty wrote:

*'As the war lengthened, it became more brutal and more savage and more hysterical and more unrelievedly black. But the worst effect was on the women. They were the first to be thrown off their base, and as the war lengthened they steadily deteriorated. They took to their hearts every catch-cry and every narrowness and every bitterness, and steadily eliminated from themselves every womanly feeling.... War, and the things war breeds – intolerance, swagger, unwomanness – captured the women, turned them into unlovely, destructive-minded, arid begetters of violence.'[40]*

The 1st Battalion, Dublin Brigade, drilled here weekly after the Rising. It was used as HQ by the Republicans/IRA from March 1922.

**25 Rutland Square**: offices of Sean T. O'Kelly, who was general secretary of the Gaelic League in 1916 and became the first President of the Republic of Ireland in 1949. On 9 September 1914 there was a meeting here of the Supreme Council of the IRB, albeit not exclusively of the IRB. (Non-IRB members were also present.) It was decided that 'England's difficulty is Ireland's opportunity' (Wolfe Tone) and there would be a Rising before the end of the war. Among those present were Eamonn Ceannt, Thomas Clarke, James Connolly, Arthur Griffith, John McBride, Sean MacDermott, Sean McGarry, William O'Brien, Sean T. O'Kelly, Padraig Pearse, Joseph Plunkett, and a man named

40. O'Hegarty, P. S., *The Victory of Sinn Féin*, 1924, 1998, p. 38.

Tobin. The Volunteer 'Advisory Committee' was formed; original members were Pearse and Plunkett and 'a considerable number of Volunteer Officers'. By December 1914, with its attendant risks of leakage, the committee was discontinued. Pearse proposed two resolutions:

1. *Volunteer action during the war should be confined to the defence of Ireland*
2. *Volunteers should announce their intention to occupy the ports, in the event of shortages, to pre-vent food from being exported.*

Early in the summer of 1915, the Executive of the IRB approved Ceannt, Pearse and Plunkett as a 'Military Committee' (Diarmuid Lynch asserts repeatedly that the 'Military Council' was instituted not by the Supreme Council, but by the IRB Executive Council).[41] P. S. O'Hegarty wrote that the Supreme Council, at its last meeting in January 1916, was not convinced an offensive insurrection was warranted.[42] Desmond Ryan has asserted that the resolution that 'we fight at the earliest date possible' apparently was adopted with some reservations on the part of some members of the Supreme Council.[43] Yet Denis McCullough has said: 'The decision by the Supreme Council to call a Rising at the earliest possible date, after prolonged discussion under my chairmanship, was unanimous. I know my worth. I was there all the time, working and building up the IRB. But the actual Rising was the work mainly of four men – Pearse, MacDermott, Connolly and Clarke.'[44] Some months later when MacDermott was released from prison, he and Clarke acted as ex-officio members of the Military Committee. After the last meeting of the Supreme Council on 16 January 1916, all additions to the re-named Military Council were at the discretion of the Executive. After Connolly's 'disappearance and reappearance,' he was co-opted onto the Council. In the second week of April, MacDonagh was co-opted onto the Council, and it thereafter consisted of the seven signatories to the Proclamation.

**28 Rutland Square** (and Granby Lane): Rutland High School

**29-30 Rutland Square**: Vaughan's Hotel; owned by Mrs Vaughan of Clare who sold it to Tom McGuire, formerly of Limerick; 'Joint No 1'. Unsafe for Volunteers after mid-1920. Christy Harte was the usual night porter. It was said he was offered many thousands of pounds by the British to turn in Michael Collins and others; he'd be given the money, protection, transportation out of Ireland and a new name. Irish wags said he'd have to change his name to Christy 'Eleyison'! Conor Clune was arrested here on 20 November 1920. He was an Irish scholar from the west who had nothing to do with the Volunteers but who had to come to see Piaras Béaslaí about Irish language projects. Béaslaí and Sean O'Connell escaped out the back on 20 November. Above the number '30' one could still see the name 'Vaughan's' for many years.

**31 Rutland Square**: Ancient Order of Hibernians Hall; the AOH was very much closer to the ICA than were the Volunteers. Joseph Scollan, from Derry, was the National Director after 1911; he bought thirty rifles from the ICA for £30 in 1915.

41. Lynch, Diarmuid, *The IRB and the 1916 Revolution*, 1957, p. 30, 150–151, and footnotes on p. 131–132.
42. O'Hegarty, P. S., *The Victory of Sinn Féin*, 1924, 1998, p. 3.
43. Ryan, Desmond, *The Rising: The Complete Story of Easter Week.* 1949, 1957, p. 9.
44. Coogan, Tim Pat, *Ireland Since the Rising*, 1966 p. 10.

**39 Rutland Square**: home of Dr Paddy Browne of Maynooth College (later President of University College Galway), from which Michael Collins watched the raid on Vaughan's on 20 November 1920 (during which Conor Clune was arrested). Earlier that evening, Michael Collins had a meeting at the Gaiety Theatre bar.

**41 Rutland Square**: Irish National Forester's Hall (now Kevin Barry Memorial Hall). The GAA often met here. Padraig O'Riain's father was the caretaker and let the Fianna and Volunteers use the hall. Watching the Ulster Volunteer Force arm, the IRB began drilling here in secret prior to the meeting in Wynn's Hotel, supervised by members of the Fianna Éireann (see also 35–37 Abbey Street Lower). The Fianna 'teachers' were primarily Con Colbert, Michael Lonergan, Eamon Martin and Padraig O'Riain. Irish Volunteers learned military drill here prior to the Rising. On 23 April 1916, Volunteers met here for a concert after the Rising was 'cancelled'. On Easter Sunday night the 3rd Battalion officers and men met here under the command of de Valera. On Easter Monday, the 1st Battalion mustered here. In 1922 the IRB held conferences here for the express purpose of endeavoring to save the IRB from disruption on the Treaty issue. Michael Collins and Liam Lynch were the principal protagonists of the opposing views. On 10 January 1922 those in favour of the Treaty argued that to accept would be in line with well-accepted IRB policy, that it was a matter of expedience and not of principle. Those opposed to the Treaty argued that the Republic was 'established' and acceptance of the Treaty would disestablish it. On 18 March (postponed from 12 March) Collins determined to accept the Treaty and to do whatever was necessary to operate it and tried to convince all of the necessity for it. Lynch decided that even if the people voted for the Treaty the Army could not be committed to it. On 19 April once again Collins and Lynch squared off, but neither side was able to convince the other. Attendees were (at least) Michael Collins, Harry Boland, Eoin O'Duffy, Diarmuid O'Hegarty, Michael Staines, Sean O'Murthille, Gearóid O'Sullivan, Martin Conlon, Sean McKeown, Liam Lynch, Humphrey Murphy, Pax Whelan, Florence O'Donoghue, Joe McKelvey, Sean Boylan, Michael Sheehan, Larry Brady, Patrick Mullaney and Tom Larkin.

**44 Rutland Square**: the Ancient Order of Hibernians Meeting Rooms. It became HQ of the Irish National Volunteers and was used as a Drill Hall. After the Rising, it was the second meeting place of K Company, 3rd Battalion of Volunteers. In August 1917, Col Maurice Moore (a member of the Connaught Rangers) presided over a Convention of 176 companies and called for the re-unification of the National Volunteers with the Volunteers. It is currently the Dublin Sinn Féin HQ.

**46 Rutland Square**: Gaelic League HQ (Conradh na Gaeilge). On Easter Sunday night the 2nd Battalion officers and men met here under the command of Thomas MacDonagh. Arms were hidden here and taken by The O'Rahilly to the GPO on Monday in his blue De Dion Bouton motorcar, which was later used as a part of a barricade and burned. 'The Squad' was initiated here, 19 September 1919; a meeting was held by Michael Collins and Richard Mulcahy, at which 'The Squad' was officially formed, though its original meeting had been in July. Ben Barrett, Paddy Daly, Sean Doyle, Tom Keogh, Joe Leonard, Mick McDonnell, and Jim Slattery attended. Barrett, Daly, Doyle and Leonard were told to leave their jobs as they would become full time employees. In August 1917 a meeting was held here to establish a National Executive of Oglaigh na hÉireann (IRA). It was decided to have the meeting at the same time as the Sinn Féin Ard Fheis, which met on 27 October 1917: present were Thomas Ashe, Cathal Brugha, Michael Collins, Eamon de

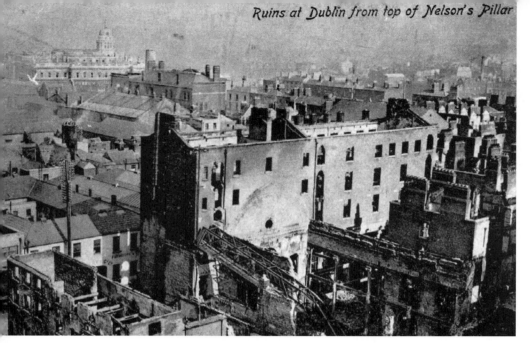

*The ruins of Dublin from the top of Nelson's Pillar*

Valera, Diarmuid Lynch, Richard Mulcahy, Diarmuid O'Hegarty, Michael Staines. In April 1918 Joe Good wrote that there was a meeting here chaired by Cathal Brugha and Dick Mulcahy. At this meeting it was decided to send Volunteers to London to assassinate the British Cabinet. Brugha led the team to London in May and it stayed there until August, but he never received Dáil approval for the assassinations. Those on the team included Tom Craven, Joe Good, Matt Furlong, Martin Gleeson, James 'Ginger' McNamara, James Mooney, Peter Murtagh, Sam Reilly and Bill Whelan.

**27 Rutland Street Upper**: home of Sean T. O'Kelly in 1916. Padraig and Willie Pearse stayed here for the two nights preceding the Rising.

**29 Rutland Street Upper** home of Oscar Traynor at the time of the Rising.

**Ryder's Row**: O'Flanagan Sinn Féin Club. This was where Volunteers, including Kevin Barry, mustered on the morning he was captured.

**Sackville Lane**: The O'Rahilly crawled up here after being wounded, and died here. He died slowly – four hours after he was shot he was heard calling for water, and at the moment of surrender nineteen hours later a British ambulance came across him, barely alive. A British officer was then said to remark: 'The more of them that die naturally, the fewer we'll have to shoot'. The O'Rahilly wrote this note to his wife: 'Written after I was shot, Darling Nancy I was shot leading a rush up Moore Street, took refuge in a doorway. While I was there I heard the men pointing out where I was + I made a bolt for the lane I am in now. I got more than one bullet I think. Tons + tons of love dearie to you + to the boys + to Nell + Anna. It was a good fight anyhow. Please deliver this to Nannie O'Rahilly, 40 Herbert Park, Dublin. Good bye darling.' His body was seen by Elizabeth O'Farrell when she returned from her first meeting with Gen Lowe in Tom Clarke's shop.

**Sackville Place**: six buildings were burned here during the Rising.

*1916 – The Geneeral Post Office*

**Sackville Street** (formerly Drogheda Street, now O'Connell Street): reputed to be Europe's widest street at 150 feet, with a 50-foot wide central mall and two-50 foot wide roadways. Originally developed in the 1700s by Henry Moore, Earl of Drogheda, and named after Lionel Cranfield Sackville, 1st Duke of Dorset, Lord Lieutenant of Ireland, 1731–37 and 1751–55. In the early years of the twentieth century, it was unofficially 'divided,' with the west side being given over to the British military and their girls, and the east side to the Dublin civilians. Its name was officially changed in 1924 to honour Daniel O'Connell. A previous attempt to change it in 1885 was prevented by Hedges Eyre Chatterton, the Vice-Chancellor of Ireland, who got an injunction preventing it. The citizens started using the O'Connell name, though, and the old street plates disintegrated without replacement.

**Sackville Street**: Carlisle Bridge/Sackville Bridge/O'Connell Bridge; 154 feet wide, almost square and wider than it is long. The present structure was built in 1880.

**Sackville Street (now O'Connell Street)**: on 31 March 1912, there was a monster meeting to welcome the Home Rule Bill. The first speaker was John Redmond: 'Trust the old party and Home Rule next year'. The second speaker was Eoin MacNeill: 'There is no government so very bad that it would not be better for the Irish people to accept it if they themselves were in charge of it. If the English people have sense, they will not endeavor to keep back from Ireland as much as one inch of her rights, especially in regard to the financial question and the question of taxation. We are not asking for charity but demanding our rights.' Padraig Pearse appeared third. He, like MacNeill, spoke in Irish: 'We have no wish to destroy the British, we only want our freedom. We differ among ourselves on small points, but we agree that we want freedom, in some shape or other. There are two sections of us – one that would be content to remain under the British Government in our own land, another that never paid, and never will pay, hom-

*1916 – The Last Stand inside the Geneeral Post Office*

age to the King. I am of the latter, and everyone knows it. But I should think myself a traitor to my country if I did not answer the summons of this gathering, for it is clear to me that the Bill we support today will be for the good of Ireland, and that we will be stronger with it than without it. Let us unite and win a good Act from the British: I think it can be done.' He concluded with the following words however: 'If we are tricked this time, there is a party in Ireland, and I am one of them, that will advise the Gael to have no counsel or dealing with the Gall but to answer henceforward, with the strong arm and the sword's edge .... If we are cheated once more there will be red war in Ireland.'45 In the early years, Pearse's 'nationalism' was more cultural than political, but by this time he had come to the conclusion that force was needed in the face of Unionist opposition to Home Rule. With the passage of just four years he would read the Proclamation from about the same spot on the street.

**Sackville Street Lower**: this ran from Henry Street on the west and North Earl Street on the east to O'Connell Bridge. All buildings from 1 to 47 were burned during the Rising. Some were burned as a result of British artillery fire, and some from fires started by looters; both fireworks and lamp-oil were set alight by the looters.

**Sackville Street Lower**: James 'Big Jim' Larkin's Statue. Larkin led the workers during the Lockout of 1913 and was exiled to America: it was then that James Connolly formed the Irish Citizen Army for the protection of the workers. Larkin was in America during the Rising and returned in 1923. His statue was sculpted by Oisin Kelly. The words 'The great appear great because we are on our knees: let us be free' were attributed to Larkin, but they were probably written by Camille Desmoulins during the French Revolution

---

45. Macardle, Dorothy, *The Irish Republic*, 1937, 1965, p. 82.

in 1789. On the west side of the plinth the following lines appear, written by Patrick Kavanagh:

*And tyranny trampled them in Dublin's gutter*
*Until Jim Larkin came along and cried*
*The call of Freedom and the call of Pride*
*And Slavery crept to its hands and knees*
*And Nineteen Thirteen cheered from out the utter*
*Degradation of their miseries.*

On the east side of the plinth are the words of Sean O'Casey: 'He talked to the workers as only Jim Larkin could speak, not for an assignation with peace, dark obedience or placid resignation; but trumpet-tongued of resistance to wrong, discontent with leering poverty, and defiance of any power strutting out to stand in the way of their march onward'.

**Sackville Street Lower**: Nelson's Pillar, between Henry Street and North Earl Street, distinguished Upper Sackville Street from Lower Sackville Street. The original stone was laid on 15 Feb 1808 and the monument was completed in 1809; it was the first such monument to Lord Nelson and cost £6,858, raised by public subscription. It stood 134 feet tall, carved out of white Portland stone, with 168 winding steps to the lookout balcony. It was blown up by the IRA at 1.32 am on Tuesday, 8 March 1966.

**Sackville Street Lower**: the General Post Office (GPO); opened in 1818, it was 200 feet long and 150 feet wide, with a height of 50 feet in three storeys. Its architect was Francis Johnston. A major edifice of Dublin's eighteenth-century and nineteenth-century classical architecture, it was built from mountain granite with a portico of Portland stone. The portico is 50 feet long, an Ionic portico of six fluted columns, a pediment surmounted with statues of Hibernia, Fidelity and Mercury, and a tympanum decorated with the Royal coat of arms. The Proclamation of the Irish Republic was read on the steps at 12.45 pm on Monday, 24 April 1916 (some reports erroneously cite 12.04 pm). Florrie O'Donoghue wrote:

*It was considered essential that the Proclamation should be in such terms and issued in such circumstances that, no matter how the Rising ended, the event would take an authentic place in historic succession to earlier efforts to achieve freedom, and that it re-define in modern terms the unchanging aspiration of the Irish people for sovereign control over their own destinies. That aspiration had to be set on the highest moral plane and expressed publicly in a definite form.* (For the text of the Proclamation see Appendix III.)

There is a plaque on the building displaying the following message:

*Here on Easter Monday 1916, Padraig Pearse read the Proclamation of the Irish Republic. From this building he commanded the forces that asserted in arms Ireland's right to freedom. It is they who keep the fire alive.*

After the Rising, and before the GPO was reconstructed, a temporary 'GPO' was located at 14 Sackville Street. The GPO was re-opened in 1929 after renovation.

**Sackville Street Lower**: the Daniel O'Connell Monument; O'Connell lived between 1775 and 1847; he was known as 'The Liberator'. His monument was designed by John Henry Foley and was unveiled in 1882. One of the higher female figures holds a copy of the 'Catholic Emancipation' Act of 1829. The lower figures represent Patriotism, Fidelity, Courage, and Eloquence. There are many bullet holes in the statue, relics of the Rising.

**1 Sackville Street Lower** (and Eden Quay): Hopkins and Hopkins, jewellers and silversmiths. Held by Seamus Robinson, Seamus Lundy and Cormac Turner alone until Connolly sent ICA member Andy Conroy, a crack shot as a sniper. Made the Sam Maguire Trophy for the GAA in 1928; fashioned to the design of the Ardagh Chalice.

**2 Sackville Street Lower**: William Scott, tailor: burned during the Rising.

**3 Sackville Street Lower**: Hamilton, Long & Co, apothecaries: burned during the Rising.

**4 Sackville Street Lower**: The Waverley Hotel: burned during the Rising.

**6, 7 Sackville Street Lower**: Dublin Bread Co; its glass roof was described by James Stephens as a 'Chinese-like pagoda'. The initials D.B.C. were worn on the uniforms in the restaurant, leading one waitress to tell a questioning English officer they represented: 'Death Before Conscription!'. A detail under the command of Fergus O'Kelly held it during the Rising.

**8 Sackville Street Lower**: Grand Hotel and Restaurant: burned during the Rising.

**10, 11 Sackville Street Lower** (corner Abbey Street Lower) Reis & Co Building. The Irish School of Wireless Telegraphy was situated here; it was closed in 1914 and all its apparatus was dismantled then. Fergus O'Kelly led six men to take and restore the wireless equipment to get the 'story out to the world'. The first 'broadcast' was at 5.30 pm on Tuesday, but the receiver could not be repaired. Johnny 'Blimey' O'Connor was the telegrapher. The building was burned out on Wednesday.

**12, 13 Sackville Street Lower** (corner of Abbey Street Lower): Hibernian Bank; burned during the Rising.

**15 Sackville Street Lower**: City and County of Dublin Permanent Building Society; burned during the Rising.

*St John Ambulance Brigade, 'First Aid' Hut, outside the Hamman Hotel, O'Connell Street, Dublin, June 29th 1922.*
*The 'First Aid' hut wasn't dismantled until many years later.*

**17 Sackville Street Lower**: Hoyte & Son, druggists and oilworks; 'The City of Dublin Drug Hall'. This premises housed a lot of chemicals, methylated spirits, turpentine, oils etc. It burst into flames during the Rising and many oil drums exploded, giving extra fuel to the flames: 'The most wonderful fireworks show ever'.

**18 Sackville Street Lower**: True-Form Boot Co, looted during the Rising.

**20 Sackville Street Lower**: Clery's Department Store (first floor of the Imperial Hotel); founded by Limerick businessman Michael Clery in 1853.

**21-27 Sackville Street Lower**: Imperial Hotel, owned by William Martin Murphy. On Sunday, 31 August 1913, Jim Larkin addressed the crowd in Sackville Street as he promised. He did so from a window of the Imperial Hotel. Following his appearance, police entered the room and arrested him. In Sackville Street there were riots and a police 'baton charge'. The majority of the police 'baton work' was at the Prince's Street corner, and was carried out by both RIC and DMP constables. Sgt Richardson was in charge of the DMP constables as well as the RIC members. Countess Markievicz was one of those injured and she named it 'Bloody Sunday'. From Sackville Street, the rioting spread to the Liberties, Clanbrassil Street, Aungier Street and the Quays. Thereafter, the Dublin Employer's Federation, headed by Murphy, locked out all the workers who would not sign the following pledge: 'I hereby undertake to carry out all instructions given to me by or on behalf of my employers, and, further, I agree to immediately resign my membership of the Irish Transport and General Workers' Union (if a member); and I further undertake that I will not join or in any way support this union.'[46] All those who refused to sign were locked out and the 1913 Lockout was underway. M. W. O'Brien was in com-

---

46. Yeates, Padraig, *Lockout – Dublin 1913*, 2000, p. 114.

mand of the unit which occupied this building during the Rising and the Plough and the Stars flag was raised over it. Volunteer Cpt Weafer died in the fire here. Mrs Thomas Dillon (nee Geraldine Plunkett) watched the storming of the GPO from here on Easter Monday. She had been married on Sunday in what was to be a double wedding with Grace Gifford and Joseph Plunkett.

**28 Sackville Street Lower**: Richard Allen, gentlemen's attire and 'supplier of motor garments and servant's livery': burned during the Rising.

**29 Sackville Street Lower**: burned during the Rising, the building housed O'Farrell Freres, tobacconist; Norman Dewar, photographer; the National Standard Life Insurance Company; and Peter Donnelly, coal merchant.

**30 Sackville Street Lower**: The Munster and Leinster Bank: burned during the Rising.

**31 Sackville Street Lower**: burned during the Rising, the building housed the Cable Boot Company; Cole's dental surgery; and the Irish Pig Dealer's Association.

**32 Sackville Street Lower**: burned during the Rising, the building housed Dunne's & Co, hat makers; W. F. Brown, window ticket and show card writer; the All-Ireland Servants Registry Office, Kathleen Garrity, proprietress; and Mary Brady, ladies' clothing.

**33 Sackville Street Lower**: burned during the Rising. The building housed the Pillar Café, restaurant and tea rooms, at the corner of Talbot Street. Miss McFarland was the manager. Cmdt Brennan-Whitmore was charged with taking the building and building barricades. He tried fruitlessly to stop the looting, until he shot into the air. It was his command that set up the 'string and can' communication system and when Brennan-Whitmore was captured he met the Australian sniper, stationed in Trinity, who hit one of his cans and tried to hit the string.

**34 Sackville Street Lower**: Noblett's, confectioners, looted during the Rising.

**35-39 Sackville Street Lower** (corner of Prince's Street): Hotel Metropole, demolished during the Rising. Grace Gifford often attended the Nine Arts Balls held here. Michael Collins came here to escort Joseph Plunkett to the GPO. Harry Boland came here from the GPO, under the command of Oscar Traynor, then returned to the GPO prior to the surrender.

**40 Sackville Street Lower**: Eason's bookshop; British Army training manuals were on sale here; Volunteers bought and used them from before the Rising until the Truce.

**55 Sackville Street Lower** (corner of Bachelor's Walk): Chancellor and Son Photographic Studio, next to Kelly's; the slogan 'Photographer to the King' was painted on the Sackville Street wall.

**56 Sackville Street Lower** (corner of Bachelor's Walk): Kelly's gun and ammunition shop, 'Kelly's Fort'. The sign on the building announced: 'Fishing Tackle and Gunpowder Office'. The garrison here was commanded by Peadar Bracken; Joe Good was a member.

**Sackville Street Upper**: eight buildings were burned here during the Rising. Two of the 1916 garrisons were mustered here after their surrender: the Four Courts garrison, and the GPO/Moore Street garrison.

**Sackville Street Upper** (at Parnell Street): Charles Stewart Parnell Monument. The obelisk was commissioned in 1900 and completed in 1910, and the statue was sculpted by Augustus St Gaudens. It bears Parnell's declaration 'No man shall have the right to fix the boundary to the march of a Nation'.

**1, 2 Sackville Street Upper**: Tyler's Boot Merchants; destroyed during the Rising.

**5, 6, 7 Sackville Street Upper** (corner of Cathedral Street): William Lawrence's Bazaar, a photo, toy and stationery shop; it was looted and burned during the Rising. The shop contained fireworks which were set off, starting fires elsewhere in the street.

**9 Sackville Street Upper**: Dublin United Tramways Offices; destroyed during the Rising

**10 Sackville Street Upper**: Hibernian Bible Society; destroyed during the Rising.

**11-22 Sackville Street Upper**: the so-called 'Block' was the location which included the Crown, Granville, Gresham and Hammam hotels; it was taken by Republicans/IRA in late June 1922 and held until 5 July.

**11 Sackville Street Upper**: Gleeson & Co, tailors and outfitters. The company advertisement stated: 'Irish goods only'. During the War of Independence it ran an ad with a man in a trench coat (the 'usual' IRA 'uniform'): 'Don't Hesitate to Shoot – straight to Gleeson & Co'!

**12-13 Sackville Street Upper**: the Hammam Hotel; Republican/IRA HQ. It was noted for its Turkish Baths. Part of 'The Block' of buildings held by Republicans/IRA, it was taken on 29 June 1922 by Republicans/IRA under Oscar Traynor. The billiard room became the Republican/IRA hospital. De Valera, Oscar Traynor and Austin Stack left on 3 July and went to a safe house, intending to start a guerilla war; they were led to safety by Sean M. Glynn. The Hammam Hotel was held finally by seventeen men and three women to nurse the wounded. Cathal Brugha was fatally shot leaving here on 5 July 1922. Twice he had been ordered to surrender by Oscar Traynor, and he refused. On 5 July Brugha ordered the others out and after some reluctance they left under a flag of truce and surrendered to the Free State soldiers who had sealed off the rear laneway, Thomas's Lane. Linda Kearns and Dr J. P. Brennan, Dublin County Coroner, suspecting what Brugha was about to do, secured his permission to remain. He ran out and the Free State soldiers were ordered to 'fire low' but he was hit by several bullets. A bullet severed his femoral artery, and he was driven to the Mater Hospital with Linda Kearns holding the artery's end in her fingers. Finally, he died of the effects of loss of blood. A Republican/IRA garrison was commanded here by Cecil Malley, a brother of Ernie O'Malley (Ernie used the O' form). He was captured and imprisoned at Portlaoise and Mountjoy.

**17 Sackville Street Upper**: Granville Hotel; 'Jameson,' a British spy whose real name was John Charles Byrne, stayed here during the War of Independence.

**21-22 Sackville Street Upper**: Gresham Hotel; surrender point for the Volunteers under Daly's command. On 21 November 1920 (Bloody Sunday) Cpt Patrick MacCormack in Room 22 (the IRA had asked for Room 24) was killed by mistake. He was really a member of the Royal Medical (Veterinary) Corps. Also killed was L. E. Wilde (Room 14) who had no connection with the Army or Intelligence. Hugh Callaghan was the doorman who led the IRA to the rooms, and he mistakenly took them to Room 22 instead of Room 24. The Volunteers were under the command of Paddy Moran. (He was hanged on 14 March 1921 in Mountjoy for participation in the Bloody Sunday executions at Upper Baggott St. He was not there, and while he was a prisoner at Kilmainham Gaol he had an opportunity to escape, but refused it knowing he was not guilty of the crime with which he was charged.) Also in the Volunteer team was Paddy Kennedy. On Christmas Eve, 1920, Michael Collins, Gearóid O'Sullivan, Rory O'Connor and Tom Cullen met here to celebrate (David Neligan was invited, but declined: of him, Collins said 'Dave's getting windy!'). The private dining room Collins had arranged was not available, so they took a table in the public dining room. A raid by Auxies took Collins to the cloakroom where he was 'compared' with his 'official' photo. It was his closest escape ever.

After the raid, they were released; they got drunk and went up to Rutland Square to Vaughan's and then to Devlin's, there Cullen and Piaras Béaslaí borrowed a car and drove them to Mrs O'Donovan's where they slept until Christmas morning. In April 1921 Lord Derby stayed here, disguised by horn-rimmed glasses and under the name 'Edwards'. He met with de Valera to begin negotiations for a truce. There was little progress at these meetings.

**23 Sackville Street Upper**: Sir James Mackey's, seeds and bulbs

**24 Sackville Street Upper**: offices of the Catholic Truth Society; it was the Gaelic League premises at the turn of the century.

**25 Sackville Street Upper**: Power's Irish Lace; also the Dublin HQ of the St Vincent de Paul Society

**42 Sackville Street Upper**: The Catholic Commercial Club. In 1914 Cumann na mBan held a meeting here to determine what action to take on the Redmond/Volunteer split after Redmond's Woodenbridge speech. There was a large majority for the Redmond position, and this led to a split in Cumann na mBan too. The members of the Executive Committee who stayed with the Volunteers included: Kathleen Clarke, Áine Ceannt, Lily O'Brennan, Sorcha MacMahon, Mrs Martin Conlon, Mrs Joseph McGuinness, Maire Tuohy, Mrs Reddin, Maura McCarron, the two Misses O'Sullivan, the two Misses Elliott. Sorcha MacMahon subsequently acted as secretary.

**43 Sackville Street Upper**: YMCA, opposite the Gresham Hotel, it was burned during the Civil War.

**44 Sackville Street Upper**: burned during the Civil War

**46-47 Sackville Street Upper**: Gilbey's wine shop, opposite the Gresham Hotel

**50 Sackville Street Upper**: M. H. Gill & Son, Catholic publishing house. Dick McKee worked here, and had a firing range in the basement with a full-size figure of George V as a target.

**56 Sackville Street Upper**: Edinburgh Temperance Hotel, opposite the Gresham Hotel

**63, 64 Sackville Street Upper**: Royal Bank of Ireland

**65, 66 Sackville Street Upper**: Northern Banking Co, burned during both the Rising and the Civil War

**68 Sackville Street Upper**: the GAA held meetings here, often attended by Harry Boland. Dublin Castle held this to be the 'Central Council of the GAA' prior to the Rising.

**8 St Columba's Road Upper, Drumcondra**: home of Emmet Dalton. During WWI he fought with the Royal Dublin Fusiliers, winning the Military Cross at Ginchy; at the time, he believed he was fighting for Ireland. He joined the Irish Volunteers in 1914, and rejoined them again in 1919, after his WWI service.

**9 St Edward's Terrace, Rathgar**: Countess Markievicz moved here in 1909.

**82 St George's Avenue, Blackrock**: James Stephens died here in 1901.

**St James's Gate**: Guinness Brewery. 'The Brewery Award' was given every year to the best dray horse, usually a Clydesdale.

**2 St John's Terrace, Blackrock**: home of the poet Kickham Budd

**St George's Villa, Sandymount**: home of the Pearse Family

**122 St Lawrence Road, Clontarf**: Arthur Griffith's home; he moved here in 1910 after he married Maud Sheehan. Raided on the evening of 26–27 November 1920, and Griffith was arrested and imprisoned at Mountjoy Prison. Griffith only occasionally stayed at his home at this time, but he was here that night because it was his wedding anniversary.

**St Mary's Place**: St Mary's Church (officially St Mary's Chapel of Ease): the church is in the middle of the road and it is said if one runs around it three times at night one will meet the devil on the third round.

**St Mary's Place**: Christian Brothers School. Arthur Griffith and Sean O'Kelly attended here.

**6 St Mary's Road**: home of Laurence J. Kettle (son of A. J. Kettle, an aide to Charles Stewart Parnell); first Hon Secretary of the Irish Volunteers and head of Dublin Corporation's electrical department

**St Mary's Terrace, Rathfarnham**: home of Cpt Seamus Murphy

**St Stephen's Green**: it covers about sixty acres and has eight gates; named after St Stephen's Church and Leper Hospital, sited from 1224 to 1639 in the vicinity of Mercer Street. In 1877 Sir Arthur Guinness paid for it to be refurbished; it was placed under the management of the Board of Works, and it was re-opened in 1880. During the Rising, both sides stopped firing twice a day so the park-keeper, Jack Kearney, could leave his cottage in one corner to feed the ducks. The cottage is still there, as are the ducks! There are monuments here to Countess Markievicz, the Fianna, Robert Emmett, James Clarence Mangan, Thomas Kettle, James Joyce, O'Donovan Rossa, Wolfe Tone; there is also a famine memorial. The Fusilier's Arch is at the Grafton Street entrance (a Boer War monument to the Dublin Fusiliers); the entrance was known as 'Traitor's Gate'.

**8 St Stephen's Green (north)**: Hibernian United Services Club

**11 St Stephen's Green (north)**: the Loreto Convent School was originally here, and later moved to 21 St Stephen's Green. School run by Louise Gavan Duffy – she formerly ran St. Ita's. Michael Collins used this school for meetings. Collins met Archbishop Joseph Patrick Clune of Perth, Western Australia, here on 4 December 1920, at Lloyd George's behest, to discuss peace feelers.

**17 St Stephen's Green (north)**: Dublin University Club (now Kildare Street and University Club). The page boy, Walter McKay, aged seventeen, testified that he had seen Countess Markievicz aim and fire through the windows at the members of the club. It was this testimony that was used by the courtmartial to convict her on the two charges: 'took part in an armed rebellion against His Majesty the King and did attempt to cause disaffection among the civilian population of His Majesty.' She always denied that she shot at the club.

**27-32 St Stephen's Green (north, corner of Kildare Street)**: Shelbourne Hotel; opened in 1824 by Martin Burke, originally of County Tipperary. The General Manager from 1904 to 1930 was G. R. F. Olden. During the Rising, the British were under the command of Cpt Carl Elliotson and Cpt Andrews. There were over a hundred troops in the garrison. It was left undefended by the Volunteers not because they did not recognise its importance, but because 50 Volunteers and ICA men who were to have taken it were simply not there. Paddy Kelly, a Shelbourne porter, made stealthy access to the roof at frequent intervals to signal with flags to the Rebels in St Stephen's Green, as did Eileen Costello. In May 1916, The Commission to Inquire into the Rising met here under the Chairmanship of Lord Hardinge. A strike from April-June 1920 basically closed the Hotel, and only the assistant manager, Mr Powell, remained in residence. On Bloody Sunday, 21 November 1920, a squad entered and tried to kill some officers but the officers all escaped. The squad climbed a staircase, turned a corner and fired at armed men, only to find they had fired at their reflection in a large mirror! From February to May, 1922, the drafting of the Constitution of the Free State took place in Room 112, renamed

The Constitution Room. By the time it was replaced in 1937, 41 of its 83 Articles had been amended. The Drafting Committee was composed of Michael Collins (Chairman), James Douglas, Darrell Figgis (actually did most of the drafting), C. J. France, James MacNeill, R. J. P. Mortished, James Murnihan, John O'Byrne, Professor Alfred O'Rahilly, P. J. O'Toole, and E. M. Stephens.

**32 St Stephen's Green (north)**: Oliver St John Gogarty's consulting rooms

**44 St Stephen's Green (east)**: the United Arts Club moved here from Lincoln Place; founded in 1907 by Count Casimir Markievicz, Countess Markievicz and Ellen Duncan. The members included William Butler Yeats, Jack Yeats, Frank Cruise O'Brien, Thomas Bodkin, Dermot O'Brien, Lennox Robinson, Katherine Tynan Hinkson; most of the members were Unionists who opposed the Home Rule Bill.

**56 St Stephen's Green (east)**: home to Henry Grattan, the 18th century orator whose name is given to Grattan's Parliament.

**73 St Stephen's Green (south)**: home of Maud Gonne MacBride; her son, Sean, was sent by IRA headquarters to Wicklow to organise during the War of Independence. He fought for the Republicans/IRA in the Civil War, and was sent to Donegal with C. S. Andrews. Much later he was awarded the Nobel Peace Prize as one of the founders of Amnesty International (see also Roebuck House, Clonskeagh).

**78-81 St Stephen's Green (east)**: Iveagh House; originally two houses; donated to the state by the Guinness family in 1939; now the Department of Foreign Affairs.

**85–86 St Stephen's Green (south)**: The Catholic University (now Newman House) was founded here in two superb Georgian houses, and opened in 1854 with John Henry Newman as the founding Rector. It is now part of University College Dublin. James Grace (Northumberland Road ) reported here at 11.00 on Easter Monday; the Company CO was Simon Donnelly, but only about thirty-four members of the company showed up.

**90 St Stephen's Green (south)**: home of Irish historian Alice Stopford Green, daughter of Sir Charles Gavan Duffy, widow of the British historian John Richard Green. When she lived in London, she was responsible for raising most of the funds for the purchase of the Howth Rifles, which cost £1,500. The largest single contributor was George Fitz Hardinge Berkeley, with Mrs Green the next largest subscriber – Roger Casement, and Erskine Childers and his wife subscribed the rest of the money. Erskine Childers stayed here following his service in the British Army during WWI. IRA members often stayed here during the War of Independence, and the house was repeatedly raided. Maire Comerford worked here as a secretary.[47]

**93 St Stephen's Green (south)**: Centenary (Methodist) Church; Rev F. E. Harte was the Minister, Alfred (Alfie) Deale was the choirmaster and Edwin Deale was the organist.

**94 St Stephen's Green (south)**: Wesley College, Rev T. J. Irwin was the principal.

**113 St Stephen's Green (west)**: home of Michael Donnelly. He approved the occupation of his home during the Rising. A lieutenant in the ICA, he pressed for more involvement of the ICA in the War of Independence.

**123 St Stephen's Green (west)**: Royal College of Surgeons in Ireland. There are three statues atop the Royal Coat of Arms: Athena, Goddess of Wisdom and War; Asklepios, God

---

47. See Griffith, Kenneth and O'Grady, Timothy, *Curious Journey: an oral history of Ireland's Unfinished Revolution*, Mercier, Cork.

of Medicine; and Hygeia, Goddess of Health. It was opened to women in 1885. Countess Markievicz and Michael Mallin surrendered to Maj deCourcy Wheeler on nearby York Street. She removed her Mauser and kissed it before handing it over! This type of Mauser pistol converted into a rifle and was nicknamed a 'Peter the Painter'. Peter Piaktow was a Latvian anarchist in London, a painter, and was sought but never caught following a 1911 London riot. The weapon he used was nicknamed after him and it was as such that the Volunteers called it. George Jameson Johnston was Professor of Surgery in the Royal College.

**124 St Stephen's Green (west)**: birthplace of Robert Emmet (since demolished); his family moved here in 1779.

**140 St Stephen's Green (west)**: home of Thomas Henderson, grandfather of Frank and Leo Henderson; Frank's *Recollections of a Dublin Volunteer* has been published by Cork University Press.

**Sallymount Avenue**: 'Brookville'; home of the Pearse family in 1907

**Sampson's Lane** (and Moore Street): where The O'Rahilly was fatally wounded in front of Kelly's Shop, shot by troops of the Sherwood Foresters. He actually died of blood loss (see Sackville Lane).

**Sandyford, Co Dublin**: Maire Comerford's home. She was turned away from St Stephen's Green during the Rising because of her youth. She was active in the fighting in Dublin, and carried dispatches between the Four Courts and O'Connell Street during the Civil War. She was the most 'energetic' of Cumann na mBan members during the Civil War and was passionately Republican. She was shot in the leg while imprisoned in Mountjoy, but escaped. She was subsequently imprisoned in Kilmainham after recapture, where she endured a hunger strike.

**Sandyford, Co Dublin**: Lamb Doyle's; this well-known public house was used for Volunteer and IRA meetings.

**Sandymount**: Fairfield House (corner of Herbert Road and Newbridge Avenue); home of James Stephens

**Schoolhouse Lane**: The Model School; attended by Peadar Kearney

**3 Seafield Road, Clontarf**: home of Arthur Shields at the time of the Rising

**Seville Place**: home of Dan Head, killed in the Custom House fire

**100 Seville Place**: Gaelic Football Club; raided by the Black and Tans and one man killed

**Shelbourne Road**: Beggar's Bush Barracks. The Free State Army was officially established here on 31 January 1922.

**Sherrard Street**: home of Frank Molony, brother of Helena Molony. In August 1909, Bulmer Hobson and Countess Markievicz met here and discussed the establishment of Fianna na hÉireann in Dublin. Hobson had earlier founded the Fianna in Belfast in 1902.

**Sir John Rogerson's Quay**: home of 'Sheila Grennan'. *Who's Who* claims she conveyed the instruction for the surrender along with Elizabeth More O'Farrell, but most commentators agree that the woman's name was Julia Grenan, although Brian O'Higgins has it spelled 'Grennan'.[48] For example *Last Words* by Piaras MacLochlainn, published by the Kilmainham Jail Restoration Society in 1971, names her as Julia Grenan.[49]

---

48. O'Farrell, Padraic, *Who's Who in the Irish War of Independence and Civil War*, 1997, p. 19.
49. MacLochlainn, Pieras, *Last Words, Letters and Statements of the Leaders Executed after the Rising at Easter 1916*, 1971, p. 183.

**Skerries, Co Dublin**: Grand Hotel; Harry Boland, sharing a room with Joe Griffin, was shot here on 30 July 1922 and taken to St Vincent's Hospital, where he died after surgery.

**13 Stafford Street**: City Printing Works; it printed *The Irish Worker* for James Connolly as well as many ICA posters and handbills.

**44 Stafford Street**: birthplace of Theobald Wolfe Tone (since demolished); the street is now named in his honour.

**Steevens' Lane**: Dr Steevens' Hospital; named for Dr Richard Steevens, a wealthy doctor who willed his estate to his sister Grizel on condition that a hospital was to be built for the poor in Dublin after her death – she built the hospital during her lifetime however. It was built between 1721 and 1733, making it the oldest public hospital in Ireland. It is now the HQ of the Eastern Health Board (Health Service Executive).

**165 Strand Road**: Loughnavale, de Valera's office from January until April 1921; owned by Mrs MacGarry.

**Strand Street**: Inghinidhe na hÉireann used an empty loft here as a classroom in the early 1900s.

**15 Strandville Avenue**: home of George Norgrove; he and his wife and daughters, Annie and Emily, were in Dublin's City Hall during the Rising.

**Suffolk Street**: Quill's photo-engraving shop; the family lived upstairs. It was close to Dublin Castle. Michael Collins used to have documents brought here from the Castle and 'copied' overnight, then returned before they were missed.

**22-23 Suffolk Street**: Republican/IRA HQ, Sinn Féin Party HQ during the Civil War. De Valera often used this as an office during the period between the Treaty debates and the outbreak of the Civil War. In June 1923, the Organising Committee of Sinn Féin decided to contest seats in the general election and in August the party put up 87 candidates on an abstentionist policy. Their election manifesto stated: 'The Sinn Féin candidates in this election stand as they have stood in every election since 1917, for the unity and untrammelled independence of Ireland'. Of the 87 candidates, 64 were in prison or 'on the run'. Forty-four Sinn Féin candidates were elected, and two further seats were won in bye-elections in November 1924; Dublin (Seán Lemass) and Mayo (Dr Madden).

**10 Summer Street, North Circular Road**: home of Cpt Jack White at the time of the Rising.

**30 Summerhill Parade**: home of Frank Flood, 1Lt of the Dublin Brigade during the War of Independence. A student at UCD he led the abortive Drumcondra Ambush, and was hanged in Mountjoy Prison on 14 March 1921.

**42 Summerhill Road**: home of C. S. (Todd) Andrews, author of *Dublin Made Me*. He was sent by IRA headquarters to Donegal to organise during the War of Independence, but spent most of the time in Dublin and was imprisoned in Mountjoy, Arbour Hill and finally in the Rath Internment Camp in the Curragh (he was prisoner number 1569 in hut 32). He escaped from the camp after the Truce on 9 September 1921. He fought for the Republicans/IRA in the Civil War, and again was sent to Donegal to train the senior officers of the Donegal Brigade, then became an ADC to Liam Lynch before Lynch was killed. He was captured in Cork and was imprisoned there, then transferred to Newbridge where he was again interned (he was prisoner number 2571 in Newbridge and was in army hut number 60 with many other Dubliners). In January 1924 he was transferred to an internment center at the Curragh Camp, Tintown Number 2 (where he became prisoner number 876 and was with Jack Plunkett). He was released in April 1924.

**25 Sydney Parade**: last home of Gen Emmet Dalton; he died here on his eightieth birthday in 1978.

**16-17 Synge Street**: Christian Brothers School. Harry Boland attended here for a while but left after a clash with one of the brothers. C. S. Andrews attended, as did George Reynolds (Clanwilliam House garrison) and Gerald Keogh, who was killed in front of Trinity during the Rising. Michael Hayes was a teacher here; he was Minister of Education in the First Dáil and became the first Ceann Comhairle of the post-treaty Dáil. He became a Senator later and was Professor of Irish at UCD.

**33 Synge Street**: boyhood home of George Bernard Shaw (it was 3 Upper Synge Street when he lived here). It was later the home of a DMP police officer. Michael Collins arranged rooms here for Kevin O'Higgins, who stayed as 'Mr Casey'. The house is now the Shaw Museum.

**Talbot Street**: Tara Hall; it was used by Cumann na mBan as an auxiliary hospital during the Civil War fighting in Dublin.

**82 Talbot Street**: home of Sean Milroy

**94 Talbot Street**: Republican Outfitter's, owned by Peadar Clancy and Tom Hunter. Sean Treacy (Sean O'Treasaigh) was killed in front of this shop on 14 October 1920. Lt Price and G Division Sgt Francis Christian were also killed. Two civilians, Patrick Carroll and Joseph Carrington, were killed, and a DMP constable was wounded by indiscriminate Auxie firing. Treacy was followed here by RIC Sgt Christian after he attended Professor Carolan's funeral (see also Whitehall, 'Fernside', Drumcondra). RIC Sgt Roche was brought up from Tipperary to identify Treacy, and gloated over his body in the street. Treacy was the Vice-Brigadier of the Tipperary Brigade. Treacy was meeting with Dan Breen, Tom Cullen, Dick McKee, Joe Vyse (a former English Naval officer who was Michael Collins' Director of Purchases and was arrested after the raid), Frank and Leo Henderson, George and Jack Plunkett, and Liam Tobin. Volunteer Sean Brunswick went to 'help' Treacy and emptied his pockets of all documents before the RIC and DMP could get to him. Treacy was to have married May Quigley on 25 October 1920, within a fortnight of being killed.

**Tara Street**: (corner of Townsend Street): Central Fire Station opened in 1900. British 18-pounders were taken out of Trinity College, placed on top of the tower, and fired across the Liffey at Liberty Hall. It became the offices of *The Irish Press*, newspaper founded by Eamon de Valera.

**Temple Bar**: Irish Volunteers broke glass on the streets here to inhibit cavalry during the Rising.

**9 Temple Bar**: printer Robert Latchford was prosecuted and fined £5 under DORA in June 1916 for printing a statement purportedly made by Thomas MacDonagh in the dock.

**12 Temple Lane**: printer Paul Curtis was similarly prosecuted and fined under DORA for printing the same statement.

**Temple Street**: Temple Street Children's Hospital, where Dr Ada English worked; she was later a member of the Second Dáil.

**Temple Street**: D Company of the 1st Battalion, Dublin Brigade, mustered here under Cpt Heuston for the Rising.

**14 Temple Street**: home of Charles Stewart Parnell

**8 Temple Villas, Palmerston Road, Rathmines**: Grace Gifford Plunkett's home. It was this address she listed on her wedding engagement announcement.

**Terenure**: first home of Mr and Mrs Kevin O'Higgins after their marriage. It was attacked by the Republicans/IRA during the Civil War and Mrs O'Higgins moved to the safety of Government Buildings.

**Thomas Street**: St Catherine's Church (C of I). The gibbet where Robert Emmett was executed on 20 September 1803 once stood in front of the church. The block on which he was beheaded is now in St Enda's.

**Thomas Street**: the Church of Saints Augustine and John; erected by the Augustinian Fathers in the late 1800s on the site of one of the first hospitals in Europe, built by the Danes in the twelfth century. It has the tallest spire in Dublin, visible all over the city. James Pearse (father of Padraig) was responsible for some of the statues and stone work. It contains the Chapel of Our Lady of Good Counsel.

**Thomas Street**: Fr Eugene McCarthy found lodgings here for Grace Gifford Plunkett on the morning of 4 May, after he presided at the wedding between Grace and Joseph Plunkett.

**Thomas Street**: Irish Volunteers used a home here to make 'Mills Bombs' during the War of Independence.

**1 Thomas Street**: home of Arthur Guinness. He bought Rainsford's Brewery at James's Gate in 1750 with a lease for 9,000 years! His home is now part of the main gate of the Brewery. 'Porter' was so named because it was the favourite libation of London porters and from 1799 his brewery concentrated on this.

**Townsend Street** (corner of Great Brunswick Street): this was the HQ of the detective division of the Dublin Metropolitan Police.

**Townsend Street**: James Larkin founded the Irish Transport and General Workers Union (ITGWU) in a tenement here.

**Townsend Street**: DMP Sgt Morris was seriously injured here during the 1913 Lockout riots on 21 September. He returned to work, but died on 1 February 1914 of pneumonia. He is the only DMP or RIC member to be listed as 'killed' as a result of the Lockout.

**Usher's Island**: Mendicity Institute, directly across the Liffey from the Royal Barracks. This was formerly Moira House, home of Lord and Countess Moira; he was an opponent of the Union, and was a Governor-General of India. He was a friend, supporter and protector of Robert Emmet and Wolfe Tone, Lord Edward and Lady Pamela Fitzgerald, and Michael Dwyer. They and other 'rebels' often dined here. It was given to the citizens of Dublin as an 'Institution for the Suppression of Mendicancy in Dublin' in 1826. In the days of the Rising, and before, mendicants were not permitted to enter through the front door. It was held by D Company, 1st Battalion, Dublin Brigade, under Cpt Sean Heuston; approximately 30 Volunteers, all between the ages of 18 and 25, were in the garrison (13 Volunteers from Swords, under the command of Richard Coleman, and 17 Fianna held out against approximately 400 Dublin Fusiliers). Heuston was only 25 years old. He was instructed to hold this position for two hours to delay British deployment – they held for three days! They started with two weapons and one box of ammunition. There were 28 survivors and 2 killed. The Volunteers and Fianna only surrendered when they ran out of ammunition on Wednesday, infuriating the British that so few youngsters held them off for so long. Peter Wilson from Swords was killed by a British sniper in Roe's Distillery as the men were being formed up after the surrender. Dick Balfe and Liam Staines were badly wounded.

**12 Vernon Avenue, Clontarf**: childhood home of Arthur Shields and William Joseph Shields (Barry Fitzgerald), noted Abbey Theatre actors at this time and during the twenties. Arthur was in the GPO. *The Spancel of Death*, by Mayo Fenian T. H. Nally, was to have starred Arthur, and was scheduled to open on 25 April at the Abbey. Because of the Rising, it failed to open and because no script survived it was never produced.

**8 Victoria Terrace, Rathgar**: home owned by May Langan (later Mrs Kilbride); it was Erskine Childers' Ministry of Propaganda office. The staff included Lily O'Brennan and Moira O'Byrne.

**9 Vincent Street**: Gerald Boland's home

**12 Villiers Road, Rathmines**: home of H. J. Tipping; he was the Controller of the GPO and was in charge of opening accounts and funding after the Rising.

**1 Walworth Road, Portobello**: (see also 12 Vernon Avenue) birthplace of Arthur and William Joseph Shields. William Joseph became known as Barry Fitzgerald, born 10 March 1888. Educated to enter the banking business, he was bitten by the acting bug and joined Dublin's Abbey Players. He famously starred in the Abbey Theatre production of Sean O'Casey's *Juno And The Paycock* and, many years later, in John Ford's film *The Quiet Man*. Arthur Shields was born on 15 February 1896. He was in the GPO during the Rising.

**Waterford Street**: 'house' of Becky Cooper, a 'Monto' madam. British agents were alleged to use her as a front to pass on information.

**Waterloo Road**: Erskine Childers' home. Michael Collins often came here.

**Weaver Square**: home of James Connolly and his family during his first stay in Dublin; his daughter Nora wrote that it was 'the first that we did not have to share with anyone'.

**2-7 Wellington Quay**: Clarence Hotel; Dave Neligan stayed here when he returned to Dublin to re-join the DMP. Liam Lynch was sleeping here when the attack on the Four Courts commenced; he left to go to the South and was captured with Liam Deasy. They were taken for questioning by Eoin O'Duffy, who let them go. They subsequently went to Kingsbridge station and caught a train to the South with Seamus Robinson.

**Wellington Road**: home of Louise Murphy; Frank Gallagher stayed in this safe house (David Hogan was his pseudonym as the author of *Four Glorious Years*).

**Wellington Road**: Erskine Childers lived here after he left the home of Mrs Green on St Stephen's Green and before he moved to Bushy Park.

**41 Wellington Road**: this was the last home of James Larkin, where he died.

**55 Wellington Road**: home of Sean T. O'Kelly. On 5 January 1922 a committee of five, from all sides of the Treaty question, met here. Proposals were made that if the Dáil voted in favour of the Treaty, de Valera should remain as President, the Dáil should retain ultimate authority, and that only members of the Provisional Government would be called upon to declare allegiance to the Treaty. Collins and Griffith agreed, but de Valera turned them down, and the recommendations were never forwarded to the Dáil. Eoin MacNeill and Liam Mellowes dissented at the meeting. Sean T. became the first President of the Republic of Ireland in 1949.

**Werburgh Street**: St Werburgh's Church. Lord Edward FitzGerald is buried in this church; his implacable enemy Major Sirr is interred in the churchyard outside.

**17 Wesley Road**: Susan Mitchell, an avid Republican and Cumann na mBan member, moved here on 7 June 1917.

**Westland Row**: St Andrew's Church. Built with the assistance of Daniel O'Connell between 1832 and 1837, it was the first church built on a main road after Catholic

Emancipation. The Mater Dolorosa statue here was sculpted by Willie Pearse. Kevin Barry was baptised here.

**20 Westland Row**: office of Daniel Maher, solicitor. Pearse left letters with Maher 'to be opened in case of my death', including his will, and other documents/instructions of a financial character.

**21 Westland Row**: birthplace of Oscar Wilde, this address is given in the register of his baptism in St Mark's Parish Church, in nearby Great Brunswick Street (now Pearse Street).

**36 Westland Row**: Oriel House; HQ of Special Branch, a unit of the Irish Free State's detectives section. It was the nucleus of a special detection and intelligence unit. Dave Neligan, Ned Broy, James McNamara and Tom Cullen worked in the unit after the Civil War. It was under the command of Liam Tobin in the early years, of a semi-military character. Reached a strength of about 125 by the end of the Civil War. In February 1923, all units were merged under Joe McGrath with a complement of about 350. In February 1923 the unit moved to 68 Merrion Square. The building now houses the Royal Irish Academy of Music

**45-46 Westland Row**: Christian Brothers School; Brother Maunsell, from Co Kerry, and Brother Craven were noted teachers here. It was attended by Padraig and Willie Pearse (starting in 1891) and by Desmond Ryan in 1907.

**48-52 Westland Row**: Westland Row Railway Station, now Pearse Station, the terminus for the Dublin-Kingstown Railway

**Westmoreland Street**: the British placed 18-pounders here to shell Lower Sackville Street during the Rising. Some buildings in this street were damaged or destroyed, including Kennedy & McSharry, men's outfitters at no. 24.

**38 Westmoreland Street**: James Duffy & Co Ltd, publishers; it published many history books by 'revolutionary' authors.

**28 Wexford Street**: Boland's tobacco shop; run by Harry's mother, Catherine, after his father died.

**Whitefriar Street**: Church of Our Lady of Mount Carmel (Carmelite Church). Erected in 1825, this church occupies a site acquired by the Carmelites in 1280. It contains the statue of Our Lady of Dublin. St Valentine's remains are in a wine cask here, given by Pope Gregory XVI to Fr Spratt in 1835. Father McCabe was the prior in 1916. Harry Boland was buried from here; his remains arrived here from St Vincent's Hospital on 3 July 1922. Michael Browne of Maynooth (later Bishop of Galway) was the principal celebrant of the Requiem Mass. As the cortege proceeded up O'Connell St to Glasnevin, a Lancia armored car containing Free State troops stopped, the troops disembarked, laid down their arms in the street, removed their caps and stood at attention until the hearse had passed. The government had allowed the funeral to proceed without interruption. Many thought the armored car incident was the only way Michael Collins could pay his last respects.

**Whitehall**: 'Fernside', Drumcondra; Professor Carolan's house. On 11 October 1920, the Cairo Gang surprised Dan Breen and Sean Treacy here (Sean O'Treasaigh). They escaped (killing two, including Maj G. O. S. Smythe) but Breen was wounded several times and badly cut on a broken window pane in making his escape. Professor Carolan was put up against wall and shot. Before he died, he was able to give a full account of what happened.

**Wicklow Street**: Fergus Brian Molloy was a British spy who offered to take Cullen, Thornton, and Tobin into Dublin Castle to obtain information, but they never took up the offer. His body was found here in March 1920 (see also Parkgate Street).

**1-3 Wicklow Street**: (corner of Grafton Street) Weir and Sons, jewellers. It was next door to the Wicklow Hotel. Michael Collins bought Kitty Kiernan's 'unofficial' engagement present, a watch, here.

**42 Wicklow Street**: Wicklow Hotel, next to Weir's, one building away from Grafton Street. John MacBride was on his way to have lunch here with his brother (who was to be married) on Easter Monday when he accidentally met a Volunteer column led by Thomas MacDonagh at St Stephen's Green and was told the Rising was underway. He was 'invited' to participate and that is how he ended up at Jacob's. It was a complete accident. This was a usual meeting place for Cullen, Neligan, Tobin and Michael Collins. Paddy O'Shea, from Kerry, was the waiter and often passed messages. William Doran, porter, betrayed IRA men and was killed outside the hotel on the order of Collins. Joe Dolan, a member of the Squad, arrived at the hotel in a taxi, and when Doran picked up the luggage he was shot. When Doran's wife put in a 'claim' on behalf of herself and her children, Collins arranged for her to be paid from Sinn Féin funds and they never knew the true circumstances of his betrayal.

**William's Lane**: rear of Independent House (*The Independent* newspaper owned by William Martin Murphy was a fairly moderate paper prior to the Rising). Also on the premises was *The Freeman's Journal*. James Connolly was seriously wounded in his ankle upon returning from here to the GPO late on Thursday afternoon.

**North William Street**: National School; attended by Sean Connolly

**39 North William Street**: home of Sgt, then Lt Frank Robbins of the ICA. He was in the Stephen's Green/College of Surgeons garrison.

**58 South William Street**: William Street Courthouse; Kathleen Clarke was President of the Children's Court and the Court of Conscience which were held here. For many years the building housed the Dublin Civic Museum and the Old Dublin Society.

**5 Windsor Villas, Clontarf**: childhood home of the Henderson family. Some of the Howth rifles were hidden under the floorboards here. Frank wrote *Narratives: Frank Henderson's Easter Rising*: He was in the GPO, and was later a captive at Frongoch. Leo was also in the GPO, became a leading Republican/IRA figure and led the raid on the garage which was the prelude to the attack on the Four Courts in 1922, and spent the rest of the Civil War in Mountjoy Prison. Nora was a member of Cumann na mBan, and was in the Four Courts garrison in 1922. Gertie married Major Leech of the British Army and moved to England. Maurice was involved post-1916 and was interned by the Free State in 1923. Robert did not participate in the military struggle

**Winetavern Street**: the first artillery fired on the Four Courts came from here at 4.29 am on 28 June 1922. Cpt Johnny Doyle fired the first round.

**Wood Quay**: the British shelled the Four Courts from here during the Rising. Free State troops also placed 18-pounder guns here to shell the Four Courts in June 1922 at the start of the Irish Civil War.

**Yarnhall Street**: Linenhall Barracks; burned down in 1916. The fires were lit by Ned Daly's men retreating from the Four Courts. The site now contains housing. In 1916 it was the HQ of the British Army Pay Department.

**3 Yarnhall Street**: Patrick Mahon, printer, printed *Irish Freedom* here.

**York Street** (and St Stephen's Green): Royal College of Surgeons in Ireland, garrisoned during the Rising under the command of Mallin and Countess Markievicz. Maj de Courcy Wheeler accepted their surrender in York Street.

**41 York Street**: Dublin Conservative Workingmen's Club. Many Protestant workers belonged to this club. The Southern Battalion of the Dublin Brigade met here before the Rising. It was the third meeting place of K Company, 3rd Battalion of Volunteers, after the Rising. Those speaking against conscription often used the hall here for rallies. David Hogan spoke here in 1918. It became the HQ of the Fianna after the Rising. It was a meeting place for Anti-Treatyites, Republicans/IRA.

# Appendix I:
## Historic locations outside Dublin, 1913–1923

**Ballagh, Goold's Cross, Co Tipperary**: *The Gael*; Edward Dwyer, owner and editor

**Ballinasloe, Co Galway**: *The Toiler*; Patrick MacIntyre, editor. He opposed the ICA. *The Toiler* was printed by the Western News Company, also at Ballinasloe, Co Galway.

**Belfast, Falls Road**: Catholic Boys' Hall. Bulmer Hobson founded Fianna na hÉireann here on 26 June 1902. In 1905, he and Denis McCullough founded the Dungannon Clubs (named after the meeting place of the Volunteers in 1778) and engaged Sean MacDermott as their full-time organiser.

**Belfast, 117 Victoria Street**: Fianna Hall; it became the Belfast HQ of the Fianna.

**Carrigaholt, Co Clare**: O'Curry College (Irish College); Brian O'Higgins was the Secretary from January 1917 until he was imprisoned (again) in May 1918.

**Connemara, Co Galway**: Renvyle House; this was Oliver St John Gogarty's house in the west. It was built by the Blakes, a Protestant family, in 1680. During the Land League wars of the late 1800s, the Blake widow who owned the house at the time converted it to a hotel. Gogarty bought it in the early 1900s. It was burned by the Republicans/IRA on 22 January 1922 during the Civil War. St John Gogarty received compensation for it's burning from the Irish Free State government.

**Connemara, Co Galway**: Rosmuc, near Roundstone, Padraig Pearse's summer cottage

**Cork, Co Cork**: Winthrop Street; Wren's Hotel. 'Quinlisk', a British double agent, was told Michael Collins was here and when he subsequently gave the Cork RIC this information he (Quinlisk) was killed on 19 February 1920. Sgt Timothy Quinlisk was a former member of the Casement Brigade in Germany before the Rising.

**Greystones, Co Wicklow**: a fashionable resort about twenty miles south of Dublin. De Valera's family lived there while he was in the US.

**Greystones, Co Wicklow**: Grand Hotel; this was the hotel where Kitty Kiernan often stayed. She and Michael Collins often met here.

**Kilcoole, Co Wicklow**: arms were landed here on 1 August 1914. Sir Thomas Myles, a life-long nationalist, took part in the running of guns to Ireland, picking up 600 guns from Conor O'Brien's *Kelpie*, which had delivered them from Germany to the Welsh coast. Myles sailed them in his vessel, *Chotah*, to Kilcoole. He was helped by James Creed Meredith, who became President of the Supreme Court. The *Chotah* landed 600 rifles and 19,000 rounds of ammunition.

**Killorglin, Co Kerry**: Ballykissane Pier; Con Keating, Charles Monaghan and Domhnall (Donal) Sheehan were killed here when their car went off the pier on Good Friday, 21 April, just prior to the Rising. Keating was a wireless expert who had previously tried to set up a wireless at Count Plunkett's home in Kimmage. He was carrying a lamp he had received from Eamonn Ceannt, which was to have been used to signal the *Aud*. They were in Kerry attempting to meet up with Casement.

**Limerick, Co Limerick**: Frederick Street; Daly family home

**Lisburn, Co Antrim**: Detective Inspector Oswald Ross Swanzy was shot outside a church here on 22 August 1920. Swanzy was one of those responsible for the murder of Thomas MacCurtain, Mayor of Cork, and one who was indicted for 'wilful murder' by the investigating jury. Michael Collins had him traced to Lisburn and sent a special team to kill him.

**Tralee, Co Kerry**: Fenit Pier

# Appendix II:
# Addresses associated with Michael Collins
# (Micheal O'Coileain)[1]

**Abbey Street, Middle** (O'Connell Street corner): Dáil Secretariat; on the second floor there was an office, usually called 'The Dump'.
**Abbey Street, Upper**: Higgins's Pub
**Abbey Street, Upper**: Bannon Brothers' Pub; Collins first met Dave Neligan here.
**Abbey Street, Upper**: George Moreland, cabinet makers; meeting place for 'The Squad'
**16 Airfield Road, Rathgar**: home of Mrs O'Donovan; Collins stayed here often. He ate dinner here on the night of Bloody Sunday.
**Amiens Street**: Phil Sheridan's Coolevin Dairies
**3 Andrew Street**: used as an office

**32 Bachelor's Walk**: second office of the Irish National Aid and Volunteers' Dependents' Fund. Collins worked here as Secretary for the fund from February 1917 to 1918 at a salary of £2 10s per week. The address was also an intelligence office from 1917 to 1921. Liam Tobin and Tom Cullen were in charge of intelligence directly under Collins. Members included: Charlie Byrne, Paddy Caldwell, Charles Dalton, Joe Dolan, Joe Guilfoyle, Ned Kelleher, Patrick Kennedy, Dan McDonnell, Peter Magee, Frank Saurin, Frank Thornton. Another office here was Collins's Finance Office. He was arrested outside this office on 2 April 1918, and he was taken to the DMP's Brunswick Street Station accompanied by Detectives Smith and Thornton. From there he was taken to the Longford Assizes where he refused to recognise the court and since it was not Volunteer policy to accept bail he was then imprisoned in Sligo on 10 April 1918. Ultimately he was set free on bail from Sligo (see Ballinamuck, Co Longford).
**Baggot Street, Croke Park, Earlsfort Terrace, Jones Road, Morehampton Road, Mount Street, Pembroke Road, Sackville Street**: Bloody Sunday, Dublin (21 November 1920). In 1920 'The Cairo Gang' had been recruited and formed by Col Ormonde Winter, KBE, CB, CMG, DSO, Chief of the British Combined Intelligence Services in Ireland from the spring of 1920 until the Truce. He was known to the IRA/Volunteers as the 'Holy Terror'. The Cairo Gang was ruthless and efficient, and set out specifically to eliminate Michael Collins and his Intelligence Department. It had been primarily responsible for tracking down Dan Breen and Sean Treacy, and had killed Treacy in Talbot Street, Dublin. Over twenty officers had been sentenced by Michael Collins, Brugha and others at their 35

---

1. The addresses cover the period 16 October 1890 to 22 August 1922 (Collins's Glasnevin tombstone indicates his birthday as 12 October 1890).

Lower Gardiner Street meeting. (The publicised and 'official' figures stated that 11 officers were killed and 4 escaped, but Frank Thornton's memoirs listed 19 killed, at 8 different addresses in Dublin.) In fact 15 British officers were killed in 8 locations as follows:

*92 Lower Baggot Street: Cpt W. F. Newbury*
*119 Lower Baggot Street: Cpt George T. Baggally*
*28 Earlsfort Terrace: Cpt John Fitzgerald*
*117 Morehampton Road: Cpt Donald L. McClean, T. H. Smith*
*22 Lower Mount Street: Lt H. R. Angliss (Patrick McMahon), Auxiliary Cadets Garner and Morris*
*38 Upper Mount Street: Lt Peter Ames, Cpt George Bennett*
*28 Upper Pembroke Road: Maj Dowling, Cpt Leonard Price*
*Upper Sackville Street, Gresham Hotel: Cpt Patrick MacCormack, L. E.. Wilde*

Dave Neligan stated that the incident: 'caused complete panic in Dublin Castle.'[2] Prime Minister David Lloyd George: 'They got what they deserved – beaten by counter-jumpers!' 'Ask Griffith for God's sake to keep his head, and not to break off the slender link that had been established. Tragic as the events in Dublin were, they were of no importance. These men were soldiers, and took a soldier's risk.'[3]

Michael Collins said: 'My one intention was the destruction of the undesirables who continued to make miserable the lives of ordinary decent citizens. I have proof enough to assure myself of the atrocities which this gang of spies and informers have committed. Perjury and torture are words too easily known to them. If I had a second motive it was no more than a feeling I would have for a dangerous reptile. By their destruction the very air is made sweeter. For myself, my conscience is clear. There is no crime in detecting and destroying, in wartime, the spy and the informer. They have destroyed without trial. I have paid them back in their own coin..'[4]

Services for six of the Protestant officers were held at Westminster Abbey and services for the Catholic men, Peter Ames, George Bennett and Patrick McMahon, were held at Westminster Cathedral.

Thirteen Irish were killed in 2 locations:

*Jones Road/Croke Park: Mick Hogan, Jane Boyle (26), James Burke, Daniel Carroll, Michael Feery, Thomas Hogan, James Matthews, Patrick O'Dowd, Jerry O'Leary (10), Willie Robinson (11), Thomas Ryan (he was shot dead while whispering the Act of Contrition in Hogan's ear), John Scott (14), Joseph Traynor, and James Teehan*

*Lincoln Place: 7 civilians shot, 2 died.*

Sixty-two people were injured in Croke Park, and another 12 were injured in the stampede out. Maj Mills commanded the Regular Army back-up troops and reported adversely on the actions of the Black and Tans. Dick McKee and Peadar Clancy were killed, along with Conor Clune, in Dublin Castle. McKee and Clancy were captured in Sean Fitzpatrick's house in Lower Gloucester Street – supposedly a 'safe house'. James (Shankers) Ryan, the tout who turned them in, was later killed in Hyne's Pub in Gloucester Place.

---

2.  Neligan, David, *The Spy in the Castle*, 1968, 1999, p. 123.
3.  Gleeson, James, *Bloody Sunday*, 1962, p. 181.
4.  Gleeson, James, *Bloody Sunday*, 1962, p. 191.

**Ballinamuck, Co Longford** (near Granard): Legga Chapel; on 3 March 1918 Michael Collins made a speech here which was 'calculated to cause disaffection':

*You will not get anything from the British Government unless you approach them with a bullock's tail in one hand and a landlord's head in the other .... Do not participate in raids for arms of useless old shotguns and old swords – go where you will find arms that will be of some use to you [RIC Barracks], and we call on the Irish Volunteers to defend their arms until death.[5]*

This speech led to a warrant for his arrest sworn on 11 March 1918 to return him 'to the locality pending his trial at assizes'. This warrant led to his arrest outside his Bachelor's Walk office on 2 April 1918, and he was taken to the DMP's College Street Station, and then transported to Longford and brought before the magistrate M. Johnson who: 'took depositions and returned the accused for trial at the next assizes for the county. The accused, who was very abusive and insulting, refused to recognise the court or give bail and was remanded to Sligo gaol'. He was conveyed to Sligo Gaol on 10 April 1918, and released on 20 April. The magistrate granted the adjournment but required bail of £50 and two sureties of £25 each. Michael Doyle of Main Street, Longford, and Michael Cox of Ballymahon Street, Longford, went as Collins's sureties.

The official charges, noted as the 'Outrage' on RIC forms were:

*Unlawfully incited to riot.*
*Unlawfully incited the public to raid for arms.*
*Unlawfully incited forcible entry.*
*Unlawfully incited to assault on persons.*
*Unlawfully incited to steal arms.[6]*

A change of venue to the 'Londonderry' Assizes issued on 28 June 1918, with his appearance scheduled for 17 July 1918, but Collins did not appear. A bench warrant was executed on that date. As a consequence of this, 'his description was inserted in *Hue and Cry* and first appeared in the issue of 4 April 1919 under Co Longford. After that, Collins was officially 'on the run' and remained so until the Truce.[7]

**Barnsbury Hall, London**: in November 1909, Collins was sworn in here as a member of the IRB by his fellow post office worker, Sam Maguire. He went on to become the treasurer for the IRB of London.

**Beal na mBlath, Co Cork**: Collins's fatal itinerary, 20–22 August 1922. Collins's party left the Victoria Hotel, Cork, at 6.16 am on 22 August 1922. The convoy included the following:

*A motorcyclist, Lt John Smyth (from Enniscorthy). He was shot in the neck while helping to move Collins's body, but continued on his motorcycle.*

*A Crossley Tender under the command of Cmdt Sean (Paddy) O'Connell (he said the Act of Contrition in Collins's ear), Cpt Joe Dolan, John O'Connell (the driver) and eight riflemen.*

*Collins and Emmet Dalton in a yellow Leland Thomas touring car. The driver was Private Smith Corry (English born) and the reserve driver was M. Quinn.*

---

5.   Stewart, A. T. Q., *Michael Collins: The Secret File*, 1997, p. 82.
6.   Stewart, A. T. Q., *Michael Collins: The Secret File*, 1997, p. 141.
7.   From the RIC files on Collins in the National Archives.

*A Rolls Royce Whippet Slievenamon armoured car. The Vicker's gunner on the armoured car was John (Jock) McPeake (he deserted on 2 December 1922 with Pat and Mick O'Sullivan and took the armoured car to the IRA; he said he did it for a woman; he was arrested in Glasgow in July 1923 and was imprisoned in Portlaoise where he endured a hunger strike). Cooney and Monks were the other members of the armored car crew.*

The convoy went through Macroom (Collins met Florrie O'Donoghue here) and Crookstown and having passed through Bael na mBlath at 8 am it stopped to get directions. At Bandon Collins met with Gen Sean Hales. At Clonakilty the convoy stopped for lunch at Callinan's Pub (*Who's Who* claims it was White's Pub). In the afternoon the convoy went to Roscarberry and Collins had a drink in the Four Alls Pub (owned by his cousin Jeremiah) at Sam's Cross where Collins declared: 'I'm going to put an end to this bloody war'. The convoy left Skibbereen at 5 pm and headed back to Cork. Collins met his great friend John L. Sullivan on this journey.[8] The convoy detoured around Clonakilty on the way back because of a roadblock. It stopped at Lee's Hotel (Munster Arms) in Bandon for tea. Major General Sean Hales was in command here. His brother Tom Hales was the column leader on the other side and led the IRA ambush.[9] The ambush party met in Long's Pub: Daniel Holland, Jim Hurley, Jim Kearney, Tom Kelliher (not Tom Kelleher, Cmdt Gen 1st Southern Division), John O'Callahan, Denis (Sonny) O'Neal (from Maryborough, Co Cork, was to provide covering fire to retreating IRA ambush members). The ambush took place at Bael na mBlath (between Macroom and Bandon but closer to Crookstown than Bandon) at 7.45 pm. Denis (Sonny) O'Neal almost surely fired the fatal shot.

Collins's body was taken to Shanakiel Hospital in Cork. Sean Galvin was the courier who brought the news to Cork. Collins's body was brought here by Commandant Frank O'Friel and he assisted in its cleaning. Dr Patrick Cagney was the doctor who examined the body and only spoke of his examination after his retirement. In 1966 he told Sean McGarry that he always felt Collins was killed by a .303 bullet. The bullet entered behind his left ear, making a small entry wound, and exiting above the left ear making a 'ragged wound'. He said Collins's long hair partially hid the entry wound. Eleanor Gordon, Matron of Shanakiel Hospital, cleaned and attended to Collins's wounds and also later testified to the nature of the wounds. Comdt Gen Dr Leo Aherne examined Collins's body when it was brought to the Imperial Hotel, Cork.

The steamship *SS Classic* (*SS Innisfallen* according to *Who's Who*) brought Collins's body from Cork to Dublin. In Dublin, Oliver St John Gogarty embalmed the body, and had Sir John Lavery paint Collins's portrait. Albert Power sculpted the death mask.

Collins died intestate, leaving an estate of £1,950 9s 11d. Shane Leslie wrote the following lines:

---

8.  see Griffith, Kenneth and O'Grady, Timothy, *Curious Journey: an oral history of Ireland's Unfinished Revolution*, Mercier, Cork
9.  There is no consensus who or even how many were in the ambush party. The party set an ambush with a cart across the road, and a mine, and waited all day for the column's return, but then dismantled the mine and was in the process of moving the cart when Collins's column came upon them. It has been said there were many more Republicans/IRA in the ambush party during the day, but by the time of the arrival of Collins it is thought there were only 4 members left in the ambush party with 3 other groups of 2–3 men 'passing through'.

*What is that curling flower of wonder*
*As white as snow, as red as blood?*
*When Death goes by in flame and thunder*
*And rips the beauty from the bud.*

*They left his blossom white and slender*
*Beneath Glasnevin's shaking sod;*
*His spirit passed like sunset splendour*
*Unto the dead Fianna's God.*

*Good luck be with you, Michael Collins,*
*Or stay or go you far away;*
*Or stay you with the folk of fairy,*
*Or come with ghosts another day.*

**Beggar's Bush**: the Free State Army was officially established at Beggar's Bush Barracks on 31 January 1922.

**1 Brendan Road, Donnybrook**: Batt O'Connor's home. Collins often lunched here, stayed here, and used it for meetings. 'Jameson' (John Charles Byrne) was lured here to see if he was a spy. Collins hid £25,000 in gold in a baby's coffin under the floor here.

**6 Brendan Road, Donnybrook**: this house was owned by the Dáil and was often used by Collins.

**23 Brendan Road, Donnybrook**: this house was owned by Susan (Sinead) Mason and her aunt, Mrs Donovan. Collins often stayed here. She was Collins's personal and private secretary, and endured an enormous workload as well as dangerously carrying dispatches from location to location. For a while their friends, the O'Connors and Sister Margaret Mary, thought they'd marry.

**5 Cabra Road**: Michael Foley's home, where Collins first met Ned Broy

**Camden Street**: Mrs Padraig O'Keefe's restaurant. Collins often lunched here and used it as an 'office' between 76 Harcourt Street and 22 Mary Street.

**3 Crow Street**: the Department of Intelligence office was on the second floor, above J. F. Fowler's, printers. Though it was technically the head office of his Ministry, Collins infrequently came here. Under the name of Irish Products Company, Liam Tobin, Collins's Chief of Intelligence, had his office here, assisted by Tom Cullen and Frank Thornton. Principal Staff: Charlie Dalton, Joe Dolan, Joe Guilfoyle, Frank Saurin.

**Dame Street**: Craig Gardiner & Co, Chartered Accountants; Collins worked here before the Rising.

**Dawson Street**: P. S. O'Hegarty's bookshop; it was used as a 'drop' for Collins.

**21 Dawson Street**: Eileen McGrane's home where Collins kept many papers; it was raided on 31 December 1920.

**Denzille Lane**: Batty Hyland owned a garage here; Batty was Collins's regular driver, and his brother, Joe, also drove for him.

**Dublin Castle**: the Castle was handed over to Collins on 16 January 1922 by Lord Edward Talbot Fitzallen, Lord Lieutenant of Ireland.

**Dun Laoghaire, Co Dublin**: Royal Marine Hotel; Collins and Kitty Kiernan were dancing here when Joe O'Reilly came to tell them of the truce. John and Hazel Lavery stayed here when they came to Ireland so that John could work on his painting on the subject of the Civil War in August 1922. They were in residence when Collins was killed.

**10 Exchequer Street**: first 'real' Irish National Aid and Volunteers' Dependents' Fund office. Collins worked for Kathleen Clarke here after his release from Frongoch.

**Frongoch, North Wales**: Collins was Irish Prisoner 1320 here. M. W. O'Reilly was the camp's first O/C. Collins smoked 30 cigarettes a day – he gave them up in 1921, after the Tans arrived, saying he would not be a slave to anything.

**Furry Park, Raheny**: home of Crompton and Moya Llewellan Davies; Collins often stayed here. He ate dinner here on 17 August 1922 with the Laverys, Sir Horace and Lady Plunkett, Piaras Béaslaí, Joe O'Reilly and others. A man named Dixon (formerly a marksman with the Connaught Rangers) was apprehended with a rifle, and was taken and shot by Collins's guards.

**35 Gardiner Street, Lower**: Typographical Society's Rooms/HQ of theDublin Printer's Union. On 20 November 1920 Collins met Cathal Brugha, Peadar Clancy, Paddy Daly, Dick McKee, Dick Mulcahy and Sean Russell here to finalise plans for Bloody Sunday.

**Gardiner Row**: Linda Kearns' home; Collins used the house for meetings and stayed here occasionally.

**65 Great Britain Street**: home of Mr and Mrs Maurice Collins (no relation), where Michael Collins often stayed overnight. It was raided on 31 January 1920.

**68–69 Great Britain Street**: Liam Devlin's Pub, just off Rutland Square. It was 'Joint No 2' – the 'unofficial HQ' of Collins. He waited here for Bloody Sunday reports.

**Great Brunswick Street**: G-Division HQ. Ned Broy let Collins in on the night of 7 April 1919 (not Dublin Castle as portrayed in the film *Michael Collins*) to look over the G-Division files on the Volunteers (Collins met Sean Nunan on the way to meet Broy and took him along, so Nunan also saw the files). It was on this foray that Collins read his own file; the contents indicated that he 'belongs, to a family of 'brainy' people and of advanced Sinn Féin sympathies. That gave Collins such a hearty laugh that Broy heard him and was concerned Collins would be discovered.

**8 Haddon Road, Clontarf**: Thomas Gay's home. Gay was the librarian in Capel Street Municipal Library. Weekly conferences were held here with Broy, McNamara and Neligan.

**∗6 Harcourt Street**: Ministry of Finance office, raided on 12 September 1919.[10]

**Harcourt Street**: Ivanhoe Hotel. Collins hid on the roof here when 6 Harcourt Street was raided.

**∗76 Harcourt Street**: raided in November 1919.

**∗17 Harcourt Terrace**: used from the end of May to June 1921

**∗21, 22 Harry Street**: used as a primary office and also a Department of Intelligence office. It was not in use for long.

---

10. The addresses marked here with an asterisk ∗ indicate three of Collins's seven primary offices during the period.

**Henry Street**: Collins had an office of sorts here.

**1 Island View, Howth**: home of Mrs Quick; she rented rooms to many young women and Collins often enquired after them in letters. Susan Killeen, a London 'girlfriend' lived here following the start of WWI.

**King's Cross, London**: the 'German' Gymnasium; on 25 April 1914 Collins was enrolled here in Company No 1 of the London Branch of the Irish Volunteers. He was enrolled by his cousin, Sean Hurley. His membership card was signed by P. S. O'Hegarty.

**Malahide Road, Dublin**: Winstonville; Collins often stayed here.

*__22 Mary Street__: raided on 26 May 1921 (the day after the Custom House fire). This raid was one of Collins's closest calls. Alice Lyons, a typist, and Bob Conlan, the office messenger, were in the office when it was raided, but Collins had had a premonition and stayed away after his lunch with Gearóid O'Sullivan. Collins always said there was a traitor in the camp, always claimed he knew who it was, and knew of the details of the raid – including the fact that the tout had been paid £500 on the condition that there would be no blood-shed.[11]

*__28-29 Mary Street__: raided in June 1921. Batt O'Connor built a secret compartment in the draper's shop here.

**Mespil Road, Ballsbridge**: Mrs O'Donovan's Dairy; she was Gearóid O'Sullivan's aunt. Collins lived here after the Munster Hotel period and had meetings here every Sunday at noon.

**5 Mespil Road, Ballsbridge**: the home of secretary Patricia Hoey and her mother. It was raided on 1 April 1921 and Ms Hoey was arrested when a revolver was found. She was released when she stuck to her story that the revolver must have been left by a former lodger. When she was taken home the RIC hid in her house, waiting for Collins to appear. She had her mother fake a heart attack, and passed the word to Collins through a friendly female doctor. Still the RIC found a cache of documents and then sent Ms Hoey to prison for several months; she was not released until after the Truce.

*__5 Mespil Road, Ballsbridge__: close to Leeson Street Bridge it was used as a primary office and also a Department of Intelligence office. It was raided on 1 April 1921.

**Morehampton Road**: home of Mrs Andrew Woods; Collins often stayed here.

**Mountjoy Street**: Sean McGarry's home; Collins stayed here on the night the Volunteer Cabinet was arrested for the purported 'German Plot', and after McGarry had been arrested (17–18 May 1918).

**30 Mountjoy Street**: across from Aras na nGael; this was the home of Madeline 'Dilly' Dicker, a 'girlfriend' of Collins's before Kitty Kiernan.

**1 Mountjoy Square**: home of Alderman Walter Coles. The Dáil met here in 1919 and 1920. Collins sometimes stayed here.

**44 Mountjoy Square**: Munster Private Hotel, known as Aras na nGael. Miss Myra T. McCarthy was the owner. It was Collins's first residence after Frongoch and his primary residence until it was raided in December 1919. He stayed here infrequently thereafter, but he still left his laundry here and collected it on Saturday mornings.

---

11. The addresses marked here with an asterisk * indicate four of Collins's seven primary offices during the period.

**Oakley Road, Ranelagh**: Cullenswood House; the first location of St Enda's. Collins had a basement office here and Richard Mulcahy and his wife had the top-floor flat, 'The Dug-Out'. It was raided on 20 January 1920.

**Portobello Road**: Portobello Barracks (renamed Cathal Brugha Barracks). It was Collins's office during the Civil War. He left Dublin from here on his fatal journey.

**16 Rathdown Road**: the Belton family home. Sean Hurley found Collins a room here on his return from London in January 1916. This was the address he gave to the British after the Rising and when sent to Frongoch.

**Richmond Road, Drumcondra**: Walter House; Collins often stayed overnight.

**109 Richmond Road, Drumcondra**: the home of Michael Lynch (across from Walter House)

**29-30 Rutland Square**: Vaughan's Hotel; 'Joint No 1'– unsafe after mid-1920

**39 Rutland Square**: the home of Dr Paddy Browne of Maynooth College; Collins watched the raid on Vaughan's from here on the night of 20 November 1920.

**46 Rutland Square**: The Squad was 'officially' established on 19 September 1919 at this address (though by that time it had been in operation for two months and had already carried out two killings). Members were paid £4 10s per week. The first four members were: Ben Barrett, Paddy Daly (Paddy O'Dalaigh, sometimes said to have succeeded Mick McDonnell as leader, but usually considered the leader; he became a major general in the national army), Sean Doyle and Joe Leonard (came right behind Daly in the chain of command). Other 'original' members were Mick McDonnell (described by some as the first leader), James Conroy, Jim McGuinness, Jimmy Slattery (a Clareman with only one hand, after being injured in the Custom House fire) and William 'Billy' Stapleton (a Dubliner). Added to the 'original' nine after a few months to form 'The Twelve Apostles' (a name first applied, derisively, by Austin Stack) were Vinnie Byrne, Tom Kehoe (from Wicklow, later killed in the Civil War) and Mick O'Reilly. Others were added in January 1920 and thereafter: and were chosen for 'jobs' as needed. Not all did many 'jobs' for Collins, and many were members of various Dublin units who were picked by Collins to assist the 'regular' Squad members; this was particularly true on Bloody Sunday. The other members were: Frank Bolster, J. Brennan, Ned Breslin, Ben Byrne, Charlie Byrne (a Dubliner called 'The Count' because of his cheerful mien in all situations), Eddie Byrne, Sean Caffrey, Paddy Colgan (from Maynooth, Co Kildare), James Connolly, Jim Conway (the 'one-man column'), Andy Cooney, Tom Cullen (a teetotaler), Charlie Dalton, Jim Dempsey (a Dubliner and an old IRB man who fought in the Rising), Joe Dolan (another Dubliner, always armed with a .45 and wore a British Army badge in his lapel), Joe Dowling, Pat Drury, John Dunne, Tom Ennis, Paddy Flanagan (the oldest member of The Squad), Paddy Griffin, Jack Hanlon, Sean Kavanagh (a Dubliner and later a prison governor), Ned Kelliher (a Dubliner), Mick Kennedy, Paddy Kennedy (from Tipperary), Martin Lavan, Paddy Lawson, Seán Lemass (the future Taoiseach), Pat McCrae (a great driver), Pat McKeon, Peadar McMahon (later Chief of Staff of the Free State Army), Diarmuid O'Hegarty (a Corkman; Director of Organisation of the Volunteers), Bob O'Neill (a Clareman), Albert Rutherford, Frank Saurin (a Dubliner, known as the best-dressed Volunteer), Frank Teeling, Liam Tobin, George White and Johnny Wilson.

**Sam's Cross, Clonakilty, Co Cork**: the birthplace of Michael Collins. There is a memorial to Collins here. Woodfield was the name given by Collins's mother to the new house she built in 1908. It was burned by the Essex Division, under the command of Major Arthur Emmett Percival, in 1920.

**3 St Andrew Street**: owned by Batt O'Connor; Collins hid some gold here and also conducted some financial business here.

**St Stephen's Green**: school run by Louise Gavan Duffy; Collins used the school for meetings.

**Stafford Detention Barracks**: Collins arrived here on 1 May 1916, Irish Prisoner 48F.

# Appendix III:
## Statements and documents 1913–1923

## Contents

# 1   Manifesto of the Irish Volunteers, 25 November 1913

## Ulster

At a time when legislative proposals universally confessed to be of vital concern for the future of Ireland have been put forward, and are awaiting decision, a plan has been deliberately adopted by one of the great English political parties, advocated by the leaders of that party and by its numerous organs in the Press, and brought systematically to bear on English public opinion, to make the display of military force and the menace of armed violence the determining factor in the future relations between this country and Great Britain.

## The Tories

The party which has thus substituted open force for the semblance of civil government is seeking by this means not merely to decide an immediate political issue of grave concern to this nation, but also to obtain for itself the future control of all our national affairs. It is plain to every man that the people of Ireland, if they acquiesce in this new policy by their inaction, will consent to the surrender, not only of their rights as a nation, but of their civic rights as men.

## Act of Union

The Act of Union deprived the Irish nation of the power to direct its own course and to develop and use its own resources for its own benefit. It gave us, instead, the meager and seldom effective right of throwing our votes into the vast and complicated movement of British politics. Since the Act of Union a long series of repressive statutes has endeavored to deal with the incessant discontent of the Irish people by depriving them of various rights common to all who live under the British Constitution. The new policy goes farther than the Act of Union, and farther than all subsequent Coercion Acts taken together. It proposes to leave us the political franchise in name, and to annihilate it in fact. If we fail to take such measures as will eventually defeat this policy, we become politically the most degraded population in Europe, and no longer worthy of the name Nation.

## Our Rights

Are we to rest inactive, in the hope that the course of politics in Great Britain may save us from the degradation openly threatened against us? British politics are controlled by British interests, and are complicated by problems of great importance to the people of Great Britain. In a crisis of this kind, the duty of safeguarding our own rights is our duty first and foremost. They have rights who dare maintain them. If we remain quiescent, by what title can we expect the people of Great Britain to turn aside from their own pressing concerns to defend us? Will not such an attitude of itself mark us out as a people unworthy of defence?

## Our opportunity

Such is the occasion, not altogether unfortunate, which has brought about the inception of the Irish Volunteer movement. But the Volunteers, once they have been enrolled, will form a prominent element in the national life under a National Government. The Nation will maintain its Volunteer organisation as a guarantee of the liberties which the Irish people shall have secured.

If ever in history a people could say that an opportunity was given to them by God's will to make an honest and manly stand for their rights, that opportunity is given us to-day. The stress of industrial effort, the relative peace and prosperity of recent years, may have dulled the sense of the demands of civic duty. We may forget that the powers of the platform, the Press, and the polling booth are derived from the conscious resolve of the people to maintain their rights and liberties. From time immemorial, it has been held by every race of mankind to be the right and duty of a freeman to defend his freedom with all his resources and with his life itself. The exercise of that right distinguishes the freeman from the serf, the discharge of that duty distinguishes him from the coward.

*Citizen Army*
To drill, to learn the use of arms, to acquire the habit of disciplined and concerted action, to form a citizen army from a population now at the mercy of almost any organised aggression – this, beyond all doubt, is the programme that appeals to all Ireland, but especially to young Ireland. We begin at once in Dublin, and we are confident that the movement will be taken up without delay all over the country. Public opinion has already and quite spontaneously formed itself into an eager desire for the establishment of the Irish Volunteers.

*Our Object*
The object proposed for the Irish Volunteers is to secure and maintain the rights and liberties common to all the people of Ireland. Their duties will be defensive and protective, and they will not contemplate either aggression or domination. Their ranks are open to all able-bodied Irishmen without distinction of creed, politics, or social grade. Means will be found whereby Irishmen unable to serve as ordinary Volunteers will be enabled to aid the Volunteer forces in various capacities. There will also be work for women to do, and there are signs that the women of Ireland, true to their record, are especially enthusiastic for the success of the Irish Volunteers.

*Widest Basis*
We propose for the Volunteers' organisation the widest possible basis. Without any other association or classification, the Volunteers will be enrolled according to the district in which they live. As soon as it is found feasible, the district sections will be called upon to join in making provision for the general administration and discipline, and for the united cooperation. The provisional Committee which has acted up to the present will continue to offer its service until an elective body is formed to replace it.

*Freemen*
A proportion of time spared, not from work, but from pleasure and recreation, a voluntary adoption of discipline, a purpose firmly and steadily carried through, will renew the vitality of the Nation. Even that degree of self-discipline will bring back to every town, village, and countryside a consciousness that has long been forbidden them – the sense of freemen who have fitted themselves to defend the cause of freedom.

*Unity: Liberty*
In the name of National Unity, of National Dignity, of National and Individual Liberty, of Manly Citizenship, we appeal to our countrymen to recognise and accept without hesita-

tion the opportunity that has been granted to them to join the ranks of the Irish Volunteers, and to make the movement now begun not unworthy of the historic title which it has adopted.

## 2   Address of Padraig Pearse at the grave of Jeremiah O'Donovan Rossa, 1 August 1915

It has seemed right, before we turn away from this place in which we have laid the mortal remains of O'Donovan Rossa, that one among us should, in the name of all, speak the praise of that valiant man, and endeavor to formulate the thought and the hope that are in us as we stand around his grave. And if there is anything that makes it fitting that I, rather than some other, I rather than one of the grey-haired men who were young with him and shared in his labour and in his suffering, should speak here, it is perhaps that I may be taken as speaking on behalf of a new generation that has been re-baptised in the Fenian faith, and that has accepted the responsibility of carrying out the Fenian programme. I propose to you then that, here by the grave of this unrepentant Fenian, we renew our baptismal vows; that, here by the grave of this unconquered and unconquerable man, we ask of God, each one for himself, such unshakable purpose, such high and gallant courage, such unbreakable strength of soul as belonged to O'Donovan Rossa.

Deliberately here we avow ourselves, as he avowed himself in the dock, Irishmen of one allegiance only. We of the Irish Volunteers, and you others who are associated with us in to-day's task and duty, are bound together and must stand together henceforth in brotherly union for the achievement of the freedom of Ireland. And we know only one definition of freedom: it is Tone's definition, it is Mitchel's definition, it is Rossa's definition. Let no man blaspheme the cause that the dead generations of Ireland served by giving it any other name and definition than their name and their definition.

We stand at Rossa's grave not in sadness but rather in exaltation of spirit that it has been given to us to come thus into so close a communion with that brave and splendid Gael. Splendid and holy causes are served by men who are themselves splendid and holy. O'Donovan Rossa was splendid in the proud manhood of him, splendid in the heroic grace of him, splendid in the Gaelic strength and clarity and truth of him. And all that splendour and pride and strength was compatible with a humility and a simplicity of devotion to Ireland, to all that was olden and beautiful and Gaelic in Ireland, the holiness and simplicity of patriotism of a Michael O'Clery or of an Eoghan O'Growney. The clear true eyes of this man almost alone in his day visioned Ireland as we of to-day would surely have her: not free merely, but Gaelic as well; not Gaelic merely, but free as well.

In a closer spiritual communion with him now than ever before or perhaps ever again, in a spiritual communion with those of his day, living and dead, who suffered with him in English prisons, in communion of spirit too with our own dear comrades who suffer in English prisons to-day, and speaking on their behalf as well as our own, we pledge to Ireland our love, and we pledge to English rule in Ireland our hate. This is a place of peace, sacred to the dead, where men should speak with all charity and with all restraint; but I hold it a Christian thing, as O'Donovan Rossa held it, to hate evil, to hate untruth, to hate oppression, and, hating them, to strive to overthrow them. Our foes are strong and wise and wary; but, strong and wise and wary as they are, they cannot undo the miracles of God who ripens in the hearts of young men the seeds sown by the young men of a former generation. And the seeds sown by the young men of '65 and '67 are coming to their miraculous ripening to-day. Rulers and Defenders of Realms had need to be wary if they would guard against such processes. Life springs from death; and from the graves of patriot men and women spring living nations. The Defenders of this Realm have worked well in secret and in the open. They think that they have pacified Ireland. They think that they have purchased half of us and intimidated the other half. They think that they have foreseen everything, think that they have provided against everything; but the fools, the fools, the fools! – they have left us our Fenian dead, and while Ireland holds these graves, Ireland unfree shall never be at peace.

## 3   Manifesto of the Irish Volunteers, March 1916

With regard to the recent proceedings of the Government towards the Irish Volunteers, the council of the Irish Volunteers, which met on the 26th inst., wish to warn the public that the general tendency of the Government's action is to force a highly dangerous situation. The Government is well aware that the possession of arms is essential to the Irish Volunteer organisation, and the Volunteers cannot submit to being disarmed either in numbers or detail without surrendering and abandoning the position they have held at all times since their first formation. The Volunteer organisation also cannot maintain its efficiency without organisers. The raiding for arms and attempted disarming of men, therefore, in the natural course of things can only be met by resistance and bloodshed. None of the Irish Volunteers recognise, or will ever recognise, the right of the Government to disarm them or to imprison their officers and men in any fashion. The council also draws attention to the repeated instances in which the Government's arbitrary action has been associated with the movements of hostile crowds, which are led to believe they act under the Government's approval. In this council's belief, this feature of the case is based on a deliberate policy of creating factious hostility between sections of the Irish people. Nothing need be hoped from remonstrance with the Government, but we appeal to the Irish people to look closely into the facts in every instance and keep a watch on the conduct and policy of the authorities, and to fix the responsibility for any grave consequence that may arise.

## 4   Cancellation order of Eoin MacNeill, 22 April 1916

Owing to the very critical position, all orders given to Irish Volunteers for tomorrow, Easter Sunday, are hereby rescinded, and no parades, marches, or other movements of Irish Volunteers will take place. Each individual Volunteer will obey this order strictly in every particular.

*Eoin MacNeill*
*Holy Saturday, 22 April 1916*

*Patrick H. Pearse*

## 5   MacDonagh and Pearse Order to Parade, 24 April 1916

24 April
1  The four City Battalions will parade for inspection and route march at 10 a.m. today. Commandants will arrange centres.
2  Full arms and equipment and one day's rations to be carried.

*Thomas MacDonagh*
*Brigade Commandant*

*Coy E 3 will parade at Beresford Place at 10 a.m.*
*PH Pearse*
*Comdt.*

## 6   Proclamation of the Irish Republic, 24 April 1916

POBLACHT NA HÉIREANN
THE PROVISIONAL GOVERNMENT OF THE IRISH REPUBLIC
TO THE PEOPLE OF IRELAND

IRISHMEN AND IRISHWOMEN: In the name of God and of the dead generations from which she receives her old tradition of nationhood, Ireland, through us, summons her children to her flag and strikes for her freedom.

Having organised and trained her manhood through her secret revolutionary organisation, the Irish Republican Brotherhood, and through her open military organisations, The Irish Volunteers and the Irish Citizen Army, having patiently perfected her discipline, having resolutely waited for the right moment to reveal itself, she now seizes that moment, and supported by her exiled children in America and by gallant allies in Europe, but relying in the first on her own strength, she strikes in full confidence of victory.

We declare the right of the people of Ireland to the ownership of Ireland and to the unfettered control of Irish destinies, to be sovereign and indefeasible. The long usurpation of that right by a foreign people and government has not extinguished the right, nor can it ever be extinguished except by the destruction of the Irish people. In every generation the Irish people have asserted their right to national freedom and sovereignty; six times during the past three hundred years they have asserted it in arms. Standing on that fundamental right and again asserting it in arms in the face of the world, we hereby proclaim the Irish Republic as a Sovereign Independent State, and we pledge our lives and the lives of our comrades in arms to the cause of its freedom, of its welfare, and of its exaltation among the nations.

The Irish Republic is entitled to, and hereby claims, the allegiance of every Irishman and Irishwoman. The Republic guarantees religious and civil liberty, equal rights and equal opportunities to all its citizens, and declares its resolve to pursue the happiness and prosperity of the whole nation and of all its parts, cherishing all of the children of the nation equally, and oblivious of the differences carefully fostered by an alien Government, which have divided a minority from the majority in the past.

Until our arms have brought the opportune moment for the establishment of a permanent National Government, representative of the whole people of Ireland and elected by the suffrages of all her men and women, the Provisional Government, hereby constituted, will administer the civil and military affairs of the Republic in trust for the people.

We place the cause of the Irish Republic under the protection of the Most High God, Whose blessing we invoke upon our arms, and we pray that no one who serves that cause will dishonour it by cowardice, inhumanity, or rapine. In this supreme hour the Irish nation must, by its valour and discipline, and by the readiness of its children to sacrifice themselves for the common good, prove itself worthy of the august destiny to which it is called.

*Signed on Behalf of the Provisional Government,*

*Thomas J. Clarke*

| | |
|---|---|
| *Sean Mac Diarmada* | *Thomas Mac Donagh* |
| *P. H. Pearse* | *Eamonn Ceannt* |
| *James Connolly* | *Joseph Plunkett* |

## 7   Pearse Statement from the GPO, Thursday 28 April 1916

The Forces of the Irish Republic, which was proclaimed in Dublin, on Easter Monday, 24th April, have been in possession of the central part of the Capital, since 12 noon on that day. Up to yesterday headquarters was in touch with all the main outlying positions, and, despite furious, and almost continuous assaults by British Forces all those positions were then still being held, and the commandants in charge were confident of their ability to hold them for a long time.

During the course of yesterday afternoon, and evening, the enemy succeeded in cutting our communications, with our other positions in the City, and Headquarters is today isolated.

The enemy has burnt down whole blocks of houses, apparently with the object of giving themselves a clear field for the play of Artillery and Field guns against us. We have been bombarded during the evening and night, by Shrapnel and Machine Gun fire, but without material damage to our position, which is of great strength.

We are busy completing arrangements for the final defence of Headquarters, and are determined to hold it while buildings last. I desire now, lest I may not have an opportunity later, to pay homage to the gallantry of the soldiers of Irish freedom who have during the past four days been writing with fire and steel the most glorious chapter in the later history of Ireland. Justice can never be done to their heroism, to their discipline, to their gay and unconquerable spirit in the midst of peril and death.

Let me, who have led them into this, speak in my own, and in my fellow-commanders' names, and in the name of Ireland present and to come, their praise, and ask those who come after them to remember them.

For four days they have fought and toiled, almost without cessation, almost without sleep, and in the intervals of fighting they have sung songs of the freedom of Ireland. No man has complained, no man has asked 'why?' Each individual has spent himself, happy to pour out his strength for Ireland and for Freedom. If they do not win this fight, they will at least have deserved to win it. But win it they will although they win in death.

Already they have won a great thing. They have redeemed Dublin from many shames, and made her name splendid among cities.

If I were to mention names, my list would be long.

I will name only that of Commandant General James Connolly, Commanding the Dublin Division. He lies wounded, but is still the guiding brain of our resistance.

If we accomplish no more than we have accomplished, I am satisfied. I am satisfied that we have saved Ireland's honour. I am satisfied that we should have accomplished more, that we should have accomplished the task of enthroning as well as proclaiming the Irish Republic as a Sovereign State, had our arrangements for a simultaneous Rising of the whole country, with a combined plan as sound as the Dublin plan has proved to be, been allowed to go through on Easter Sunday. Of the fatal countermanding order which prevented those plans being carried out, I shall not speak further. Both Eoin MacNeill and we have acted in the best interests of Ireland.

For my part, as to anything I have done in this, I am not afraid to face the judgment of God, or the judgment of posterity.

*Padraig H. Pearse*
*Commandant General*
*Commander in Chief of the Army*
*President of the Provisional Government*
*28 April 1916 9.30 a.m.*


## 8   Pearse Surrender Order, 29 April 1916

In order to prevent the further slaughter of Dublin citizens, and in the hope of saving the lives of our followers, now surrounded and hopelessly outnumbered, the members of the Provisional Government at present at Headquarters have agreed to an unconditional surrender, and the Commandants of the various districts in the City and County will order their commands to lay down arms.

*Padraig H. Pearse*
*29 April 1916*


## 9   Connolly Surrender Order, 29 April 1916

I agree to these conditions for the men only under my command in the Moore Street District and for the men in the Stephen's Green Command.

*James Connolly*
*April 29/16*


## 10  MacDonagh Surrender Order, 29 April 1916

On consultation with Commandant Ceannt and other officers I have decided to agree to unconditional surrender also.

*Thomas MacDonagh*
*30.IV.16*
*3.15 p.m.*

## 11 *Pearse Statement to Court Martial, 2 May 1916*

The following is the substance of what I said when asked today by the President of the Court Martial at Richmond Barracks whether I had anything to say in defence:

I desire in the first place to repeat what I have already said in letters to General Sir John Maxwell and Brigadier General Lowe. My object in agreeing to unconditional surrender was to prevent further slaughter of the civilian population of Dublin and to save the lives of our gallant fellows, who, having made for six days a stand unparalleled in military history, were now surrounded and (in the case of those under the immediate command of headquarters) without food. I fully understand now, as then, that my own life is forfeit to British law, and I shall die very cheerfully if I can think the British Government, as it has already shown itself strong, will now show itself magnanimous enough to accept my single life in forfeiture and to give a general amnesty to the brave men and boys who have fought at my bidding. In the second place, I wish it to be understood that any admissions I make here are to be taken as involving myself alone. They do not involve and must not be used against anyone who acted with me, not even those who have set their names to documents with me. [The Court assented to this.]

I admit I was Commandant-General Commander-in-Chief of the forces of The Irish Republic which have been acting against you for the past week, and that I was President of the Provisional Government. I stand over all my acts and words done or spoken in these capacities. When I was a child of ten I went down on my knees by my bedside one night and promised God that I should devote my life to an effort to free my country. I have kept that promise.

First among all earthly things, as a boy and a man, I have worked for Irish Freedom. I have helped organise, to arm, to train, and to discipline my fellow-countrymen to the sole end that, when the time came, they might fight for Irish Freedom. The time, as it seemed to me, did come and we went into the fight. I am glad that we did, we seem to have lost, we have not lost. To refuse to fight would have been to lose, to fight is to win, we have kept the faith with the past, and handed a tradition to the future.

I repudiate the assertion of the prosecutor that I sought to aid and abet England's enemy. Germany is no more to me than England is. I asked for and accepted German aid in the shape of arms and expeditionary force, we neither asked nor accepted German gold, nor had any traffic with Germany but what I state: my aim was to win Irish Freedom; we struck the first blow ourselves but I should have been glad of an ally's aid.

I assume I am speaking to Englishmen who value their own freedom, and who profess to be fighting for the freedom of Belgium and Serbia. Believe that we too love freedom and desire it. To us it is more desirable than anything else in the world. If you strike us down now we will rise again and renew the fight. You cannot conquer Ireland. You cannot extinguish the Irish passion for freedom. If our deed has not been sufficient to win freedom, then our children will win it by a better deed.

*Padraig Pearse*
*Address to his Court Martial*
*Written in Kilmainham Gaol*
*2 May 1916*

## 12  General Blackadder Statement after Pearse Court Martial, 2 May 1916

I have just done one of the hardest tasks I have ever had to do. I have had to condemn one of the finest characters I have ever come across. There must be something very wrong in the state of things, that makes a man like that a rebel.

## 13  Pearse Letter to his Mother, 2 May 1916

My Dearest Mother,

I have been hoping up to now it would be possible to see you again, but it does not seem possible. Good-bye, dear mother. Through you I say good-bye to 'Wow? Wow!', Mary Brigid, Willie, Miss B., Michael, cousin Maggine, and everyone at St. Enda's. I hope and believe Willie and the St. Enda's boys will all be safe.

I have written two papers about financial affairs and one about books which I want you to get. With them are a few poems I want added to the poems in MS. in my bookcase. You asked me to write a little poem which would seem to be said by you to me. I have written it, and a copy is in Arbour Hill barracks with other papers. [*The Mother*]

I have just received Holy Communion. I am happy, except for the great grief of parting from you. This is the death I should have asked for if God had given me the choice of all deaths – to die a soldier's death for Ireland and for freedom. We have done right. People will say hard things of us now, but later on will praise us. Do not grieve for all of this but think of it as a sacrifice God asked of me and you.

Good-bye, dear mother, may God bless you for your great love for me and for your great faith and may He remember all you have so bravely suffered. I hope soon to see papa, and in a little while we shall all be together again. I have not words to tell you of my love for you and how my heart yearns for you all. I will call to you in my heart at the last moment.

*Your son,*
*Pat*

## 14  MacDonagh Statement to his Court Martial, 2 May 1916

Gentlemen of the Court Martial

I choose to think that you have done your duty, according to your lights, in sentencing me to death. I thank you for your courtesy. It would not be seemly for me to go to my doom without trying to express, however inadequately, my sense of the high honour I enjoy in being of those predestined in this generation to die for Irish Freedom. You will, perhaps, understand this sentiment, for it is one to which an Imperial poet of a bygone age bore immortal testimony: ''Tis sweet and glorious to die for one's country'. You would all be proud to die for Britain, your Imperial patron, and I am proud and happy to die for Ireland, my glorious Fatherland.

There is not much left to say. The Proclamation of the Irish Republic has been adduced in evidence against me as one of the signatories; you think it is already a dead and buried letter, but it lives, it lives. From minds alight with Ireland's vivid intellect, it sprang; in hearts aflame with Ireland's mighty love it was conceived. Such documents do not die.

The British occupation of Ireland has never for more than one hundred years been compelled to confront in the field a Rising so formidable as that which overwhelming forces have for the moment succeeded in quelling. This Rising did not result from accidental circumstances. It came in due recurrent season as the necessary outcome of forces that are ever at work. The fierce pulsation of resurgent pride that disclaims servitude may one day cease to throb in the heart of Ireland – but the heart of Ireland will that day be dead. While Ireland lives, the brain and brawn of her manhood will strive to destroy the last vestige of British rule in her territory.

In this ceaseless struggle, there will be, as there has been, and must be an eternal ebb and flow. But, let England make no mistake. The generous high-bred youth of Ireland will never fail to answer the call of war to win their country's freedom. Other and tamer methods they will leave to other and tamer men; but they must do it or die.

It will be said that our movement was foredoomed to failure. It had proved so. Yet it might have been otherwise. There is always a chance for brave men who challenge fortune. That we had such a chance none knows so well as your statesmen and military experts. The mass of the people of Ireland will doubtless salve their consciences to sleep for another generation by the now exploded fable that Ireland cannot successfully fight England. We do not profess to represent the mass of the people of Ireland. We stand for the intellect and the soul of Ireland. To Ireland's intellect and soul the inert mass, drugged and degenerate by ages of servitude, must, in the distant day of resurrection, render homage and free service – receiving in return the vivifying impress of a free people.

Gentlemen, you have sentenced me to death and I accept your sentence with joy and pride, since it is for Ireland I am to die. I go to join the goodly company of men who died for Ireland, the least of whom was worthier than I can claim to be; and that noble band are, themselves, but a small section of that great unnumbered army of martyrs, whose Captain is the Christ Who died on Calvary. Of every white-robed knight in all that goodly company, we are the spiritual kin. The forms of heroes flit before my vision; and there is one, the star of whose destiny sways my own; there is one, the key-note of whose nature chimes harmoniously with the swan-song of my soul. It is the great Florentine, Savonarola, whose weapon was not the sword but prayer and teaching. The seed he sowed fructifies to this day in God's Church.

Take me away, and let my blood bedew the sacred soil of Ireland. I die in the certainty that once more the seed will fructify.

[The speech's authenticity was questioned but wholly accepted as true by MacDonagh's family.]

*Thomas MacDonagh*
*Address to his Court Martial*
*2 May 1916*

## 15  Final Statement of Thomas MacDonagh, 2 May 1916

I, Thomas MacDonagh, having now heard the sentence of the court martial held on me today, declare that in all my acts – all the acts for which I have been arraigned – I have been actuated by one motive only, the love of my country, the desire to make a sovereign independent state. I still hope and pray that my acts will have for consummation her lasting freedom and happiness.

I am to die at dawn, 3.30 a.m. 3rd May. I am ready to die, and I thank God that I die in so holy a cause. My country will reward my deed richly.

On April 30th I was astonished to receive by a message from P. H. Pearse, Commandant General of the Army of the Irish Republic, an order to surrender unconditionally to the British General. I did not obey the order as it came from a prisoner. I was then in supreme command of the Irish Army, consulted with my second in command and decided to confirm the order. I knew that it would involve my death and the deaths of other leaders. I hoped it would save many true men among our followers, good lives for Ireland. God grant it has done so, and God approve our deed. For myself, I have no regret. The one bitterness that death has for me is the separation it brings from my beloved wife, Muriel, and my beloved children Donagh and Barbara. My country will take them as wards, I hope.

I have devoted myself too much to national work, and too little to the making of money to leave them a competence. God help them and support them and give them a happy and prosperous life. Never was there a better, truer, purer woman than my wife, Muriel, or more adorable children than Don and Barbara. It breaks my heart to think that I shall never see my children again, but I have not wept or mourned. I counted the cost of this and I am ready to pay it.

Muriel has been sent for here. I do not know if she can come. She may have no one to take the children while she is coming. If she does.

Yesterday at my court martial in rebutting some trifling evidence, I made a statement as to my negotiations for surrender to General Lowe. On hearing it read after it struck me that it might sound like an appeal. It was not such. I made no appeal, no recantation, no apology for my acts. In what I said I merely claimed that I had acted honourably in all that I set myself to do. My enemies, in return, treated me in an unworthy manner. But that can pass. It is a great and glorious thing to die for Ireland and I can well forget all petty annoyances in the splendour of this. When my son, Don, was born I thought that to him and not to me would this be given. God has been kinder to me than I hoped.

To my son Don. My darling little boy, remember me kindly. Take my hope and purpose with my deed. For your sake and for the sake of your beloved mother and sister I wish to live long, but you will recognize the thing I have done, and see this as a consequence. I think still I have done a great thing for Ireland, and, with the defeat of her army, won the first step of her freedom. God bless you my son.

My darling daughter, Barbara, God bless you. I loved you more than ever a child has been loved.

My dearest love, Muriel, thank you a million times for all you have been to me. I have only one trouble in leaving life – leaving you so soon. Be brave, darling, God will assist and bless you. Goodbye, kiss my darlings for me. I send you the few things I have saved out of this war. Goodbye, my love, till we meet again in Heaven. I have a sure faith of our union there. I kiss this paper that goes to you. I have just heard that they have not been able to reach you. Perhaps it is better so. Yet Father Aloysius is going to make another effort to do something. God help and sustain you, my love. But for your suffering this would all be joy and glory.

*Your loving husband,*
*Thomas MacDonagh*

I return the darlings' photographs. Goodbye, my love.

*Thomas MacDonagh*
*Written at midnight, 2 May 1916*
*Kilmainham Gaol*
*Executed 3 May 1916*

## 16 Clarke Statement

This is the beginning, our fight has saved Ireland. The soldiers of tomorrow will finish the task.

*Thomas J. Clarke*

## 17 Clarke Letter to Kathleen, 30 April 1916

Dear K,

I am in better health and more satisfied than for many a day – all will be well eventually – but this is my good-bye for now – you are ever before me to cheer me – God bless you and the boys. Let them be proud to follow the same path – Sean is with me and McG, all well – they all heroes. I'm full of pride my love.

*Your*
*Tom*

Love to John & Madge Etc.

*Written to Kathleen from Richmond Barracks*
*30 April 1916*

## 18 Clarke Statement, 3 May 1916

I and my fellow signatories believe we have struck the first successful blow for Freedom. The next blow, which we have no doubt Ireland will strike, will win through. In this belief we die happy.

*Thomas J. Clarke*
*3 May 1916*
*Kilmainham Gaol*
*Executed 3 May 1916*

## 19  Plunkett Will, 23 April 1916

Will of Joseph Mary (Patrick) Plunkett made this day April 23rd 1916.

I give and bequeath everything of which I am possessed or may become possessed to Grace Evelyn (Mary Vandeleur) Gifford.

*Signed Joseph Mary Plunkett*
*Witnessed George Oliver Plunkett*

## 20  Plunkett Letter to Grace Gifford, 29 April 1916

To Miss Grace Gifford, 8 Temple Villas
Palmerston Rd.
6th Day of the Irish Republic
Saturday April 29th 1916. About noon.
Somewhere in Moore St.

My Darling Grace,

This is just a little note to say I love you and to tell you that I did everything I could to arrange for us to meet and get married but that it was impossible.

Except for that I have no regrets. We will meet soon.

My other actions have been as right as I could see and make them, and I cannot wish them undone. You at any rate will not misjudge them.

Give my love to my people and friends. Darling, darling child, I wish we were together. Love me always as I love you. For the rest all you do will please me. I told a few people that I wish you to have everything that belongs to me. This is my last wish so please see to it. Love xxxx

*Joe*

## 21  Will of Michael O'Hanrahan, 4 May 1916

I, Micheal O hAnnrachain, give and bequeath all my rights in 'A Swordsman of the Brigade' to my mother & after her to my sisters.

*Michael O hAnnrachain*
*Kilmainham*
*4/5/16*
*May 4th 16*
*T.Wright, S.M*
*MPSC*
*B.L.Barnett, Lieut.*
*59th Sig Co. RE*

*Will of Michael O'Hanrahan*
*Kilmainham Gaol*
*Executed 4 May 1916*

## 22 General Blackadder Statement after MacBride Court Martial, 4 May 1916

All the men behaved well, but the one who stands out and the most soldierly was John MacBride. He, on entering, stood to attention facing us and in his eyes I could read: 'You are soldiers. I am one. You have won. I have lost. Do your worst'.

*Brigadier General Charles Blackadder*

## 23 MacDermott Letter to his sister, 7 May 1916

Let there be no talk of 'foolish enterprises'. I have no vain regrets. If you really love me, teach the children the history of their own land and teach them that the cause of Caitlin ni h-Uallachain never dies. Ireland shall be free from the centre to the sea as soon as the people of Ireland believe in the necessity for Ireland's freedom and are prepared to make the necessary sacrifices to obtain it.

*Sean MacDermott's letter to his sister, a Dominican nun*
*Written in Kilmainham Gaol*
*7 May 1916*

## 24 Ceannt Statement, 7 May 1916

I leave for the guidance of other revolutionaries, who may tread the path which I have trod, this advice, never to treat with the enemy, never to surrender to his mercy, but to fight to a finish. I see nothing gained but grave disaster caused, by the surrender which has marked the end of the Irish Insurrection of 1916 – so far at least as Dublin is concerned. The enemy has not cherished one generous thought for those who, with little hope, with poor equipment, and weak in numbers, withstood his forces for one glorious week. Ireland has shown she is a Nation. This generation can claim to have raised sons as brave as any that went before. And in the years to come, Ireland will honour those who risked *all* for her honour at Easter in 1916. I bear no ill will against whom I have fought. I have found the common soldiers and the higher officers human and companionable, even the English who were actually in the fight against us. Thank God soldiering for Ireland has opened my heart and made me see poor humanity where I expected to see only scorn and reproach. I have met the man who escaped from me by a ruse under the Red Cross. But I do not regret having withheld my fire. He gave me cakes!

I wish to record the magnificent gallantry and fearless, calm determination of the men who fought with me. All, all were simply splendid. Even I knew no fear nor panic and shrank from no risk as I shrink not now from the death which faces me at daybreak. I hope to see God's face even for a moment in the morning. His will be done. All here are very kind. My poor wife saw me yesterday and bore up – so my warden told me – even after she left my presence. Poor Áine, poor Ronan. God is their only shield now that I am removed. And God is a better shield than I.

I have just seen Áine, Nell, Richard and Mick and bade them a conditional good-bye. Even now they have hope.

*Eamonn Ceannt*
*7 May 1916*
*Kilmainham Gaol – Cell 88 before he was moved to Cell 20*
*Executed 8 May 1916*

## 25 Ceannt Letter to his wife Áine, 8 May 1916

My Dearest Wife Áine,

Not wife, but widow before these lines reach you. I am here without hope of this world, and without fear, calmly awaiting the end. I have had Holy Communion, and Fr. Augustine has been with me, and will be back again.

Dearest silly little Fanny! My poor little sweetheart of how many years now? Ever my comforter, God comfort you now.

What can I say? I die a noble death for Ireland's freedom. Men and women will vie with one another to shake your dear hand.

Be proud of me, as I am and ever was of you. My cold exterior was a mask. It served me in these last days. You have a duty to me and to Ronan – that is to live.

My dying wishes are that you remember your state of health. Work only as much as may be necessary, and freely accept the little attentions which in due course will be showered upon you.

You will be, you are, the wife of one of the leaders of the Revolution. Sweeter still, you are my little child, my dearest pet, my sweetheart, of the hawthorn hedges, and summer eves. I remember all, and I banish all, so that I may die bravely. I have but one hour to live; then God's judgment, and through His infinite mercy, a place near your poor Grannie and my mother and father and Jem, and all the fine Irish who went through the scourge of similar misfortune from this vale of tears into the Promised Land.

Biodh misneach agat a stóirín mo chroide. Tog do cheann agus mo chroide. Tog do cheann agus biodh foighde agat go bhfeicfimid a chéile arís i bhFlaithis Dé —Tusa, agus mise agus Ronan beag beag bocht.

*Adieu*
*Eamonn*

Have courage the love of my heart. Take your head and my heart and have hope that we will be together again in the vision (kingdom or joy) of God. Poor you, and me and poor little Ronan.

*Eamonn Ceannt*
*Letter to his wife – 8 May 1916*
*Kilmainham Gaol*
*Executed 8 May 1916*

## 26 Connolly Written Statement to Court Martial, 9 May 1916

The evidence went mainly to establish the fact that the accused, James Connolly was in command at the General Post Office, and was also Commandant-General of the Dublin division.

Two of the witnesses, however, tried to bring in alleged instances of wantonly risking the lives of prisoners. The court held that this charge was irrelevant, and could not be placed against the prisoner.

I do not wish to make any defence except against the charges of wanton cruelty to prisoners. These trifling allegations that have been made, if they record facts that really happened, deal with the almost unavoidable incidents of a hurried uprising against long established authority, and nowhere show evidence of set purpose to wantonly injure unarmed persons.

We went out to break the connection between this country and the British Empire, and to establish an Irish Republic. We believe the call that we then issued to the people of Ireland was a nobler call, in a holier cause, than any call issued to them during this war, having any connection with the war. We succeeded in proving that Irishmen are ready to die endeavouring to win for Ireland those national rights which the British Government has been asking them to die for in Belgium. As long as that remains the case, the cause of Irish Freedom is safe.

Believing that the British Government has no right in Ireland, never had any right in Ireland, and never can have any right in Ireland, the presence of any one generation of Irishmen of even a respectable minority, ready to die to affirm that truth, makes that government forever a usurpation and crime against human progress.

I personally thank God that I have lived to see the day when thousands of Irish men and boys, and hundreds of Irish women and girls were ready to affirm that truth and attest it with their lives, if need be.

*James Connolly*
*Commandant-General, Dublin Division*
*Army of the Irish Republic*

*Written Statement to Court Martial*
*9 May 1916*
*Executed 12 May 1916*

## 27 Connolly Quotation at Execution, 12 May 1916

Father Aloysius: 'Will you pray for the men who are about to shoot you?'

James Connolly: 'I will say a prayer for all brave men who do their duty. Forgive them for they know not what they do'.

*James Connolly to Fr Aloysius*
*Kilmainham Gaol – Stonebreaker's Yard*
*12 May 1916*

## 28 MacDermott Statement to Court Martial, 12 May 1916

I have been sentenced to a soldier's death – to be shot tomorrow morning. I have nothing to say about this only that I look on it as a part of the day's work. We die that the Irish nation will live. Our blood will re-baptise and reinvigorate the old land. Knowing this it is superfluous to say how happy I feel. I know now what I have always felt – that the Irish nation can never die. Let present-day placehunters condemn our actions as they will, posterity will judge us aright from the effects of our action.

*Letter from Sean MacDiarmada to John Daly*
*Kilmainham Prison*
*11 May 1916*

KILMAINHAM PRISON
12 MAY 1916
3.30 A.M

I, Sean Mac Diarmada, before paying the penalty of death for my love of Ireland, and abhorrence of her slavery, desire to make known to all my fellow-countrymen that I die, as I have lived, bearing no malice to any man, and in perfect peace with Almighty God. The principles for which I give my life are so sacred that I now walk to my death in the most calm and collected manner. I meet death for Ireland's cause as I have worked for the same cause all my life. I have asked the Rev. E. McCarthy who has prepared me to meet my God and who had given me courage to face the ordeal I am about to undergo, to convey this message to my fellow-countrymen.

*God Save Ireland*
*Sean MacDiarmada*
*Executed 12 May 1916*

## 29 George Bernard Shaw Letter to Hannie Collins, 23 August 1922

So tear up your mourning and hang up your brightest colours in his honour; and let us all praise God that he had not to die in a snuffy bed of a trumpery cough, weakened by age, and saddened by the disappointments that would have attended his work had he lived.

*George Bernard Shaw in a letter to Hannie Collins*
*on the day after Michael Collins's funeral*

## 30  Irish Declaration of Independence, 21 January 1919

IRISH DECLARATION OF INDEPENDENCE
21ST JANUARY 1919
FIRST DÁIL ÉIREANN

### ENACTED BY THE PARLIAMENT OF THE REPUBLIC OF IRELAND

Whereas the Irish People is by right a free people:

And whereas for seven hundred years the Irish People has never ceased to repudiate and has repeatedly protested in arms against foreign usurpation:

And whereas English rule in this country is, and always has been, based upon force and fraud and maintained by military occupation against the declared will of the people:

And whereas the Irish Republic was proclaimed in Dublin on Easter Monday, 1916, by the Irish Republican Army, acting on behalf of the Irish People:

And whereas the Irish People is resolved to secure and maintain its complete independence in order to promote the common weal, to re-establish justice, to provide for future defence, to ensure peace at home and good will with all nations, and to constitute a national policy based upon the people's will with equal right and equal opportunity for every citizen:

And whereas at the threshold of a new era in history the Irish electorate has in the General Election of December, 1918, seized the first occasion to declare by an overwhelming majority its firm allegiance to the Irish Republic:

Now, therefore, we, the elected Representatives of the ancient Irish People in National Parliament assembled, do, in the name of the Irish Nation, ratify the establishment of the Irish Republic and pledge ourselves and our people to make this declaration effective by every means at our command:

We ordain that the elected Representatives of the Irish People alone have power to make laws binding on the people of Ireland, and that the Irish Parliament is the only Parliament to which that people will give its allegiance:

We solemnly declare foreign government in Ireland to be an invasion of our national right which we will never tolerate, and we demand the evacuation of our country by the English Garrison:

We claim for our national independence the recognition and support of every free nation in the world, and we proclaim that independence to be a condition precedent to international peace hereafter:

In the name of the Irish People we humbly commit our destiny to Almighty God Who gave our fathers the courage and determination to persevere through long centuries of a ruthless tyranny, and strong in the justice of the cause which they have handed down to us, we ask His Divine blessing on this the last stage of the struggle we have pledged ourselves to carry through to freedom.[2]

---

2.  Dáil Éireann, Minutes of the Proceedings of the First Parliament of the Republic of Ireland, 21 January 1919.

# Appendix IV:
## Organisations and garrisons, songs, plays, uniforms, flags and emblems

*Songs and Plays*

**A Nation Once Again**: Thomas Davis 1848

**God Save Ireland**: Timothy Daniel (T. D.) Sullivan

**A Soldier's Song/Amhrán na bhFiann**: Peadar Kearney wrote the lyrics and is usually given 'credit' (1907). Paddy Heaney wrote the music (there is some evidence Sean Rogan may have assisted with the music). By 1907 Kearney wanted to write something more rousing and original and produced the words of *A Soldier's Song*. According to Seamus de Burca, Kearney's nephew, Heaney 'worked on the melody for a week and gave up in despair when half way through the chorus – his inspiration had failed. When Kearney called round to see him on a Sunday morning, Heaney was dejected. Kearney asked him anxiously how the music was coming along and for a reply Heaney threw the manuscript in the fire. Kearney snatched it out, smoothed it on the table. The tune was all right, but the chorus was all wrong. They went over the words and Kearney suggested they go back on the melody of the verse. So Heaney toned out the tune and Kearney lilted the words. And thus *A Soldier's Song* was born.' The song lyrics were published by Bulmer Hobson in *Irish Freedom* in 1912. It was first published in sheet form in 1916 with the image of a rifle entwined with Celtic designed lettering: Words by Peadar Kearney, Music by Patrick Heaney, arranged by Cathal MacDubhghaill and published by Whelan & Son, 17 Upper Ormond Quay, Dublin. Following the Rising the music was arranged and published by Victor Herbert in New York in December 1916, with the proceeds going to Ireland. It was officially recognised as the Irish National Anthem in 1926.

**Caitlin Ni Uallachain**: Written by William Butler Yeats. The manifestation of the Irish ideal in womanhood and nationhood – beautiful, sanctified, romantic and not quite attainable. First produced in St Teresa's Hall, Clarendon Street, 2, 3, 4 April 1902. The lead actress was Maud Gonne (MacBride).

> *They shall be remembered forever*
> *They shall be alive forever*
> *They shall be speaking forever*
> *The people shall hear them forever.*

## Organisations

### The Irish Republican Brotherhood

In Peter Lanigan's timber yard, Lombard Street, Dublin, on St Patrick's Day, 1858, James Stephens formally established the Irish Republican Brotherhood. (It was originally named the Irish *Revolutionary* Brotherhood, but soon came to be known as the Irish Republican Brotherhood.) John O'Mahony and Michael Doheny had sent Owen Considine to Ireland on behalf of the exiled Young Irelanders in America. The Irish Republican Brotherhood (IRB) was a small, secret, revolutionary body whose sole object was to 'establish and maintain a free and independent Republican Government in Ireland'. It became known as the Fenian movement in the 1850s and 1860s, and was committed to the use of force to establish an independent Irish republic. After organising an abortive rising in March 1867, it suffered deep internal divisions over leadership and strategy in both the US and Ireland – whether it was best to strike at England, in Ireland or in Canada. The issue was resolved after a series of failed interventions in Canada in 1866, 1867 and 1871, and bombings in England which did not lead Ireland closer to independence.

In the US, the IRB's reorganisation was begun after the release from prison in 1871 of two of its most effective leaders – Jeremiah ODonovan Rossa and John Devoy.

Riven by continuing internal squabbles, in Ireland the IRB was unable to exploit the weakness and divisions in the constitutional movement following Parnell's divorce scandal, 1890–1891.

The unit of organisation was the 'Circle' which could be sub-divided into groups of not more than ten. Each Circle was under the command of an elected 'Centre'. Circles were grouped to form Districts under District Centres, and these were grouped into County Circles under a County Centre. The whole organisation was divided into eleven Districts, eight in Ireland, two in England and one in Scotland.

It was eventually rejuvenated in Ireland, in about 1907, led by Bulmer Hobson and Tom Clarke, thus preparing the way for all that followed. The governing body was the Supreme Council. Before 1916, this consisted of eleven members, and after the 1917 reorganisation it contained fifteen members. Constitutionally, this body met at least once every four months. When not in session, all powers of the Supreme Council, except for declaring war, devolved onto an executive of three: the President, Secretary and Treasurer. The Constitution provided for the establishment of a Military Council, subordinate to the Supreme Council. (The seven signatories of the 1916 Proclamation constituted the entire Military Council at that time.) Its members spoke of it as 'The Organisation' according to Bulmer Hobson. The organisation's oath was as follows:

*I, _____, in the presence of Almighty God, do solemnly swear allegiance to the Irish Republic, now virtually established; and that I will do my very utmost, at every risk, while life lasts, to defend its independence and integrity; that I will bear true allegiance to the Supreme Council of the Irish Republican Brotherhood and Government of the Irish Republic and implicitly obey the Constitution of the Irish Republican Brotherhood and, finally, that I will yield implicit independence in all things, not contrary to the laws of God, to the commands of my superior officers and will preserve inviolable the secrets of the organisation. So help me God! Amen.*

Its constitution was dedicated to force against England at any favourable opportunity, but this was to be a democratic decision: 'The IRB shall await the decision of the Irish Nation as expressed by a majority of the Irish people as to the fit hour of inaugurating a war against England and shall, pending such an emergency, lend its support to every movement calculated to advance the cause of Irish independence, consistent with the preservation of its own integrity.' The IRB planned the Rising. The Irish Volunteers and the Irish Citizen Army made it possible. The establishment of the Irish Volunteers gave the IRB the great opportunity to 'train and equip its members as a military body for the purpose of securing independence for Ireland by force of arms' and securing 'the cooperation of all Irish military bodies in the accomplishment of its objects' (IRB Constitution, 1920). Numerically, the IRB probably never exceeded two thousand members. However, they were all extremely loyal and well trained, and there was very tight security. The executions of 1916 just about wiped out the Supreme Council, and after the prisoners were released the IRB had to reconstitute itself. In 1917, Sean McGarry was elected President, Michael Collins was elected Secretary, and Diarmuid Lynch was elected Treasurer.

### Cumann Luthcleas Gael/Gaelic Athletic Association (GAA)

In the 1880s, many, including Dr Thomas W. Croke (Archbishop of Cashel), maintained that 'ball-playing, hurling, football kicking according to Irish rules ... may now be said to be not only dead and buried, but in several localities to be entirely forgotten. What the country needed was an Irish organisation to bring order and unity to sport on a nationwide basis.' In August 1884 Michael Cusack, at a meeting in Loughrea, Co Galway, outlined his plans to a group of local athletic enthusiasts to establish a national organisation for Irish athletes and to revive hurling. On 1 November 1884 the Gaelic Athletic Association was founded at Miss Hayes's Commercial Hotel, Thurles, Co Tipperary by Michael Cusack (Clareman, teacher, sportsman and nationalist) and Maurice Davin (Tipperary man who at the time was Ireland's most famous athlete). Other founding members present were John Wyse-Power, John McKay, J. K. Bracken, Joseph O'Ryan and Thomas St George McCarthy. Many of the seven men who attended the meeting were Fenians. Not present at the Thurles meeting was P.W. Nally, a keen athlete and leading IRB organiser who also played a prominent role in bringing about the birth of this new Association: he was the one who suggested the organisation to Cusack. Maurice Davin was elected president of the new organisation. Three secretaries were elected: Cusack, Wyse-Power and McKay. Davin in a brief speech called for a body to draft rules to help revive Irish games and to open athletics to the man in the street. The meeting also agreed to invite Archbishop Croke of Cashel, Charles Stewart Parnell and Michael Davitt to become patrons. All three accepted, although Dr Croke resigned after conflicts with Cusack. The GAA drew up its first set of rules in 1885. The essential objectives of the Association were: 1) to bring about the organisation of Irish sport by Irish men; 2) to draft new rules for Irish games; 3) to devise schemes of recreation for Irish people. Patrick W. Nally was the first to organise a national athletic sports meeting on his father's farm in Balla, Co Mayo.

### Connradh na Gaeilge/the Gaelic League

Founded by Douglas Hyde (first President of Ireland), Fr Eugene O'Growney, and Eoin MacNeill on 31 July 1893. Douglas Hyde became its first President and Eoin MacNeill was

Vice-President and Hon Secretary. Its original purpose was not revival but to help Irish speakers where Irish was still spoken. Its first official newspaper was *Fainne an Lae* (Dawn) which was edited by Eoin MacNeill. By 1906 Connradh na Gaeilge had 900 branches with 100,000 members.

### An Claidheamh Soluis

This ('The Organ of Militant Freedom') was the official newspaper of the Gaelic League. It was also known by the one word *Claidheamh*. Padraig Pearse was the editor from 1903 to 1909, then Sean Forde. The O'Rahilly was the manager. Eoin MacNeill's article 'The North Began,' on 1 November 1913, suggested that the rest of Ireland would do well to imitate the Ulster Volunteers and form citizen forces. Afterwards he was approached by Bulmer Hobson to 'head' the Irish Volunteers.

### Inghinidhe na hÉireann/Daughters of Ireland

Founded by Maud Gonne MacBride in October 1900; she became the first President with Maire T. Quinn as Hon Secretary (the organisation eventually merged with Cumann na mBan). Ironically the organisational meeting took place at Easter 1900. The first meeting determined to give Arthur Griffith a new blackthorn stick for the one he supposedly broke over the head of the editor of the society paper *Figaro*. It was also at this meeting that it was determined to give sweets to all children who did *not* go to the Phoenix Park to see Queen Victoria. The objectives of Inghinidhe na hÉireann were: the re-establishment of the complete independence of Ireland; to encourage the study of Gaelic, of Irish literature, history, music, and art especially among the young (by organising and teaching classes dedicated to the above aims); to support and popularise Irish manufacture; to discourage the reading and circulation of low English literature, the singing of English songs, the attending of vulgar English entertainments at the theatres and music halls, and to combat in every way English influence, which was seen to be doing so much injury to the artistic taste and refinement of the Irish people; to form a fund called the National Purposes Fund, for the furtherance of the above objectives.

In 1908, the organisation initiated *Bean na hÉireann*, the first nationalist-feminist journal to be produced in Ireland. *Bean na hÉireann* was edited by Helena Molony. The staff comprised: Madeline ffrench-Mullen, Sydney Gifford, Bulmer Hobson, Maud Gonne MacBride, Dr Pat MacCartan, Sean McGarry, Countess Markievicz. The contributors were Sir Roger Casement, Maeve Cavanagh, Padraic Colum, Madeline ffrench-Mullen (as 'M O'Callaghan' or 'Dectora'), Sydney Gifford (as 'John Brennan' or 'Sorcha Ni Hanlon'), Arthur Griffith, Maude Gonne MacBride (as 'Maidbh'), Terence MacSwiney, Helena Maloney (as 'Emer', 'E', or 'A Worker'), Count Markievicz, Countess Markievicz (as 'Armid' or 'Macha'), Susan Mitchell, Padraic O'Conaire, Seamus O'Sullivan, Joseph Plunkett, George Russell (AE), James Stephens, Katherine Tynan.

### Cumann na nGaedheal

Not to be confused with the party founded by W. T. Cosgrave in 1923. This organisation was founded by Arthur Griffith in 1900, with the Celtic Literary society as its nucleus. It was in fact a federation of literary societies aimed at the sovereign independence of Ireland. Its purpose was to promote a 'Buy Irish' campaign. It combined with the Dungannon Clubs in April 1907 to create the Sinn Féin League.

IRB; Eamon Martin, IRB; Liam Mellowes, IRB; Col Maurice Moore, United Irish League/Irish Parliamentary Party; Seamus O'Connor, IRB; Colm O'Lochlainn; The O'Rahilly; Peter O'Reilly, Ancient Order of Hibernians; Padraig O'Riain, IRB; Robert Page, IRB; P. H. Pearse, IRB; Joseph Plunkett; George Walsh, Ancient Order of Hibernians; Peadar White.

In February 1914, it issued a provisional constitution, embodying the objects of the Volunteers: '1. To secure and maintain the rights and liberties common to all the people of Ireland; 2. To train, discipline, arm and equip a body of Irish Volunteers for the above purpose; 3. To unite for this purpose Irishmen of every creed and of every party and class.'

## Cumann na mBan/Irishwomen's Council
The first meeting to discuss its founding was held on 25 November 1913, the same night as the first meeting of the Volunteers. Its first 'official' meeting was at Wynn's Hotel on 2 April 1914. Agnes O'Farrelly was its first President and Mary Colum was one of its first organisers. The time-lag between the formation of the Irish Volunteers and the activation of its counterpart, Cumann na mBan, was due to disagreement on whether the women would be part of the Volunteers, or whether they would be content to perform tasks like fund-raising when requested by the men. Many men envisioned the women's role to be totally subordinate to the needs of the Volunteers. Its initial appeal was to women who could give time to the establishment of the organisation, women who did not need to work. There were forty-three affiliated branches before the Rising. In 1916 Kathleen Clarke was President (some books claim Countess Markievicz was president in 1916 – *Kathleen Lynn*, Marie Mulholland, p. 34) and Sorcha McMahon was Secretary. Members included: Elizabeth Bloxham, Winifred Carney (she won one of its first shooting competitions), Áine Ceannt, Nora Connolly, Margaret Dobbs, Louise Gavan Duffy, Agnes MacNeill, Una O'Brien, Nancie O'Rahilly, Niamh Plunkett, Jenny Wyse-Power, Mrs Tuohy. Its objects were:

- to advance the cause of Irish liberty
- to organise Irishwomen in the furtherance of this object
- to assist in arming and equipping a body of Irishmen for the defence of Ireland
- to form a fund for these purposes, to be called 'The Defence of Ireland Fund' (Policy for 1917–1918)
- to continue collecting for the 'Defence of Ireland Fund' and any other fund to be devoted to the arming and equipping of the men and women of Ireland
- to assist in the movement to secure representation of Ireland at the Peace Conference by the election of Republican candidates, etc
- to follow the policy of the Republican Proclamation by seeing that women take up their proper position in the life of the nation (Policy for 1918–1919)
- to develop the suggested military activities in conjunction with the Irish Volunteers
- to organise opposition to conscription along the lines laid down in the two anti-conscription pledges.

In August 1916 Cumann na mBan held a convention in Dublin presided over by Louise Gavan Duffy. Countess Markievicz was elected President, though she was still in prison.

Cumann na mBan played a larger role in the Civil War than in the Rising. The members held their own Convention on the Treaty on 5 February 1922, and voted 419 to 63 against the Treaty. Countess Markievicz was elected president. Pro-Treaty members were asked to resign, and they formed their own group, called Cumann na Saoirse (Society of Freedom), which was not militarily active during the Civil War.

### Cumann na dTeachaire/League of Women Delegates
Founded in April 1917 as the League of Women Delegates. At a meeting on 16 October the name was Gaelicised and a constitution was drawn up with the following aims: to safeguard the political rights of Irishwomen; to ensure adequate representation for them in the Republican Government; to urge and facilitate the appointment of women to Public Boards throughout the country; to educate Irishwomen in the rights and duties of citizenship. The primary focus was to promote the representation and participation of women in the reorganisation of Sinn Féin

## Political parties

### Fine Ghaedheal
Founded at the Convention of the Irish Race in Paris on 27 January 1922; DeValera was President.

### Womens' Prisoners' Defence League
Founded by Maud Gonne MacBride in 1922. Known as 'The Mothers', its members gathered at prison gates and helped inmates and relatives in various ways. Operated throughout the Civil War and afterwards.

### Cumann na Poblachta/The Republican League
Anti-Treaty Party founded by Eamon deValera on 15 March 1922. The Republican Party comprised TDs who were anti-treaty.

### Cumann na nGaedheal
Treaty Party Founded by William T. Cosgrave in March 1923. It was the Free State Party succeeded by Fine Gael.

### Fianna Fáil
'Soldiers of Destiny;' founded by Eamon deValera on 16 May 1927. Incorporated most of the Republicans who were to sit in the Dáil. (On 11 March 1926 de Valera proposed at the Sinn Féin Ard Fheis a motion that it would be a matter of principle for Republicans to enter the parliaments in Dublin and Northern Ireland if the Oath of Allegiance was removed. This motion was defeated 223-218, and deValera resigned from Sinn Féin in 1927.)

### Clann na Poblachta
Radical Republican Political Party. Headed by Sean MacBride. Became part of a coalition government in 1948.

The geographical areas for the training of the Volunteer Brigades prior to the Rising were as follows:

1st Battalion:    North of the Liffey and West of Sackville Street
2nd Battalion:   North of the Liffey and East of Sackville Street
3rd Battalion:    South of the Liffey
4th Battalion:    South townships, Rathmines etc
5th Battalion:    Engineers only
6th Battalion:    South Co Dublin, Kingstown

## Dublin Brigade

- *Thomas MacDonagh* (Tomás MacDonnchada, executed 3 May 1916, aged 38).* In Kilmainham, he was seen by Fr Aloysius. He was also visited by his sister, Sister Mary Francesca, who gave him their mother's rosary. He put it around his neck, and she received it back the next day from Fr Aloysius, though it had had six beads shot off!
- *M. W. O'Reilly* (Vice-Commandant, Camp O/C at Frongoch and subsequently director of Training for IRA)
- *Eamon de Valera* (Adjutant)

## GPO Headquarters Battalion, Men†

They mustered at Liberty Hall; garrison total approximately 250–300 at any one time; killed, 13; executed, 6.

- *Padraig Pearse* (Pádraic MacPiarais, executed 3 May 1916, aged 36).* In Kilmainham, he was attended by Fr Aloysius.
- *Tom Clarke* (Tomás O Clerigh, executed 3 May 1916, aged 59).* In Kilmainham, he was seen by Fr Columbus who told him he had to 'admit that he had done a great wrong' in order to get absolution. Clarke threw him out: 'I'm not a bit sorry for what I did. I glory in it. And if that means I'm not entitled to absolution, then I'll have to go to the next world without it. To say I'm sorry would be a lie and I am not going to face my God with a lie on my tongue.' To Kathleen, he said of MacNeill: 'I want you to see to it that our people know of his treachery to us. He must never be allowed back into the national life of the country, for sure as he is, so sure he will act treacherously in a crisis. He is a weak man, but I know every effort will be made to whitewash him.'
- *James Connolly* (Seamus Ó Conghile, executed 12 May 1916, aged 46).* In Dublin Castle, he recounted the story of the escape to Nora and said: 'We can't fail now. Such lads will never forget.' In Dublin Castle and at Kilmainham, he was attended by Fr Aloysius. The doctor in Dublin Castle was Surgeon Richard Tobin.
- *Sean MacDermott* (Seán MacDiarmada, executed 12 May 1916, aged 32; crippled by polio in June 1911).* In Kilmainham, he was visited by the Ryan sisters, Mary and Phyllis. He was attended by Fr McCarthy and Fr Augustine. He was shot sitting on a soapbox according to Fr. Augustine's statement.

---

†    Names followed by an asterisk ∗ signify those executed and names followed by two asterisks ∗∗ signify those who died during the Rising. Officially, sixty-four Volunteers died in addition to those executed.

- *Joseph Mary Plunkett* (Ioseph Ó Pluingcéad, executed 4 May 1916, aged 29).\* He carried a sword that belonged to Robert Emmet. In Kilmainham, he was seen by Fr Sebastian. He and Grace Gifford were married by Fr McCarthy, who also brought Grace back to see him.
- *Willie Pearse* (Liam MacPiarais, executed 4 May 1916).\* In Kilmainham, he was attended by Fr Augustine, and saw his mother and his sister, Margaret.
- *Arthur Agnew;* from Liverpool, he was part of the Kimmage garrison; he had originally been assigned to O'Connell Bridge at the outset of the Rising.
- *Harry Boland:* he had come in from Fairview with the group led by Cpt Frank Henderson. He and Dairmuid Lynch were underground making the ammunition safe, unknown to Pearse and the others, so Boland was the penultimate person to leave the GPO. He was imprisoned in Mountjoy, then Dartmoor, then Lewes in Sussex, and finally in Maidstone Prison.
- *Lt Michael Boland;* in command on the roof. He had been in the Boer War and thought it 'madness' to take and hold buildings. 'Shut in here with our leaders, and the flags over our heads to tell the enemy just where to find us when they want us. We should have taken to the hills like the Boers.'
- *Edmund (Ned) Boland,* Harry's brother; he was in the Imperial Hotel and escaped to Cathedral Street. The priests of the Pro-Cathedral told some Volunteers that if they wanted to leave their guns in the vaults they could do so – some did and escaped capture.
- *Peadar Bracken;* one of the Kimmage garrison. He had originally been in charge of three others at O'Connell Bridge at the outset of the Rising, then he led the men in 'Kelly's Fort'.
- *Cpt Liam Breen;* detailed to the Reiss's Building.
- *Seamus Brennan,* from Tullamore; he was posted at the Tower Bar directly across Henry Street from the GPO. He came in from Kimmage with George Plunkett.
- *Comdt W. J. Brennan*-Whitmore; aide to Joseph Plunkett (*Is Dublin Burning?*). He helped Michael Collins get Joseph Plunkett to the GPO, and led some Volunteers in North King Street. He was wounded escaping from the Imperial Hotel.
- *Edward (Eamon) Bulfin;* a member of the Rathfarnham Company, he was posted on the roof of the GPO.
- *Frank Burke;* a teacher at St Enda's. He was imprisoned at Frongoch. He became a second lieutenant in E Company during the War of Independence.
- *Joe Byrne;* an IRB member, he was *not* a Volunteer, but reported to the GPO on Tuesday.
- *Tom Byrne;* a member of the Kildare Volunteers, he travelled from Kildare, joined the Maynooth Volunteers and came to the GPO. He fought in the Boer War and was thereafter known as 'The Boer'.
- *Ignatius Callendar;* when he went off to fight, his mother pinned a badge of the Little Flower of Jesus on his chest with the remark 'You're all right now – the Little Flower will protect you'. A courier, he made ten trips between the GPO and the Four Courts garrison.
- *Lt Liam Clarke;* badly wounded when a home-made bomb exploded prematurely. When he got to the hospital, one Volunteer remarked: 'So much for those bloody canisters. If it didn't blow Liam's head off, the divil use it is to us'.
- *Harry Colley*

- *Dick McKee*
- *Pat McCrea;* went with M. W. O'Reilly to an arms depot in Rutland Square to get more weapons.
- *Sean McGarry*
- *Seamus McGowan;* ICA member, he supervised the removal of the war stores from Liberty Hall on Monday afternoon.
- *Tom McGrath*
- *Dan McLaughlin;* attended medical school for ten years without earning a degree, assisted Jim Ryan
- *John (Sean) McLoughlin* (16); he was a messenger, often shuttling between the Mendicity Institute and the GPO. He was appointed a Commandant by Connolly and was in command of a group of thirty assigned to take the *Irish Independent* offices on Thursday afternoon. Connolly led them to the *Independent.* It was on this foray that Connolly was wounded in the ankle
- *Liam McNeive;* IRB member from Liverpool, he led a company of Volunteers from Liverpool in the GPO.
- *John McQuaid*
- **Francis Macken;* taught Irish at St Enda's.
- *Sean Milroy*
- *Paddy Moran;* from Glasgow, he was part of the Kimmage garrison. He had originally been assigned to O'Connell Bridge at the outset of the Rising.
- *Ned Morgan*
- *'Steenie' Mulvey;* a Volunteer in Bray.
- *Michael Murphy;* married Martha Kelly. He was imprisoned in Frongoch.
- *Seamus Murphy*
- *Paddy Murray;* from Galway, imprisoned in Frongoch.
- **John Neale;* cockney member of the ICA, often used the term 'comrade'. He took 'potshots' at Nelson's nose on the Pillar until Connolly told him to desist.
- *Harry Nicholls*
- *Ernest* and *Sean Nunan* (brothers); had been sent by their father from London to join the Rising. They were taken from Frongoch and handed over to the English military for desertion, and eventually discharged as 'persons not likely to give loyal and faithful service to His Majesty'. Sean later accompanied Michael Collins when Ned Broy let them in to see the G-Division files.
- *Domhnall O Buachalla*
- *Kevin O'Carroll;* was next to The O'Rahilly when he was killed, and was himself badly wounded in the stomach.
- *Lt Johnny 'Blimey' O'Connor;* originally from London, he had been at Kimmage. An electrician, he installed many communications throughout the GPO; he and others had attempted to restore wireless equipment from the Telephone Company School opposite the GPO. They broadcast 'Ireland Proclaims Republic' from Monday night until later in the week when they were driven out by fire. He fought on the Republican side during the Civil War.
- *Rory O'Connor;* he was an assistant to Joe Plunkett before the Rising.
- *Paddy O'Donoghue;* he was taken from Frongoch and handed over to the British military for desertion, and eventually discharged as 'a person not likely to give loyal and faithful service to His Majesty'.

- *Brian O'Higgins* (*The Soldier's Story of Easter Week*); one of the party who moved the explosives into the GPO basement. He was imprisoned in Frongoch, became a TD and fought on the side of Republicans/IRA in the Civil War.
- *Paudeen O'Keefe;* led some men to the GPO from the Imperial Hotel.
- *Fergus O'Kelly;* in command of the detail in the wireless school and then the Dublin Bread Company.
- *Sean T. O'Kelly* (future President); he was Pearse's adjutant during the Rising. He was sent to release Hobson on Monday evening from Sean Harling's home in Cabra Park.
- *Lt Ted O'Kelly;* a member of the Kildare Volunteers, he travelled from Kildare, joined the Maynooth Volunteers and came to the GPO where he was slightly wounded.
- *O'Laughlin;* wounded in the breakout and taken to the McKane house in Moore Street.
- *Diarmuid O'Laoghaire*
- *Jim O'Neill;* ICA officer who acted as QM during the Rising. He was primarily responsible for the issuance of 'bombs'.
- \*\**The O'Rahilly* (Michael Joseph, aged 41); munitions officer. He said to Countess Markievicz at Liberty Hall just before marching off: 'It is madness, but it is glorious madness'. Left the GPO about 8.00 pm on Friday night to find a way to Williams and Woods: 'It will either be a glorious victory or a glorious death'. Another Volunteer in the GPO reported: 'I heard the burst of fire, then the sound of feet running, then the sound of one's man feet, then silence'. The O'Rahilly wrote this note to his wife: 'Written after I was shot – Darling Nancy I was shot leading a rush up Moore Street, took refuge in a doorway. While I was there I heard the men pointing out where I was + I made a bolt for the lane I am in now. I got more than one bullet I think. Tons + tons of love dearie to you + to the boys + to Nell + Anna. It was a good fight anyhow. Please deliver this to Nannie O'Rahilly 40 Herbert Park, Dublin. Good bye darling.' He wrote this on a note he'd received from his son, Aodghan; it had a bullet hole through it! (Some commentators have his party as comprising 12, some 30, others 40 men. G. A. Hayes-McCoy writes in *Studies in the History of the Rising* that he led an advance guard of 40 men. Max Caulfield in *The Easter Rebellion* has O'Rahilly leading 12 men. Jack Plunkett's memoir indicates there were a dozen men in the party.)
- *Joe O'Reilly;* became Michael Collins's 'assistant' after Frongoch.
- *Cpt Martin O'Reilly;* led the party of wounded and women to Jervis Street Hospital. The party consisted of Fr Flanagan, Cpt Mahoney, sixteen wounded men and twelve women.
- *Cpt Michael W. O'Reilly;* QM on the Brigade Staff.
- *Gearóid O'Sullivan;* cousin of Michael Collins. He was a few months younger than Michael Collins, and moved to Dublin in 1909 to attend St Patrick's Training College on his way to becoming a teacher, then he attended the Royal University. He was the youngest officer in the GPO. He raised the flags on the roof between 1 and 2 pm on 24 April. He ran with a mattress around himself from Clery's to the GPO, fell, got up and made it across unscathed. He was sent to Frongoch and was released in the general amnesty on 21 December 1916. On 19 October 1922 he married Maud Kiernan, Kitty's sister, in what was to be a double wedding with Kitty and Michael Collins. Kitty was a bridesmaid, but dressed all in black. He became Adjutant-General of the Free State Army. He died on Good Friday 1948 and was buried in Glasnevin on Easter Monday.
- *Cpt George Plunkett*
- *Jack Plunkett*

- *Julia Grenan* (sometimes named as 'Shelia Grennan': see Sir John Rogerson's Quay)
- *Annie Higgins*
- *Martha Kelly;* married Michael Murphy. She was imprisoned in Kilmainham.
- *Sorcha MacMahon*
- *Mary McLoughlin;* she was Sean's school-girl sister.
- *Elizabeth More O'Farrell*
- *Rose Ann Murphy*
- *Mae Murray*
- *Molly O'Reilly* (became one of Michael Collins's best 'sources')
- *Leslie Price;* she married Tom Barry. Tom Clarke sent her to the Pro-Cathedral to fetch a priest on Thursday – she brought Fr Flanagan back.
- *Mollie Reynolds;* was very active in the later anti-conscription campaign.
- *Phyllis (Eilis Ni) Rian;* she was a sister of Jim, later Mrs Sean T. O'Kelly.
- *Mary (Min) Ryan;* sister of Jim, Sean MacDermott's fiance, later married Richard Mulcahy. She and her sister, Phyllis, were the last two to see Sean MacDermott in Kilmainham Gaol: 'He preferred to talk of casual matters, asking about different people we knew, enjoying little jokes almost as though we were in Bewley's. He had worked and planned for Irish Independence since boyhood. His last words, save for his prayers, were 'God Save Ireland'. At four o'clock , when the shooting was done, a gentle rain began to fall – the tears of Dark Rosaleen.'
- *Effie Traaffe*
- *Martha Walsh;* later Mrs Murphy.

## British prisoners in the GPO
2nd Lt A. D. Chalmers; a British officer from the 14th Royal Fusiliers who was using the postal facilities in the GPO at the time the Rising began. He was 'trussed up' with telephone cord by Michael Collins and remained captive all week. The O'Rahilly 'appointed' him to keep a watch to note that nothing had been 'stolen' by the Volunteers. He was shot in the thigh when the prisoners were let go in advance of The O'Rahilly's escape bid.
- *Pvt James Doyle,* Royal Irish Regiment; escaped and hid in the Coliseum Theatre, and was discovered only on 3 May.
- *Sgt Henry,* School of Musketry; escaped and hid in the Coliseum Theatre, and was discovered only on 3 May.
- *2nd Lt King,* Royal Irish Fusiliers
- *Lt George O'Mahoney,* a doctor in the English Indian Army Medical Corps. He was on convalescent leave after injuring his leg in a fall in the Himalayas. He was originally from Cork. As a prisoner he helped take care of the wounded, and treated Connolly's leg wound; Connolly told him: 'You are the most valuable thing we've captured!'

## 1st Battalion, Men
A, B and C Companies mustered in Blackhall Place under Cmdt Daly and proceeded to Brunswick Street. D Company mustered in Temple Street under Cpt Heuston and proceeded to Liberty Hall

Garrison total 282; killed, 9; executed, 2. Brunswick Street, Four Courts, North Dublin Union, North King Street ('Reilly's Fort'), Magazine Fort

Mendicity Institute: garrison: 35. Most of the Volunteers were Fianna, and most were between 12 and 25 years old (Heuston was only 25 years old). He was instructed to hold this position for two hours to delay English deployment; they held for three days. They started with two weapons and one box of ammunition. They were reinforced with 13 reinforcements from North County and there were 23 survivors and 2 killed. The Fianna only surrendered when they ran out of ammunition on Wednesday, infuriating the British that so few youngsters held them off for so long.

- *Commandant Edward (Ned) Daly* (Eamonn Ó Dalaigh, executed 4 May 1916, aged 25):* 'I am the commander. At all events I was in charge'. In Kilmainham, he was in cell number 66 and was attended by Fr Columbus. In Kilmainham, he was seen by his sisters, Madge, Laurie (his favorite), and Kathleen (Kattie) Clarke. Madge felt Laurie falter and told her: 'Remember, you're a Daly'.
- ***Lt Thomas Allen;* ordered a policeman to turn over the keys to the Chancery Place entrance to the Four Courts and they entered at that point.
- *Liam Archer;* became Chief of Staff of the Free State Army.
- *Piaras Béaslaí,* Vice-Commandant, became editor of *An tOglach* (The Soldier). Born and educated in Liverpool, he moved to Dublin at age 23.
- *Richard (Dick) Balfe;* he was badly wounded.
- *Paddy Boland*
- *John Joseph Byrne*
- *Lt Peadar Clancy;* he became Vice-Brigadier of the Dublin Brigade and was murdered on Bloody Sunday.
- *Sean Cody*
- *Richard (Dick) Coleman;* mobilised with the Fingal Brigade at Saucers Town, went to the GPO, then was sent to the Mendicity Institute (see 5th Battalion at Ashbourne).
- *Maurice Collins;* he took up his post in Lamb's public house after he was released from guarding Bulmer Hobson on Monday evening. He was imprisoned in Wandsworth. After his release he opened a tobacconist and confectioner shop, with a billiard room.
- *Martin Conlan;* he was in charge at Fr Mathew Hall.
- *Lt Cosgrave*
- *F. X. Coughlan*
- *Paddy Daly;* a Fianna member. Some months before the Rising he got a job with a building firm making repairs at The Magazine Fort and he knew the Fort's layout. He was the engineer for the whole Brigade.
- ***John Dwan* (25); killed in North King Street. He lived on Lower Gardiner Street.
- *Cpt Frank Fahy;* later Ceann Comhairle (Speaker of the Dáil).
- ***Patrick Farrell* (19)
- *Cpt Douglas ffrench-Mullen;* he was in the Four Courts.
- *Sean Harling* (14); he was in the North Dublin Union *(Ireland's Unfinished Revolution)*. At the very beginning of the Rising he was selling race cards for the Fairyhouse Race Meeting outside the Broadstone Station. He became aide to de Valera, and witnessed the dictation of the letters appointing the plenipotentiaries to the Treaty negotiations, and delivered the letters to them. He fought for the Republicans/IRA in the Civil War.
- *Peadar Healy;* a ticket collector at the Broadstone Railway Station, he was taken by surprise and reported to his battalion position late.

- *Lt Diarmuid Hegarty*
- *Sean ('Jack') Heuston* (Seán MacAodha, executed 8 May 1916, aged 25);\* D Company, Mendicity Institution, held by Fianna Volunteers, all aged between 12 and 25. This was the first garrison to capitulate. In Kilmainham, he was in cell number 19. He was seen by Fr Albert and also his brother, Michael, who was studying to be a Dominican priest, as well as Fr Browne, the Dominican novice master. In addition, he was seen by his mother, sister, aunt and a first cousin.
- *William Hogan;* he was in North King Street.
- *Gerry Holohan;* a Fianna member. It was his assignment to buy a football for the game at Phoenix Park in the area known as the Fifteen Acres. He bought it at a shop on Ormond Quay on his way to the Park. After the Playfair family was turned loose, one of the sons ran for help and Holohan had to shoot him. With Denis O'Callahan he set Linenhall Barracks alight.
- *Cmdt Paddy Holohan;* a Fianna member, he was O/C in the North Dublin Union.
- \*\**Sean Bernard Howard* (17); a friend of Sean Harling. Member of the Fianna Pipers Band. He and a few members of the Fianna blew up a bridge to block the British.
- *Thomas Hunter*
- \*\**John Hurley* (29)
- *Patrick Kelly*
- *Cpt Nicholas Laffan*
- *Frank Lawlor;* he was interned in Frongoch.
- *Laurence Lawlor* (brother); interned in Frongoch.
- *Cpt Fionan Lynch;* he was a prisoner in Mountjoy when Tom Ashe was carried to be force-fed. Lynch cried out 'Stick it, Tom'. Ashe replied, 'I'll stick it, Fin'.
- *Andy MacDonald;* a member of the Fianna.
- *Edward (Eunan) MacGinley;* a member of the Fianna.
- *Frank McCabe;* he was in North King Street.
- *Tommy McCarthy;* he brought in a load of ammunition.
- *Lt Joseph McGuinness;* uncle of Brighid Lyons Thornton. He was in command of the first twenty Volunteers sent to take the Four Courts. He won the South Longford election on 9 May 1917: 'Put him *in* to get him *out*' was the election slogan. He was in Lewes Gaol.
- \*\**Peter Paul Manning* (25)
- *L. Marie;* a Fianna member.
- *Eamonn Martin;* a Fianna member, he was wounded with a bullet through his lung. He helped to set the Linenhall Barracks on fire.
- *William Meade*
- *Barney Mellows;* a Fianna member.
- *William Murphy;* he was in North King Street
- *Cpt Denis O'Callaghan;* a Fianna member and deputy to Daly he was sent to capture Broadstone Station, but the mission was aborted. With Gerry Holohan and Eamonn Martin he set Linenhall Barracks on fire.
- *Lt Liam O'Cearbhaill*
- *Mortimer O'Connell;* he became Chief Clerk of Dáil Éireann.
- *John S. O'Connor*
- *Tommy O'Connor* (brother)

- *Con O'Donovan;* on Holy Saturday he had been one of those detailed to guard Bulmer Hobson
- **Patrick O'Flanagan;* he was killed entering 'Reilly's Fort'.
- *Fergus O'Kelly*
- *Cpt James O'Sullivan;* Battalion Adjutant, he occupied positions on the Cabra Road and South Circular Road, then went to the GPO.
- *Tom Roche;* he commandeered the hansom cab for the Fianna escape from Phoenix Park.
- *Thomas Sherrin;* he was in North King Street.
- *Frank Shouldice;* he was in Father Mathew Hall: 'It was a terrible slaughter'.
- *Lt Jack Shouldice*
- *Liam Staines;* he was badly wounded.
- *Paddy Stephenson*
- *Paddy Swann;* deported after the Rising. His brother was in the GPO.
- *Eamonn Tierney;* from London, he 'Fetched the flag' on the retreat from North King Street, and was unscathed.
- **Philip Walsh* (28)
- *John Williamson;* he served in North King Street.
- **Peter Wilson;* a Swords Volunteer, he was killed by a sniper at the Mendicity Institute when the Volunteers were being formed up to leave after surrender.

## 1st Battalion, Women

- *Maire McCarron*
- *Áine ui Chonail*
- *Eilis Bean ui Chonaill*
- *Mrs (Martin) Conlon*
- *Marcella Cosgrave*
- *Maggie Derham*
- *Eilis Elliott*
- *Emily Elliott*
- *M. Elliott*
- *Ellen (Nellie) Ennis*
- *Mrs Frank Fahy*
- *Dora Harford*
- *Christina Hayes*
- *Kathleen Kenny*
- *Bessie Lynch* (Kelly)
- *Brighid Lyons* (Thornton) (*Ireland's Unfinished Revolution*); imprisoned in Kilmainham Gaol
- *Lt Katy McGuinness*
- *Rose McGuinness*
- *Kathleen (Kate) Martin*
- *Margaret Martin*
- *Florence (Flossie) Mead*
- *Caroline (Carrie) Mitchell*
- *Pauline Morkan*
- *Mrs Morkan*

- *Mrs Seamus Murphy*
- *Lily Murnane*
- *Áine Ní Rian*
- *Eilis O'Connell*
- *Maura O'Neill Mackay*
- *Dolly O'Sullivan*
- *Mollie O'Sullivan*
- *Eileen Parker*
- *Eileen Walsh*

## 2nd Battalion, Men

Mustered at St Stephen's Green and occupied Jacob's Biscuit Factory on Peter Street and Bishop Street, but about half the battalion went to the GPO after mustering at Fr Mathew Park in Fairview; garrison total 85; killed, 3; executed, 3.

- *Commandant Thomas MacDonagh* (Tomás MacDonnchada, executed 3 May 1916, aged 38).*
- *Michael O'Hanrahan* (Micheal O hAnnrachain, executed 4 May 1916) Vice-Commandant.* In Kilmainham, he was in cell Number 67 and was seen by his sisters, and he was attended by Fr Albert.
- *Gerald Boland;* Harry's brother, imprisoned in Frongoch with Michael Collins, where his dislike for Collins increased.
- ***James Byrne* (19)
- *Vincent Byrne* (14)
- *Jimmy Conroy;* from Dublin, it was he who bought the paraffin to burn the Custom House in 1921.
- *Mr Conroy;* quite aged, he was Jimmy's father.
- *Michael Fleming;* he later hid Sean Treacy after his escape from Professor Carolan's house.
- *Joseph Furlong;* from Wexford and an IRB member. Prior to the Rising he was engaged in undercover work for the IRB.
- *Michael Hayes* (later Senator)
- *Tom Hunter;* Battalion Vice-Commandant, he tearfully informed rank and file of their surrender. He broke his sword in two on the stairway before he informed his men.
- *Peadar Kearney;* one of a group which seized Barmacks Malthouse in Fumbally Lane. Upon being informed of the surrender, he was one of those who argued for a mass breakout to the hills (*A Soldier's Song*).
- *Maj John MacBride* (Seán MacBhríde, executed 5 May 1916, aged 51).* 'Liberty is a priceless thing and anyone of you that sees a chance, take it. I'd do so myself but my liberty days are over. Good luck, boys. Many of you may live to fight another day. Take my advice, never allow yourselves to be cooped inside the walls of a building again.' In Kilmainham, he was attended by Fr Augustine. 'Mind the Flag' reportedly were his last words before the firing squad. He had been the witness at the New York wedding of Tom and Kattie Clarke.
- John MacDonagh, brother of Thomas.
- *Dick McKee;* became O/C of the Dublin Brigade and was murdered on Bloody Sunday.
- *Patrick (Paddy) Moran;* he was hanged at Mountjoy Prison for the Bloody Sunday killings even though he hadn't taken part in the killings for which he was charged.

- *Padraig O Cellaigh*
- \*\**John O'Grady* (27); one of fifteen cyclists who set off to relieve some of de Valera's men in Boland's. They were unable to force their way in, and he was killed on the return journey: 'I fear they got me'. He had been married only eight months.
- *Henry O'Hanrahan;* he was a brother of Michael.
- *Christopher O'Malley*
- *Lt Danny O'Riordan*
- *Fred O'Rourke;* later with the St Stephen's Green garrison.
- \*\**Dennis Ross*
- *Thomas Slater;* a member of the IRB since 1905.
- *William (Bill) Stapleton;* he was the guard commander.
- *Martin Walton* (15); his parents did not want him to fight so they took the valves from his bicycle tires. He was unable to get to Jacob's until Tuesday morning. He fought for the Free State in the Civil War. A great friend of Michael Collins.

## 2nd Battalion, Women
- *Sara Kealy*
- *Kathleen Lane*
- *Annie McQuade*
- *Maire Nic Shiubhlaigh* (nee Molly Walker/Mrs Eamonn Price); in command of the women, a famous actress in the early days of the Abbey Theatre.
- *Josie Pollard*
- *Miss Pollard* (sister of Josie)

## 3rd Battalion
Boland's Bakery/Mill; A, B and D Companies mustered in Great Brunswick Street. C Company mustered in Earlsfort Terrace; garrison total 173; killed, 10 (Grand Canal Street, Westland Row Station, Mount Street Bridge).
- *Commandant Eamon de Valera;* in Kilmainham, he was in cell number 59. While on penal servitude, though, his number was Convict 95, and there was a song written with that title. (De Valera was the only commandant who did not allow women in the garrison.)
- *P. Begley* was Vice-Commandant at Boland's and left his post on Thursday.
- \*\**Joseph Byrne* (32)
- *Paddy Byrne;* 1, 2 Clanwilliam Place/25 Northumberland Road detachment, sent home because of his youth.
- *William Christian;* 1, 2 Clanwilliam Place/25 Northumberland Road detachment.
- *Joe Clarke;* 1, 2 Clanwilliam Place/25 Northumberland Road detachment.
- \*\**2 Lt John Costello*
- *Cpt Michael Cullen;* erected the flag on the distillery tower. He 'watched over' de Valera when de Valera went to sleep and Dev cried 'set the Railway on fire'.
- *Cpt Simon Donnelly;* O/C of C Company. He joined the IRB in 1914 and was part of the Howth gun-running project. He was one of the Volunteers who had bought his own rifle and bought his Martini in 1914.
- *James Doyle;* 1, 2 Clanwilliam Place/25 Northumberland Road detachment.
- \*\**Patrick Doyle* (36); 1, 2 Clanwilliam Place/25 Northumberland Road detachment.

- *Patrick J. Doyle;* O/C at St Stephen's Parochial Hall, 1, 2 Clanwilliam Place/25 Northumberland Road detachment. He was a Volunteer musketry instructor.
- **Edward Ennis* (33)
- *Lt James Fitzgerald*
- *Willie Fitzgerald* (15)
- *Paddy Flanagan*
- ***James Grace;* 1, 2 Clanwilliam Place/25 Northumberland Road detachment.
- *Lt John (Sean) Guilfoyle;* wanted to escape to the mountains and continue fighting. He tunneled into a shop across from Beggar's Bush Barracks and harrassed the Barracks *with rifle-fire.*
- *Joseph Guilfoyle;* he had been guarding a bridge on the line to Harcourt Street Station.
- *George A. Lyons;* he was a B Company officer.
- *Joe MacDermott*
- *P. McGrath;* 1, 2 Clanwilliam Place/25 Northumberland Road detachment.
- *Cpt John (Sean) McMahon;* he was O/C of B Company.
- ***Peadar Macken;* an officer, he reprimanded a Volunteer who kept ignoring the order for silence. The truculent Volunteer shot him through the heart.
- ***Lt Michael Malone* (28); O/C of the 25 Northumberland Road detachment. He was the best marksman in the Company. De Valera ended up with his Mauser and kept it for the rest of his life.
- *Cpt Frank Mullen;* halted his company on Mount Street Bridge and told them: 'Any Volunteer who wishes may hand over his rifle and leave our ranks'. Only one did.
- ***Richard Murphy;* 1, 2 Clanwilliam Place/25 Northumberland Road detachment.
- *Arthur Nolan;* he was a baker at Boland's.
- *Peter Nolan;* ripped out rails on the line to Harcourt Street Station.
- *Lt Joseph O'Byrne;* Red Cross officer, served as a doctor.
- *Cpt Joseph O'Connor;* he was Vice-Commandant and O/C of A Company. Michael Malone said to him on Good Friday: 'Well, Joe, it's pretty close to hand. I know you'll come through, but I won't.'
- *Denis O'Donoghue;* 1, 2 Clanwilliam Place/25 Northumberland Road detachment.
- *Richard Perle* (Pearl?) (16) 'Go home mother, this is no place for a woman'.
- *Lt John Quinn;* he commanded B Company at Westland Row Station.
- ***George Reynolds;* a silversmith by trade, he was O/C in Clanwilliam House, 1,2 Clanwilliam Place.
- *Willie Ronan;* 1, 2 Clanwilliam Place/25 Northumberland Road detachment.
- *Michael Rowe;* 1, 2 Clanwilliam Place/25 Northumberland Road detachment, sent home because of his youth.
- *Thomas Traynor;* executed in Mountjoy on 25 April 1921.
- *James Walsh;* 1, 2 Clanwilliam Place/25 Northumberland Road detachment.
- *Thomas Walsh;* 1, 2 Clanwilliam Place/25 Northumberland Road detachment.
- *Patrick Ward;* he'd had pneumonia earlier in the year and moved to Sandyford. He did not receive notice of the Rising and so reported only on Tuesday morning.
- ***Patrick Whelan* (23); he had been dispatched to Tralee, but returned with the discouraging news of Casement's capture, and that Robert Monteith denounced the Germans bitterly.

## 4th Battalion, Men

South Dublin Union Workhouse, mustered in Emerald Square, Dolphin's Barn; garrison total 61; killed, 8; executed: 2 (Fairbrother's Field, James's Street, Jameson's Distillery, Marrowbone Lane, Mount Brown, Roe's Distillery, Watkins Brewery, Ardee Street). Ceannt surrendered 42 (actually 43 were still active as Brugha was still there!).

- *Commandant Eamonn Ceannt* (executed 8 May 1916, aged 34);* In Kilmainham, he was in cell number 88 (upper floor) and was moved to cell number 20. He was seen by his wife Áine, Lily Brennan, and attended by Fr Augustine.
- *Cathal Brugha*; Vice-Commandant.
- *Mick Butler*
- ***W. F. (Frank) Burke*
- *Con Colbert* (Conchubhair Ó Colbaird, exected 8 May 1916, aged 23);* Watkin's Brewery/Ardee Street Brewery. In Kilmainham he was in cell number 17, and was seen by the wife of prisoner Seamus O'Murchadha. Fr Augustine attended him: 'Perhaps I'll never again get the chance of knowing when I was to die, and so I'll try and die well'.
- *Philip Cosgrave*
- *Lt William Cosgrave*; Adjutant and Brugha's deputy. First leader of the Irish Free State after the Civil War.
- ***Brendan Donnelan* (18); a Fianna member, he was killed on the very first morning of the Rising.
- *Alderman Peadar Doyle*; Ceannt's orderly, and an inhabitant of the Union.
- *James Foran*; Ceannt gave him charge of the front gate of the Union. He and Cosgrave met Thomas MacDonagh to get the terms of surrender; imprisoned in Knutsford prison.
- *Douglas ffrench-Mullen*; a talented musician, wounded at the South Dublin Union.
- *Dan Holland*; brother of Frank, Robert and Walter.
- *Frank Holland*, fought in the South Dublin Union.
- *Robert Holland*; shot an English sniper who appeared at a window dressed as a woman. His birthday was 25 April and Walter brought him a cake! He was imprisoned in Frongoch.
- *Walter (Watty) Holland* (15)
- *John Joyce*; a section-commander, he led an ambush of troops of the 3rd Royal Irish Regiment.
- *Martin Kavanagh*
- *Tom Kavanagh*; he was a brother of Martin.
- *Bill Kelly*
- *Sgt Kerrigan*
- *Mick Liston*; 'supersniper', the best shot in the battalion, he was wounded.
- ***William MacDowell* (44)
- *Cpt Thomas McCarthy*; he was in Roe's Distillery and left his post on Thursday.
- *Joe McGrath*; first Secretary of the National Aid and Volunteers' Dependents' Fund; later started the Irish Sweepstakes. He escaped after the surrender: 'Toor-a-loo, boys, I'm off'.
- Cpt James (Seamus) Murphy; he was in Jameson's Distillery in Marrowbone Lane.
- *Lt Harry Murray*
- *Lt O'Brien*
- *'Big' Jim O'Callaghan*

- *Mick O'Callaghan*
- *Cpt Seamus O'Murchadha*
- **John O'Reilly*
- **Richard O'Reilly;* a brother of John. Two other brothers were in the British Army and one of them was killed in France.
- **John Owens*
- *George Plunkett*
- *Arthur Power;* he was a brother of Billy and Liam.
- *Billy Power*
- *Liam Power*
- **James Quinn*
- *Mick Riordan*
- *Jack Saul;* he was in Marrowbone Lane.
- David Sears; he was the youngest in the garrison.
- **John J. Traynor* (17); he was the best shot in his Company.
- *Dan Troy*
- *Paddy Troy;* he was a brother of Dan.
- *Tom Young;* he led a patrol to scout the Ardee Street Brewery for Con Colbert.
- *Mick White*

**4th Battalion, Women**
- *Lily Brennan;* she was Ceannt's sister-in-law, and was imprisoned in Kilmainham after the Rising when he was there.
- *Mary (May) Byrne*
- *Three Cooney* sisters
- *Alice Corcoran*
- *Miss Cumiskey*
- *Two Flaherty sisters*
- *Margaret Hennessey;* she was later a Senator.
- *Margaret L. Kennedy*
- *Josie McGowan*
- *Two Monaghan sisters*
- *Rose (Mrs Seamus) Murphy (Ó Murchadha) McNamara;* her husband was Cpt Murphy. She cooked for the Marrowbone Lane garrison.
- *Lily O'Brennan*
- *Two O'Byrne sisters*
- *Josie O'Keefe*
- *Emily O'Keefe*

**5th Battalion, Men**
North Co Dublin, RIC Barracks at Ashbourne, Co Meath; garrison total 37 to start, then about 45; 2 killed (plus one died afterwards from his wounds); 8 RIC killed. Known after the Rising as the Finglas Brigade; foreshadowed the flying columns and barracks' attacks of the 1920 campaigns.
- *Commandant Thomas Ashe;* he was known as an inspirational, but somewhat impractical, leader. He was the great uncle of actor Gregory Peck.

- *Dick Coleman* (25); died of flu in Usk Prison, Wales, on 9 December 1918 while a candidate for parliament (see 1st Battalion at Mendicity Institute).
- **John Crinigan*
- *Jerry Golden*
- *Dr Richard Hayes;* medical officer and an intelligence officer.
- *Paddy Houlihan*
- **John Kealy (15);* killed in Phibsboro while carrying dispatches.
- *Matthew Kelly;* wounded.
- *Edmund Kent*
- *Frank Lawless Sr;* Battalion QM.
- *Jim Lawless;* one of the section leaders.
- *Joseph Lawless;* one of the section leaders, as well as quartermaster.
- *Richard Mulcahy;* Vice-Commandant, he succeeded Michael Collins as Commander in Chief of the Free State Army.
- *James O'Connor;* a member of the St Margaret's Company of the Volunteers, he was imprisoned in Wakefield Prison.
- *J. Rafferty;* wounded.
- **Thomas Rafferty (22);* died of wounds after the Rising.
- *N. Rooney;* one of the section leaders, he was wounded.
- *Mr Walsh;* wounded.
- *Charles Weston;* one of the section leaders.

## 5th Battalion, Women
- *Miss Adrian*
- *Mrs Lawless*

## Irish Citizen Army, Men
Mustered at Liberty Hall; Dublin Castle/City Hall; garrison total: 10 in City Hall and 40 others spread over the other posts; 9 women accompanied the men from Liberty Hall; killed, 5; executed, 1.
- *Commandant James Connolly* (Seamus O Conghile, executed 12 May 1916, aged 46).* In Dublin Castle 'hospital', he was seen by Fr Aloysius.
- *Christopher Brady;* he was in the detachment that seized the guardroom.
- **Louis Byrne*
- **Cpt Sean Connolly* (33, a brother of Eamonn, George and Matt); first to fire a killing shot [Constable James O'Brien] and first Volunteer/ICA to die in the Rising. He was employed in the motor tax office of Dublin Castle. James Connolly: 'Good luck, Sean, we won't meet again'.
- *Eamonn Connolly*
- *George Connolly;* he was in the detachment that seized the guardroom.
- *Matt Connolly* (14)
- *John Coyle;* he was severely wounded.
- *Tom Daly;* he was in the detachment that seized the guardroom.
- **Charles Darcy* (15); 'I'm ready, lads, where do you need me?' He was shot on the roof by a sniper.
- **George Geoghegan* (35) (*Down Dublin Streets*, Eamonn MacThomais, p. 15); he was in the City Hall garrison, and was killed in the grounds of Dublin Castle while escaping.

- *Tom Kane;* he led the men into the guardroom.
- *Michael King;* he led the contingent to take the Telephone Exchange in Crown Alley.
- *George Norgrove*
- *Philip O'Leary;* he was in the detachment that seized the guardroom.
- ***Lt Sean (Jack) O'Reilly;* he succeeded Sean Collins in command.
- *James Seerey;* he was in the detachment that seized the guardroom.

## Irish Citizen Army, Women
- *Brigid Brady*
- *Katie Connolly* (Barrett); she was Sean's sister.
- *Brigid Davis*
- *Rose Hackett;* later in charge of a Red Cross station in the College of Surgeons.
- *Dr Kathleen Lynn;* an ICA captain she was at St Stephen's Green before she was called to the Castle to treat Sean Collins. After both Connolly and O'Reilly were killed, as the Medical Officer she surrendered the garrison.
- *Helena Molony;* she was an ICA officer and Abbey actress.
- *Mrs George Norgrove*
- *Annie Norgrove* (16); she was a daughter of George and Mrs Norgrove.
- *Emily Norgrove* (Hanratty); she was a daughter of George and Mrs Norgrove.
- *Molly O'Reilly*
- *Jenny Shanahan;* not in uniform, and when passed by the English it was assumed she had been a prisoner. When asked 'how many rebels are on the roof?' she answered 'there must be hundreds of them still on the roof'. So the British left it for the morning. However, when she was taken to 'identify' some 'rebels,' she was recognised instead and welcomed by her friends, and the British then confined her!

## Liberty Hall
- *Peter Ennis;* he was the caretaker.
- *Seamus McGowan;* he commanded the rear party after the Volunteers had marched to the GPO.
- *Willie Oman;* bugler, he sounded the bugle at 11.45 am on 24 April. (He also played *The Last Post* at the funeral of O'Donovan Rossa on Sunday, 1 August 1915.)

## St Stephen's Green/College of Surgeons, Men
Mustered at Liberty Hall; garrison total 138; killed, 6; executed: 1; 110 men and 11 women surrendered.
- *Michael Mallin* (executed 8 May 1916) Commandant.* He was ICA Chief of Staff under Connolly. He had served twelve years as a drummer in the Royal Fusiliers. In Kilmainham he was in cell number 18, and was seen by his two brothers Tom and Bart, his sister Kate, his wife, and his children – Seamus (12), Sean, Una and Joseph (2 years and 6 months). He was also seen by the Dominican novice master, Fr Browne, and Fr Albert.
- *Maj Countess Markievicz* (48); Vice-Commandant, she was said to have shot RIC Michael Lahiff who approached the Grafton Street gate and told the party to clear out. She was supposed to have shouted 'I shot him! I shot him'. She was originally to liaise between the GPO and St Stephen's Green, but Mallin told her he needed her as second in command.

- **\*\***_John Adams_ (38)
- _Paddy Buttner_ (15)
- **\*\***_Philip Clarke_ (41); he sent a message with a little girl on a bicycle to his wife in Cork Street. When she returned with some cigarettes from his wife, he was already dead.
- _Joseph Connolly;_ a brother of Sean, he led rebel songs at night. He and Margaret Skinnider pushed to lob a bomb through the Russell Hotel windows. One ICA soldier, Freddie Ryan, was killed and Skinnider was wounded three times in the effort. Connolly dragged Mick Doherty off the roof after Doherty had been hit. He became Chief of the Dublin Fire Brigade.
- **\*\***_James Corcoran_ (33)
- _Lt Bob De Coeur;_ he called out 'If you are any bloody good, come in and fight for Ireland' and Liam O'Briain and Harry Nichols jumped the fence into St Stephen's Green.
- _Pvt Michael (Mick) Doherty;_ he was wounded fifteen times on the roof of the College of Surgeons ('I'm afraid you're a goner, Mick, may the Lord have mercy on your soul'). But he survived, only to die in the 1918 influenza epidemic.
- _Joseph Doyle;_ he led one detachment of sixteen men at J. & T. Davy's Pub.
- _Andy Dunn;_ he was imprisoned in Frongoch.
- **\*\***_James Fox_ (16); a member of the Fianna, he was an only child. Early on Tuesday morning he was shot in a trench opposite the United Services Club.
- _Jim Gough;_ he was imprisoned in Frongoch.
- _John Joseph Hendrick;_ he came from London specifically to participate in the Rising.
- _James Joyce_ (35); he came from J. &. T. Davy's Pub.
- _Seamus Kavanagh;_ he was leader of the reinforcements sent from Jacobs by Thomas MacDonagh.
- _Tommy Keenan_ (12); after Jimmy Fox was killed, Mallin sent him home and his parents locked him in his room, but he 'escaped' and returned to the Green.
- _Lt Michael Kelly;_ just promoted to the rank of lieutenant on the morning of 24 April, he led the other detachment of sixteen men on the railway bridge crossing the Grand Canal at J. &. T. Davy's Pub.
- _Jem Little_
- _Cpt Richard MacCormack;_ sent by MacDonagh with a section of the Citizen Army to take Harcourt Street Station. He was the one who lowered the Tricolour and raised the white flag.
- **\*\***_Daniel Murray_ (27)
- _Cpt Harry Nicholls;_ 4th Battalion, Volunteers, jumped the St Stephen's Green fence with _Liam O'Briain._ He was an Ulsterman and a Protestant.
- _Liam O'Briain;_ a Volunteer in the 1st Dublin Battalion. He was first at J. &. T. Davy's Pub at Portobello Bridge on his way to St Stephen's Green, and then just stayed at St Stephen's Green. Professor of Romance languages at the National University. He had been cycling around Dublin trying to get information for MacNeill, and carried cancellation messages from MacNeill in the days before the Rising.
- _William Oman;_ he was an ICA bugler.
- _Cpt John O'Neill;_ his men supported Michael Kelly's men, and they were assigned to the railway bridge overlooking Harcourt Road.
- _Fred O'Rourke_ (16)
- _Sgt James O'Shea;_ he had been a member of the ICA since its inception.

- *Councillor Bill Partridge;* led the rosary each night, in his sonorous voice. He was wounded in the head. Sentenced to fifteen years penal servitude, but was released in 1917 because he had Bright's disease. He died in 1918.
- *Frank Robbins;* his twenty men were to operate in Hatch Street.
- *Sgt Frank Robbins;* led a group that seized the College of Surgeons. There were only three men and three women (including Countess Markievicz) to take the College. He had sought greater cooperation between the ICA and the Volunteers.
- \*\**Freddie Ryan* (17); killed in the party in which Margaret Skinnider was wounded trying to set fire to the Russell Hotel.
- *Sullivan;* had jumped the railings with Liam O'Briain, and O'Briain was 'saddled' with him for the duration. From Tralee, Sullivan semed to be fighting Denis Coffee, President of UCD, not the British!

## St Stephen's Green/College of Surgeons, Women

- *Chris Caffrey;* captured while taking a message to the GPO, disguised as a war widow, and strip searched but ultimately released.
- *Kathleen Cleary*
- *(Maire Comerford* was turned away because of her youth)
- *Mary Devereaux*
- *Mary Donnelly*
- *Nora Foley* (O'Daly); she was the medical officer.
- *Madeleine ffrench-Mullen;* ICA Officer; she commanded the medical detachment. She was imprisoned at Richmond Barracks and Kilmainham Gaol.
- *Nellie Gifford* (Donnelly); she was in charge of the commissariat.
- *Brigid Gough*
- *Rosanna (Rosie) Hackett*
- *Mary (Molly) Hyland;* a noted actress, she commandeered food and brought it into the garrison.
- *Maggie Joyce*
- *Annie Kelly*
- *Kate (Kitty) Kelly*
- *Elizabeth Ann 'Lily' Kempson*
- *Bessie Lynch*
- *May Moore*
- *Brigid Murtagh*
- *Mrs Norgrove*
- *Molly Reynolds*
- *Margaret Ryan*
- *Kathleen Seerey*
- *Margaret Skinnider* (23); a mathematics teacher from Glasgow, she was wounded on Wednesday when she was in a party sent to set fire to the Russell Hotel. Wounded three times (once in the right arm, right side and back) she was carried back to the College by Bill Partridge. At Christmas 1915, she had brought detonators to Ireland on the boat from Glasgow. She wrote *Doing My Bit for Ireland.*
- *Maeve Ward*

## Leaders and Volunteers in Belfast

- *Jerry Barnes*
- *Frank Bootie*
- *Mr Burke*
- *Peter Burns*
- *Mick Carolan*
- *Thomas Clear*
- *Alex Connolly*
- *Joseph Connolly*
- *Alf Cotton*
- *Sean Cusack*, sent to Ballinagh
- *Patrick Dempsey*
- *Henry Dobbyn*
- *Seamus Dobbyn*
- *Mr Hackett*
- *Rory Haskins*
- *Sam Herron*
- *James Johnston*
- *John Kelly*
- *Dr Pat McCartan*
- *Denis McCullough*, President of the IRB
- *Charles McDowell*
- *Pat Nash*
- *Sean Neeson*
- *Harry Osborne*
- *Hugh Rogers*
- *Cathal Shannon*
- *James Smith*
- *Edward Tierney*
- *Thomas Wilson*
- *Ina Connolly*, daughter of James, she relayed messages from Belfast to Dublin
- *Nora Connolly*, daughter of James, she relayed messages from Belfast to Dublin, and from Dublin to Co Tyrone
- *Kathleen Murphy*
- *Miss O'Neill*
- *Miss Owens*

## Leaders and Volunteers in Co Clare

Approximately 30-40 men paraded at Ardmore on Easter Monday and began 'collecting' firearms from the surrounding area. By Wednesday, they all had a rifle or shotgun.

- *Michael Brennan*
- *Patrick Brennan*
- *Daniel Canny*
- *Mick Dynan*
- *Denis Healy*
- *Timothy Kelly*

- *J. Malone*
- *Seamus Murrihy,* cut the telephone line between Ennis and Ennistymon
- *Patrick O'Connor*
- *Arthur O'Donnell*
- *Thomas O'Loughlin,* cut the telephone line between Ennis and Ennistymon; imprisoned in *Frongoch*
- *C. O'Halloran*
- *Eamon Waldron*

## Leaders and Volunteers in Co Cork

- *Thomas MacCurtain,* O/C, followed MacNeill order to stand down; he often said of 2,000 Volunteers in the County only 80 would report for the Rising after MacNeill's order, so he stood the unit down. He was arrested on 3 May but later released.
- *Terence MacSwiney,* second in command; arrested on 3 May and imprisoned in Wakefield Prison. His sister Annie said later: 'The torment of that week to Terry was appeased only by the sacrifice [his death on hunger strike] in Brixton'.
- *Thomas Kent* (Tomas Ceannt, executed 9 May 1916, Cork)*. Fermoy, Co Cork, Bawnard House, Castlelyons, owned by Mrs Kent. On the night of 2 May, an RIC party went to the house on a 'clearing-up operation'; the fight took place between 2.45 am and 6.00 am. Constable Rowe was killed at the outset of the fighting according to RIC reports, though at his trial, Kent said he never fired a shot. The Kents had been armed with one rifle and three shotguns. The aged Mrs Kent re-loaded the weapons for her sons during the fighting. While Thomas was in Victoria Barracks, now Cork Detention Barracks, he was attended by Fr John Sexton. Executed at Victoria Barracks, Cork, for the killing of Head Constable Rowe. Rowe was killed after the rebels in Dublin had surrendered. Many thought Kent was executed not just because Rowe died, after all it was in a firefight, but to serve as a warning to all that the 'Rising was over, and no more fighting would be accepted'.
- *David Kent* (brother); he was severely wounded in the side and lost two fingers.
- **Richard Kent* (brother); he was shot while trying to escape. He had been a famous athlete in the area.
- *William Kent* (brother).

*The following men also served in Co Dublin in the Rising; all were Volunteers unless noted as members of the Irish Citizen Army (ICA).*

John Bannon (ICA)
Joseph Begley
Michael Behan
Andrew Bermingham
John Bermingham
William Berry
Joseph Billings
James Bird (ICA)
Michael Blanchfield
Peter Blanchfield
Edward Brennan
Patrick Breslin
James Broughan
William Brown
Thomas Bryan (ICA)
William Buckley
John Byrne (ICA)
Patrick Byrne
Arthur Cahill
Joseph Callan
Pat Callen
Michael Campbell
Dan Carney
Christopher Carberry
Peter Carpenter (ICA)
Walter Carpenter (ICA)
Charles Carrigan
Peter Carroll
Owen Carton (ICA)
Hugh Casey
James Cassells
T. Cassidy
P. Chaney
William Chaney
Michael Charlton (ICA)
Peter Christie
James Clarke
Pat Clinch
Peter Coates (ICA)

John Cody
Sean Cole
Walter Cole
James Conroy
James Conroy Jnr
John Conroy (ICA)
Sean Conway
Richard Corbally (ICA)
Joseph Cotter
Richard Cotter
Thomas Cotter
Bernard Courtney (ICA)
Daniel Courtney (ICA)
William Coyle
M. Croke
T. Croke
Pat Cullen (ICA)
James Cunningham
Francis Daly
Harry Colley
L. Condron
Eddie Connolly (ICA)
Herbert Conroy
James Daly
Henry Daniels (ICA)
Seamus Dempsey
Patrick Dennany
Joseph Derham
Peter Devereaux (ICA)
Dan Devitt
Henry Dixon
James Doherty
Edward Doyle (ICA)
Joe Doyle (ICA)
Thomas Doyle
Thomas Drennan
Joseph Duffy (ICA)
P. K. Duffy (ICA)
Frank Dunne

Thomas Dunne
James Dwyer (ICA)
J. Early
John Ellis
Sam Ellis
Elliott Elmes
Christopher Ennis
Michael Ennis
Denis Farrell
Michael Farrell
Stephen Farren
M. Fay (ICA)
John Finlay
Michael Finnegan
Leo Fitzgerald
Thomas Fitzgerald
John Fitzharris
M. Fitzsimmons
Maurice Flanagan
Matthew Flanagan
Michael Fleming
Sean Flood
John Furlong
Matthew Furlong
John Gavin
Gaynor
Christy Geraghty
Richard Gibson
Michael Giffney
Robert Gilligan
Thomas Gleeson (ICA)
William Gleeson (ICA)
Charles Goulding
James Goulding
Sean Gregory
John Griffin
Patrick Halpin
William Halpin (ICA)
William T. Halpin

| | | |
|---|---|---|
| James Hampton | Thomas Losty | Patrick Meagher |
| James Harmon | Michael Love | Thomas Meldon |
| John Harper | John Lynch | Seamus Melinn |
| A. Hayes | John Lynch | Michael Mervyn |
| Seamus Hayes | Martin Lynch | Patrick Mitchell |
| Diarmuid Healy | Michael Lynch | Michael Molloy |
| John Hegarty | William Lynch | Richard Molloy |
| Edward Hendrick | Charles Lyons | Philip Monaghan |
| James Heron | Edward Lyons | James Mooney |
| James Higgins | John Lyons | Jim Mooney |
| Thomas Hilton | James McArdle | John Moore (ICA) |
| Michael Howlett | Patrick McArdle | Patrick Moore |
| Patrick Hughes | Kevin McCabe | Eamon Moran |
| Robert Humphries | William McCabe | Patrick Moran |
| James J. Hunter | Christopher McCormack | Michael Mullen |
| Joseph Hutchinson | Owen McDermott | Thomas Monroe |
| Edward Joyce | John McDonald | William Murnane |
| John Joyce | Patrick McDonald | Colm Murphy |
| J. Kavanagh | Matt McDonnell | Fred Murphy (ICA) |
| Thomas Kearney | Patrick McDonnell (ICA) | John Murphy |
| Frank Kearns | Thomas McEvoy | Martin Murphy |
| Joseph Kearns | Patrick McGinley | Michael Murphy |
| Thomas Kearns | Con McGin | Michael Murphy |
| Tom Kehoe (The Squad) | Michael McGin | Michael Murphy |
| Joseph Kelly | James McGowan | Michael Murphy |
| J. Kennedy | Tom McGrath | Patrick Murphy (ICA) |
| Joseph Kennedy | Peter McMahon | Joseph Murray |
| Luke Kenny | Patrick McManus | Nicholas Murray |
| Charles Kenny | Frank McNally | Joseph Murtagh |
| Henry Kenny | Peter McPartlin | Patrick Murtagh |
| J. Kenny | Laurence Mackay | Joe Musgrave |
| Cyril Keogh | Michael Mackey | Denis Neary |
| Robert Killeen (ICA) | John Madden | Joseph Neary |
| Michael Knightly | T. McGuire | James Nelson (ICA) |
| Patrick Lawlor | John Mahon (ICA) | Thomas Nelson (ICA) |
| Ned Lane | Henry Manning | P. Nevin |
| Patrick Lannigan | Peter Martin | John Newman |
| John Larkin | Frank Mason | John Nolan (ICA) |
| John Larkin | George Mason | Patrick Nolan |
| Joseph Larkin | Thomas Mason | Patrick Nolan |
| Robert Legitt | Henry Meade | James Norton |
| Joe Leonard (The Squad) | Walter Meade | P. Nugent |

Tobias O'Breslin
John O'Brien
William O'Brien
William O'Brien
Charles O'Byrne
Christopher O'Byrne
James O'Byrne
James O'Byrne
James O'Byrne
John O'Byrne
John O'Byrne
Joseph L. O'Byrne
Joseph P. O'Byrne
William O'Byrne
Art O'Cahill
John O'Callaghan
Peter O'Carroll
Robert O'Carroll
W. O'Carroll
James O'Connor
John F. O'Connor
Thomas O'Connor
Michael O'Doherty (ICA)
Thomas O'Donoghue (ICA)
Robert O'Donoghue
Frank O'Flanagan
George O'Flanagan
Michael O'Flanagan
Liam O'Gorman
Edward O'Hanrahan
Michael O'Hehir
Brian O'Higgins
Garrett O'Holohan
  John T. O'Kelly
Joseph O'Kelly
Joseph O'Kelly
Sean O'Mahoney
Chris O'Malley
Donagh O'Moore
Sean O'Moore
John O'Neill (ICA)
John O'Neill (ICA)

John O'Neill
Joseph O'Neill
Joseph O'Neill
Michael O'Neill
Michael O'Neill
Timothy O'Neill
William O'Neill
Desmond O'Reilly
John O'Reilly
John O'Reilly
Joseph O'Reilly
Kevin O'Reilly
S. P. O'Reilly
J. F. O'Rourke
John O'Rourke
Michael O'Rourke
Albert O' Shea (ICA)
Robert O'Shea (ICA)
Matthew Parnell
Thomas Peate
Frank Pollard
Christopher Poole (ICA)
John Poole (ICA)
Patrick Poole (ICA)
Sean Price
Charles M. Purcell
Thomas Pugh
John Purfield (ICA)
Joseph Redmond
Patrick Redmond
Pat Reilly
Augustus Reynolds
John Richmond
Christopher Ring
Michael Roche
Sean Rogan (ICA)
John Rooney
William Ross
William Ryan
Philip Sargent
Fred Schweppe
F. K. Scullen

William Scully
Patrick Seery (ICA)
James Sexton
Philip Shanahan
Tom Sheils (ICA)
Denis Shelly
Thomas Shelly
Michael Sheppard
John Sheridan
James Shiels
Terence Simpson
Michael Slater
James Slattery (14) (The
  Squad)
Charles Smith (ICA)
Michael Smyth
Richard Stokes
James Stritch
C. Tallon
James Tallon
Joseph Trimble
Frank Turner
Harry Turner
Joseph Turner
John Twoomey
Joe Twoomey
Edward Tuke (ICA)
William Tully
Michael Wade (ICA)
George Ward
Gilbert Ward
Thomas Ward
— Weldon
Thomas Wheatley
James Whelan
John Whelan (ICA)
Joseph Whelan
William Whelan
Mark Wilson
James Wren

## Leaders and Volunteers in Co Galway
- *Liam Mellowes*, O/C, led Volunteers in an uprising
- *Ailbhe O'Monachain*
- *Bryan Molloy*

## Leaders and Volunteers in Co Kerry
- *Austin Stack*, O/C

## Leaders and Volunteers in Co Louth
- *Dan Hannigan*, O/C in Dundalk

## Leaders and Volunteers in Co Limerick
- *Michael P. Colivet*, O/C
- *James J. Gubbins*
- *Patrick Whelan*

## Leaders and Volunteers in Co Tipperary
- *Sean Allen*, shot in Cork jail after court martial in February 1921
- *Dan Allis*
- *William Benn*
- *Dan Breen*, IRB Tipperary Centre
- *Martin (Sparky) Breen*, killed in the Civil War
- *Michael Brennan*
- *James Brown*
- *Con Deere*
- *Frank Drohan*, O/C in Clonmel
- *Sean Duffy*, killed in an engagement with Auxies on 1 May 1921
- *Tadhg Dwyer*
- *Paddy English*
- *Michael Fitzpatrick*
- *Peter Hennessey*
- *Sean Hogan*
- *Sean Horan*
- *Jerry Kuely*, killed in the Civil War
- *Tadhg Kelly*
- *Dinny Lacey*
- *P. MacCormack*
- *Pierce McCann*, County Commandant
- *Jack McCarthy*
- *Con Maloney*
- *Patrick Maloney*, killed in an engagement with Auxies on 1 May 1921
- *Michael O'Callaghan*, shot and killed RIC Sgt O'Rourke who had come to arrest him on Wednesday of Easter Week; the 'one blow' in Tipperary during the Rising; he escaped to America
- *Eamonn O'Dwyer*, IRB County Centre
- *Seamus O'Neill*, imprisoned in Frongoch

- *Seamus Robinson*
- *Tom Rogers*
- *Packey Ryan*
- *Sean Treacy*
- *M. Sheehan*
- *T. Sheehan.*

## Leaders and Volunteers in Enniscorthy, Co Wexford

- *Commandant Robert Brennan*, O/C in Enniscorthy, led Volunteers in an uprising
- *Commandant Paul Galligan*
- *Michael de Lacy*
- *Cpt Seamus Doyle*
- *Cpt Sean Etchingham*
- *Richard King*
- *James Rafter*
- *Tom Sutton*, a Bray Volunteer, delivered a message to Brennan and stayed in *Enniscorthy*
- *Patrick Tobin*
- *Una Brennan*
- *Gretta Comerford*, she raised the Tricolour over the town
- *Eileen O'Hegarty*
- *Marion Stokes*
- *Mary White.*

## The following women also served in the Rising

- *Lizzie Allen*
- *Kate Brown*
- *Martha Brown*
- *Eileen Byrne*
- *Katie Byrne*
- *Alice Cashel*
- *Maeve Cavanagh*
- *G. Colley*
- *Annie Cooney*, Dublin, was imprisoned in Kilmainham Gaol
- *E. (Lily) Cooney*
- *Agnes Daly*, took messages to Co Kerry
- *Brid Dixon*
- *Helen Donnelly*
- *Kathy Doran*
- *Frances Downey*
- *Bridie Farrell*
- *Kathleen Fleming*
- *Brigid Foley*
- *May Gahan*, Dublin, remembered people pelting her with bottles as she walked to imprisonment in Kilmainham Gaol
- *Eilie (Betsy) Gray*
- *P. Hoey*

- *Ellen Humphreys*
- *Kathleen Kearney* (later Mrs Behan, mother of Brendan Behan)
- *Josephine Kelly*
- *Martha Kelly*
- *K. Kennedy*
- *Bridie Kennedy*
- *Catherine Liston*
- *Mary Liston*
- *May MacLaughlin*
- *Julia McAley*
- *Josephine McGowan*
- *Maggie McLaughlin*
- *Anastasia McLaughlin*
- *Agnes McNamara*
- *Kathleen Mahon*
- *Pauline Markham*
- *J. Milner*
- *P. Morecambe*
- *Lizzie Mulhall*
- *Rose Mullally*
- *Mrs E. Murphy*
- *Kathleen Murphy*
- *Mrs Martha Murphy*
- *Eilis Ni Chorra*
- *Kathleen Ni Chorra*
- *Katie O'Connor*
- *Florence O'Doherty*
- *Margaret O'Flaherty*
- *Sheila O'Hanlon*
- *Eileen (Eily) O'Hanrahan* (later Mrs O'Hanrahan O'Reilly)
- *Mary O'Hanrahan*
- *Emily O'Keefe*
- *Josephine O'Keefe*
- *Mary O'Moore*
- *Grace O'Sullivan*
- *Louisa O'Sullivan*
- *Mary Partridge*
- *Marie Perolz*, carried many messages on dangerous missions between garrisons
- *Maria Quigley*
- *Priscilla Quigley*
- *S. Quigley*
- *Barbara Retz*
- *Agnes Ryan*
- *K. Ryan*
- *Nell Ryan*
- *Phyllis Ryan*

- *Mary Shannon*
- *Tilly Simpson*
- *Miss Smith*
- *Josephine Spicer*
- *Aoife Taafe*
- *Nora Thornton*
- *A. Tobin*
- *Catherine Treston*
- *S. Twomey*
- *Bridie Walsh*
- *Margaret (Maggie) Walsh*
- *Mary Jo Walsh*
- *A. Wisely.*

## The following were also on the official list of dead
- *Frank Burke*, not killed, fought in the GPO and was imprisoned at Frongoch. *W. F. Burke* was killed at the South Dublin Union
- *Andrew Byrne*
- *John Cromean*
- *Peter Darcy*
- *Con Keating* (Ballykissane Pier, Co Kerry)
- *J. McCormack*
- *Charles Monaghan* (Ballykissane Pier, Co Kerry)
- *D. Murphy*
- *Richard O'Carroll* (deliberately shot with his hands raised after surrender; he died on 5 May)
- *Thomas O'Reilly*
- *Domhall (Donal) Sheehan* (Ballykissane Pier, Co Kerry)
- *Patrick Sheehy*
- *John Traynor.*

## Soldiers, police and civilians
'Official' estimates have 142 English soldiers and police killed
'Official' estimates have 254 civilians killed and over 2,000 wounded.

## Executions after the Rising
3 May, Tomas Clarke, Padraig Pearse, Thomas MacDonagh
4 May, Edward (Ned) Daly, Willie Pearse, Joseph Plunkett, Michael O'Hanrahan
5 May, John MacBride
8 May, Sean Heuston, Michael Mallin, Con Colbert, Eamonn Ceannt
9 May, Thomas Kent (Cork)
12 May, Sean McDermott, James Connolly
3 August, Roger Casement (Pentonville Prison).

## Sentences

Ninety-seven Volunteers were sentenced to death but had the sentences reduced to some years of penal servitude.

*Sentenced to death but commuted to penal servitude for life:*
- *Thomas Ashe*
- *Robert Brennan*
- *William T. Cosgrave*
- *Eamon de Valera*
- *Thomas Hunter*
- *Countess Markievicz*
- *Henry O'Hanrahan*
- *John (Jack) Shouldice.*

*Sentenced to death but commuted to ten years penal servitude:*
- *Thomas Bevan*
- *Peter Clancy*
- *Richard Davys*
- *John Doherty*
- *Peter Doyle*
- *Francis Fahy*
- *James T. Hughes*
- *George Irvine*
- *Frank Lawless*
- *James Lawless*
- *Finian Lynch*
- *Jeremiah C. Lynch*
- *Patrick McNestry*
- *James Melinn*
- *Michael Mervyn*
- *Bryan Molloy*
- *Denis O'Callaghan*
- *George Plunkett*
- *John Plunkett*
- *J. J. Reid*
- *P. E. Sweeney*
- *William Tobin*
- *J. J. Walsh*
- *Thomas Walsh*
- *John Williams.*

*Sentenced to death but commuted to penal servitude:*
- *Charles Bevan,* 3 years
- *Henry Boland,* 5 years
- *Michael Brady,* 3 years
- *J. Brennan,* 3 years

- *Maurice Brennan*, 3 years
- *Robert Brennan*, 5 years
- *F. Brooks*, 3 years
- *James Burke*, 3 years
- *John Joseph Byrne*, 3 years
- *J. Clarke*, 3 years
- *R. Coleman*, 3 years
- *William P. Corrigan*, 5 years
- *Philip Cosgrave*, 5 years
- *Gerald Crofts*, 5 years
- *John F. Cullen*, 3 years
- *Michael de Lacy*, 5 years
- *James Dempsey*, 3 years
- *J. Dorrington*, 3 years
- *James Downey*, 3 years
- *Gerald Doyle*, 3 years
- *James Doyle*, 5 years
- *Frank Drennan*, 10 years
- *John Etchingham*, 5 years
- *John Faulkner*, 3 years
- *Patrick Fogarty*, 3 years
- *Peter Galligan*, 5 years
- *Richard Hayes*, 20 years
- *P. Kelly*, 3 years
- *R. Kelly*, 3 years
- *James Joyce*, 5 years
- *George Levins*, 3 years
- *Philip MacMahon*, 3 years
- *John McArdle*, 3 years
- *Sean McGarry*, 8 years
- *J. Marks*, 3 years
- *W. Meehan*, 3 years
- *James Morrissey*, 3 years
- *J. Norton*, 3 years
- *John O'Brien*, 3 years
- *Fergus O'Connor*, 3 years
- *W. O'Dea*, 3 years
- *C. O'Donovan*, 5 years
- *T. O'Kelly*, 3 years
- *Richard King*, 5 years
- *James O'Sullivan*, 8 years
- *T. Peppard*, 3 years
- *Vincent Poole*, 5 years
- *John Quin*, 3 years
- *James Rafter*, 5 years
- *Michael Reynolds*, 3 years

- *Michael Scully*, 3 years
- *J. Wilson*, 2 years
- *P. Wilson*, 3 years
- *W. Wilson*, 3 years.

*Sentenced to penal servitude:*
- *Thomas Barrett*, 1 year
- *Thomas Bennett*, 1 year
- *Harry Boland*, 10 years, 5 remitted
- *Timothy Brosnan*, 20 years, 15 remitted
- *Joseph Burke*, 3 years
- *Christopher Carrick*, 3 years
- *John Carrick*, 3 years
- *Eddy Corcoran*, 3 years
- *John Corcoran*, 3 years
- *William Corcoran*, 3 years
- *J. Crenigan*, 1 year
- *Gerald Crofts*, 10 years, 5 remitted
- *William Darrington*, 2 years, 1 remitted
- *Michael Donohue*, 1 year
- *Frank Drennan*, 20 years, 10 remitted
- *Murtagh Fahy*, 1 year
- *Patrick Fahy*, 10 years
- *Thomas Desmond Fitzgerald*, 10 years
- *Patrick Flanagan*, 3 years
- *Michael Fleming*, 3 years
- *Michael Fleming Jnr*, 1 year
- *Thomas Fury*, 3 years
- *Thomas (Fred) Fury*, 3 years
- *Patrick Fury*, 3 years
- *John Grady*, 1 year
- *Michael Grady*, 1 year
- *John Greaves*, 6 months
- *J. Grenigan*, 2 years, 1 remitted
- *John Haniffy*, 1 year
- *Martin Hansbury*, 1 year
- *Michael Hehir*, 3 years
- *Michael Higgins*, 1 year
- *Michael Higgins* (Oranmore), 3 years
- *Joseph Howley*, 3 years
- *William Hussey*, 3 years
- *Patrick Kennedy*, 1 year
- *Thomas Kennedy*, 1 year
- *Joseph Ledwick*, 6 months
- *James Loughlin*, 3 years
- *Eoin MacNeill*, life

- *Conor McGinley*, 3 years
- *James Murray*, 1 year
- *Charles O'Neill*, 1 year
- *William Partridge*, 15 years, 5 remitted
- *E. Roach*, 1 year
- *Michael Scully*, 10 years, 7 remitted
- *Michael Toole*, 3 years
- *Patrick Weafer*, 6 months
- *Charles White*, 1 year.

## Women imprisoned

Though seventy-two women were taken prisoner after the Rising, most were soon released. However, among others, the following were imprisoned for some time: Winifred Carney, Annie Cooney, Brigid Foley, Madeleine ffrench Mullen, May Gahan, Dr. Kathleen Lynn, Helena Maloney, Countess Markievicz, Marie Perolz, and Nell Ryan.

## English Troops in Ireland during the Rising

- Army Service Corps
- Connaught Rangers
- Duke of Lancaster's Own Yeomen
- Grenadier Guards
- 2nd King Edward's Horse Regiment
- Kingstown Volunteer Corps
- North Staffordshire Regiment
- 6th Reserve Cavalry Regiment
- 5th and 12th Royal Lancers
- Royal Army Medical Corps
- 4th Battalion Royal Dublin Fusiliers
- 10th Battalion Royal Dublin Fusiliers
- Royal Engineers
- Royal Field Artillery
- Royal 8th Hussars
- Royal Iniskilling Fusiliers
- Royal Irish Fusiliers
- 3rd Battalion Royal Irish Rifles
- 3rd Battalion Royal Irish Regiment
- 18th Royal Irish Rifle Regiment
- Royal Leicestershire Regiment
- Royal Leinster Regiment, relieved the OTC at Trinity
- Royal Navy, HMS *Helga*
- Royal Scots
- 178th Brigade, The Sherwood Forester Regiment
- South Staffordshire Regiment
- Volunteer Training Corps (Trinity)
- Yeomanry

# Bibliography

## Manuscript and printed primary sources

British Parliamentary Archive, Papers, 'The Irish Uprising, 1914–1921'.

Dublin City Library & Archive, Pearse Street, Dublin 2.

The Easter Commemoration Digest, 1964.

Military Archives of Ireland, Cathal Brugha Barracks, Dublin 6.

National Archives of Ireland, Bishop Street, Dublin 8.

North Dublin Inner City Folklore Project, Amiens Street, Dublin 1.

Thom, Alexander, Thom's Irish Almanac and Official Directory

## Books

Adams, Gerry. *Who Fears to Speak? The Story of Belfast and the 1916 Rising.* (Belfast, 2001).

Alderman, Clifford Lindsey. *The Wearing of the Green, The Irish Rebellion 1916–1921.* (1972).

Andrews, C. S. *Dublin Made Me.* (Dublin, 2001).

Augusteijn, Joost. *From Public Defiance to Guerilla Warfare.* (Dublin, 1996).

Augusteijn, Joost, editor. *The Irish Revolution.* (Basingstoke, 2002).

Barry, Tom. *Guerilla Days in Ireland: A Personal Account of the Anglo-Irish War.* (Dublin, 1981).

Barton, Brian and Michael Foy. *The Easter Rising.* (Stroud, 1999).

Béaslaí, Piaras. *Michael Collins and the Making of the New Ireland.* (London, 1926).

Bell, J. Bowyer. *The Secret Army, The I.R.A.* (Dublin, 1997).

Bennett, Richard. *The Black and Tans.* (London, 2001).

Boyce, D. G. *Englishmen and Irish Troubles, British Public Opinion and the Making of Irish Policy, 1918–22.* (Aldershot 1994, c.1972).

Brasier, Andrew, and John Kelly. *Harry Boland, A Man Divided.* (Dublin, 2000).

Breen, Dan. *My Fight for Irish Freedom.* (Dublin, 1964).

Brennan, Robert. *Allegiance. (Dublin,* 1950).

Brennan-Whitmore, W. J. *Dublin Burning: The Easter Rising from Behind the Barricades.* (Dublin, 1996).

Briollay, Sylvain. *Ireland in Rebellion.* (Dublin, 1922).

Buckley, Margaret. *The Jangle of the Keys.* (Dublin, 1938).

Butler, Ewan. *Barry's Flying Column: The Story of the I.R.A.'s Cork No. 3 Brigade, 1919–1921.* (London, 1971).

Campbell, Colm. *Emergency Law in Ireland, 1918–1925.* (Oxford, 1994).

Carroll, Francis M. *American Opinion and the Irish Question, 1910–1923.* (Dublin, 1978).

Carty, Xavier. *In Bloody Protest, The Tragedy of Patrick Pearse.* (Dublin, 1978).

Cashman, Denis B. *Fenian Diary,* edited by C. W. Sullivan III. (Dublin, 2001).

Caulfield, Max. *The Easter Rebellion, Dublin 1916.* (Dublin, 1995).

Chavasse, Moirin. *Terence MacSwiney.* (Dublin & London, 1961).

Clarke, Kathleen. *Revolutionary Woman, My Fight for Ireland's Freedom,* edited by Helen Litton. (Dublin, 1997).

Clarke, Thomas. *Glimpses of an Irish Felon's Prison Life.* Foreword by P. S. O'Hegarty (Cork, 1970).

Clifford, Brendan. *War, Insurrection and Election in Ireland, 1914–21.* (Belfast, 1997).

Coffey, Thomas M. *Agony at Easter.* (London, 1969).

Collins, Michael. *The Path to Freedom,* edited by Tim Pat Coogan. (Cork, 1996).

Colum, Padraic. *Arthur Griffith.* (Dublin, 1959).

Comerford, Anthony. *The Easter Rising, Dublin 1916.* (New York, 1969).

Comerford, Maire. *The First Dáil, January 21st 1919.* (Dublin, 1969).

Connolly, Colm. *The Illustrated Life of Michael Collins.* (Boulder, 1996).

Conner, Rearden. *Shake Hands with the Devil.* (London, 1934).

Connolly, James. *Labour in Irish History.* (Dublin, 1983).

Connolly, Nora. *The Irish Rebellion of 1916* or *The Unbroken Tradition.* (New York, 1918).

Connolly, Nora. *Portrait of a Rebel Father.* (Dublin & London, 1975).

Coogan, Tim Pat. *Ireland Since the Rising.* (London, 1966).

Coogan, Tim Pat. *The Irish, A Personal View.* (London, 1975).

Coogan, Tim Pat. *On the Blanket, The Inside story of the I.R.A. Prisoners' dirty protest.* (Dublin, 1980).

Coogan, Tim Pat. *Michael Collins, The Man Who Made Ireland.* (London, 1992).

Coogan, Tim Pat. *De Valera: Long Fellow, Long Shadow.* (London, 1995).

Coogan, Tim Pat and George Morrison. *The Irish Civil War.* (London, 1998).

Coogan, Tim Pat. *1916: The Easter Rising.* (London, 2001).

Cooke, Pat. *Scéal Scoil Éanna.* (Dublin, 1986).

Costello, Francis. *Enduring the Most: The Life and Death of Terence MacSwiney.* (Dingle, 1995).

Costello, Francis, editor. *Michael Collins In His Own Words.* (Dublin, 1997).

Costello, Francis. *The Irish Revolution and its Aftermath, 1916–1923.* (Dublin, 2003).

Cowell, John. *Dublin's Famous People and Where They Lived.* (Dublin, 1996).

Cronin, Sean. *The Story of Kevin Barry.* (Cork, 1971).

Cronin, Sean. *Ideology of the I.R.A.* (Ann Arbor, 1972).

Cronin, Sean. *The McGarrity Papers.* (Tralee, 1972).

Crozier, General Frank P. *Impressions and Recollections.* (London, 1930).

Crozier, General Frank P. *Ireland Forever.* (London and Toronto, 1932).

Curran, Joseph M. *The Birth of the Irish Free State 1921–1923.* (University of Alabama, 1980).

Curtin, Nancy. *The Revolution in Ireland 1879–1923.* (Oxford, 1994).

Dalton, Charles. *With the Dublin Brigade.* (London, 1929).

Davis, Richard P. *Arthur Griffith and Non-Violent Sinn Féin.* (Dublin, 1974).

Deasy, Liam. *Towards Ireland Free, The West Cork Brigade in the War of Independence 1917–1921.* (Dublin, 1973).

Deasy, Liam. *Brother Against Brother.* (Cork, 1998).

De Bréadún, Déaglán. *The Far Side of Revenge: Making Peace in Northern Ireland.* (Cork, 2001).

De Burca, Padraig and John Boyle. *Free State or Republic?* (Dublin, 2002).

De Burca, Seamus, *The Soldier's Song: The Story of Peadar Kearney.* (Dublin, 1958).

De Rosa, Peter. *Rebels: The Irish Rising of 1916.* (London, 1990).

Doherty, Gabriel and Dermot Keogh, editors, *Michael Collins and the Making of the Irish State.* (Cork, 1998).

Dooley, Brian. *Choosing the Green, Second Generation Irish and the Cause of Ireland,* (Belfast, 2004).

Duff, Charles. *Six Days to Shake an Empire.* (London, 1966).

Dwyer, T. Ryle. *Michael Collins and the Treaty.* (Dublin, 1981).

Dwyer, T. Ryle. *De Valera's Darkest Hour, 1919–1932.* (Dublin,1982).

Dwyer, T. Ryle. *Michael Collins: The Man Who Won the War.* (Cork, 1990).

Dwyer, T. Ryle. *De Valera: The Man and Myths.* (Swords, 1992).

Dwyer, T. Ryle. *Tans, Terror and Troubles: Kerry's Real Fighting Story 1913–1923.* (Cork, 2001).

Dwyer, T. Ryle. *The Squad and the Intelligence Operations of Michael Collins.* (Cork, 2005).

Edwards, Owen Dudley and Fergus Pyle. *1916, The Easter Rising.* (London, 1968).

Edwards, Owen Dudley. *Eamon de Valera.* (Cardiff, 1987).

Edwards, Ruth Dudley. *Patrick Pearse: The Triumph of Failure.* (London, 1977).

Ellis, P. Beresford, editor. *James Connolly Selected Writings.* (Harmonsworth, 1973).

Farrell, Brian. *The Founding of Dáil Éireann.* (Dublin, 1971).

Farrell, Brian. *Sean Lemass.* (Dublin, 1983).

Farrell, J. G. *Troubles.* (New York, 2002).

Feehan, John M. *The Shooting of Michael Collins: Murder or Accident?* (Cork, 1991).

Figgis, Darrell. *Recollections of the Irish War.* (London, 1924).

Fitzgerald, Redmond. *Cry Blood, Cry Erin: The Fight for Irish Freedom.* (London, 1966).

Fitzpatrick, David. *Politics and Irish Life, 1913–1921: Provincial Experience of War and Revolution,* (Cork, 1998).

Fitzpatrick, David, editor. *Revolution: Ireland 1917–1923.* (Dublin, 1990).

Fitzpatrick, David. *Harry Boland's Irish Revolution* (Cork, 2003).

Flanagan, Thomas. *The End of the Hunt.* (London, 1994).

Forester, Margery. *Michael Collins: The Lost Leader.* (Dublin, 1989).

Fox, R. M. *Rebel Irishwomen.* (Dublin and Cork, 1935).

Fox, R.M. *History of the Irish Citizen Army.* (Dublin, 1944).

Fox, R. M. *James Connolly, The Forerunner.* (Tralee, 1946).

Gallagher, Frank. *The Four Glorious Years.* (Dublin, 1953). [written under the pseudonym David Hogan]

Gallagher, Frank. *The Indivisible Island, The Story of the Partition of Ireland.* (London, 1957).

Gallagher, Frank. *The Anglo-Irish Treaty.* (London, 1965).

Gallagher, Frank. *Days of Fear, A Diary of Hunger Strike.* (London, 1928).

Gaughan, J. Anthony, editor. *Memoirs of Constable J. Mee, RIC.* (Dublin, 1975).

Gleeson, James. *Bloody Sunday.* (London, 1962).

Gogarty, Oliver St John. *As I Was Walking Down Sackville Street.* (London, 1937).

Gogarty, Oliver St John. *It Isn't This Time of Year At All.* (London, 1954).

Golway, Terry. *For the Cause of Liberty: A Thousand Years of Ireland's Heroes.* (New York, 2000).

Good, Joe. *Enchanted by Dreams, The Journal of a Revolutionary,* edited by Maurice Good. (Tralee, 1996).

Grant, Neil. *The Easter Rising.* (New York, 1972).

Greaves, C. Desmond. *The Life and Times of James Connolly.* (London, 1961).

Greaves, C. Desmond. *Liam Mellowes and the Irish Revolution.* (London, 1971).

Greaves, C. Desmond. *The Irish Transport and General Workers Union: The Formative Years: 1909–1923.* (Dublin,1982).

Greaves, C. Desmond. *1916 as History: The Myth of the Blood Sacrifice.* (Dublin, 1991).

Griffith, Kenneth and Timothy O'Grady. *Ireland's Unfinished Revolution, An Oral History.* Originally published as *Curious Journey, An Oral History of Ireland's Unfinished Revolution.* (London, 1982).

Hart, Peter, editor. *British Intelligence in Ireland, 1920–21: The Final Reports.* (Cork, 2002).

Hart, Peter. *The I.R.A. at War, 1916–1923.* (Oxford, 2003).

Henry, Robert Mitchell. *The Evolution of Sinn Féin.* (Dublin, 1920).

Henry, William. *Supreme Sacrifice: The Story of Eamonn Ceannt, 1881–1916.* (Cork, 2005).

Hickey, D. J. *A New Dictionary of Irish History from 1800* (2004).

Hobson, Bulmer. *A Short History of the Irish Volunteers, 1913–1916.* (Dublin, 1918).

Holt, Edgar. *Protest in Arms: the Irish Troubles 1916–1923.* (London, 1960).

Hopkinson, Michael. *Green Against Green: a History of the Irish Civil War.* (Dublin, 1988).

Hopkinson, Michael, editor. *Frank Henderson's Easter Rising, Recollections of a Dublin Volunteer.* (Cork, 1998).

Hopkinson, Michael. *The Irish War of Independence.* (Dublin, 2004).

Horgan, J. J. *Parnell to Pearse.* (Dublin, 1948).

Hyland, J. L. *James Connolly.* (Dundalk, 1997).

Irish Free State Official Handbook. *Saorstát Éireann.* (Dublin, 1932).

Irish Times. *1916 Rebellion Handbook.* (Dublin, 1917).

Jeffrey, Keith. *Ireland and the Great War.* (Cambridge, 2000).

Kautt, William H. *The Anglo-Irish War, 1916–1921.* (Westport, Conn and London, 1999).

Kee, Robert. *The Green Flag* (combining three separate volumes entitled *The Most Distressful Country, The Bold Fenian Men* and *Ourselves Alone*). (London, 1972).

Kenny, Michael. *The Road to Freedom: Photographs and Memorabilia from the 1916 Rising and Afterwards.* (Dublin, 1993).

Kerryman, The. *Dublin's Fighting Story, 1916–1921, Told by the Men Who Made It.*

Kerryman, The. *With the I.R.A. in the Fight for Freedom, 1919 to the Truce, The Red Path of Glory.*

Killeen, Richard. *The Easter Rising.* (Hove, 1995).

Killeen, Richard. *Short History of Modern Ireland.* (Dublin, 2003).

Kostick, Conor. *Revolution in Ireland, Popular Militancy 1917 to 1923.* (London, 1996).

Kostick, Conor and Lorcan Collins. *The Easter Rising: A Guide to Dublin in 1916.* (Dublin, 2000).

Laffan, Michael. *The Partition of Ireland, 1911–1925.* (Dundalk, 1983).

Laffan, Michael. *The Resurrection of Ireland: The Sinn Féin Party 1916–1923.* (Cambridge, 1999).

Larkin, Emmet. *James Larkin, Irish Labour 1876–1947.* (London, 1965).

Lawlor, Sheila. *Britain and Ireland, 1914–1923.* (Dublin, 1983).

Laxton, Edward. *The Famine Ships: The Irish Exodus to America.* (London, 1996).

Lenihan, Eddie. *Defiant Irish Women.* (Cork, 1991).

LeRoux, Louis N. *Tom Clarke and the Irish Freedom Movement.* (Dublin, 1936).

LeRoux, Louis N. *Patrick H. Pearse.* Translated by Desmond Ryan. (Dublin, 1932).

Liam, Cathal. *Consumed in Freedom's Flame.* (Cincinatti, 2001).

Litton, Helen. *The Irish Civil War: An Illustrated History.* (Dublin, 1995).

Litton, Helen. *Irish Rebellions: An Illustrated History.* (Dublin, 1998).

Litton, Helen. *Cromwell: An Illustrated History.* (Dublin, 2000).

Llywelyn, Morgan. *1916.* (New York, 1998).

Llywelyn, Morgan. *A Pocket History of Irish Rebels.* (Dublin, 2000).

Llywelyn, Morgan. *1921.* (New York, 2001).

Luddy, Maria. *Hanna Sheehy Skeffington.* (Dundalk, 1995).

Lynch, Diarmuid. *The I.R.B. and the 1916 Insurrection.* (Cork, 1957).

Lynch, Mary C. and Seamus O'Donoghue. *O'Sullivan Burke, Fenian.* (Carrigadrohid, 1999).

Macardle, Dorothy. *Tragedies of Kerry 1922-1923.* (Dublin, 1998).

Macardle, Dorothy. *The Irish Republic.* (New York, 1937, 1965).

MacDowell, Vincent. *Michael Collins and the Irish Republican Brotherhood.* (Dublin, 1997).

MacEoin, Uinseonn, editor. *Survivors.* (Dublin, 1980).

Mackay, James. *Michael Collins: A Life.* (Edinburgh, 1996).

MacLochlainn, Pieras. *Last Words, Letters and Statements of the Leaders Executed after the Rising at Easter, 1916.* (Dublin, 1971).

MacManus, M. J. *Eamon De Valera.* (Dublin, 1944).

MacSwiney, Terence. *Principles of Freedom.* (Dublin, 1921, 1936).

Mac Thomais, Eamonn. *Down Dublin Streets, 1916.* (Dublin, 1965).

Maher, Jim. *Harry Boland, A Biography.* (Cork, 1998).

Malone, James. *Blood on the Flag, An Autobiography of a Freedom* Fighter. Translated by Patrick J. Twohig. (Ballincollig, 1996).

Marreco, Anne. *The Rebel Countess, The Life and Times of Constance Markievicz.* (London, 1967).

Martin, Francis X., O.S.A., editor, *The Irish Volunteers, 1913–1915.* (Dublin, 1963).

Martin, Francis X., O.S.A. The *Howth Gun-Running.* (Dublin, 1964).

Martin, Francis X., O.S.A., editor. *Leaders and Men of the Easter Rising.* (London, 1967).

Maye, Brian. *Arthur Griffith.* (Dublin, 1997).

McBride, Ian, editor. *History and Memory in Modern Ireland* (Cambridge, 2001).

McCoole, Sinead. *Hazel, A Life of Lady Lavery.* (Dublin, 1996).

McCoole, Sinead. *No Ordinary Women, Irish Female Activists in the Revolutionary Years.* (Dublin, 2003).

McCormack, John. *A Story of Dublin*. (Dublin, 2000).

McCormack, John. *A Story of Ireland*. (Dublin, 2002).

McDonnell, Kathleen Keyes. *There is a Bridge at Bandon*. (Cork, 1972).

McDowell, R. B. *The Irish Convention of 1917–1918*. (London, 1970).

McHugh, Roger, editor. *Dublin, 1916*. (London, 1966).

McKenna, Lambert. *The Social Teachings of James Connolly*. (Dublin, 1991).

McMahon, Sean. *Daniel O'Connell*. (Cork, 2000).

McMahon, Sean. *Charles Stewart Parnell*. (Cork, 2000).

McMahon, Sean. *Robert Emmet*. (Cork, 2001).

Moran, Sean Farrell. *Patrick Pearse and the Politics of Redemption*. (Washington, D.C. 1994).

Morgan, Austen. *James Connolly: A Political Biography*. (Manchester, 1988).

Moylan, Sean. *Sean Moylan: In His Own Words*. (Millstreet, 2003).

Moynihan, Maurice, editor. *The Speeches and Statements by Eamon de Valera, 1917–1973*. (Dublin, 1980).

Mulcahy, Risteard. *Richard Mulcahy (1886–1971), A Family Man*. (Dublin, 1999).

Mulholland, Marie. *The Politics and Relationships of Kathleen Lynn*. (Dublin, 2002).

Mulqueen, John and Jimmy Wren. *De Valera: An Illustrated Life*. (Dublin, 1989).

Murphy, Brian, P. *Patrick Pearse and the Lost Republican Ideal*. (Dublin, 1991).

Murphy, Brian, P. *John Chartres: Mystery Man of the Treaty*. (Dublin, 1995).

Neeson, Eoin. *The Civil War in Ireland*. (Cork, 1966).

Neeson, Eoin. *The Life and Death of Michael Collins*. (Cork, 1968).

Neeson, Eoin. *Birth of a Republic*. (Dublin, 1998).

Neill, Kenneth. *The Irish People*. (Dublin, 1979).

Neligan, David. *The Spy in the Castle*. London, 1999).

Nelson, Justin. *Michael Collins, The Final Days*. (Dublin, 1997).

Neville, Peter. *A Traveller's History of Ireland*. (London, 2002).

Nowlan, Kevin, editor. *The Making of 1916, Studies in the History of the Rising*. (Dublin, 1969).

O'Brien, Brendan. *History of the I.R.A.* (Dublin, 1997).

O'Brien, Conor Cruise. *States of Ireland*. (London, 1972).

O'Brien, William. *The Irish Revolution and How It Came About*. (London, 1923).

Ó Broin, Leon. *Dublin Castle and the 1916 Rising*. (London, 1970).

Ó Broin, Leon. *Revolutionary Underground: The Story of the I.R.B., 1858–1924*. (Dublin, 1976).

Ó Broin, Leon. *Michael Collins*. (Dublin, 1980).

Ó Broin, Leon. *In Great Haste: Letters of Michael Collins and Kitty Kiernan*. (Dublin, 1983).

Ó Buachalla, Séamus, editor. *The Letters of P. H. Pearse*. (London, 1980).

O'Callaghan, Seán. *Execution*. (London, 1974).

O'Casey, Seán (writing as P. Ó Cathasaigh). *The Story of the Irish Citizen Army*. (Dublin and London, 1919; re-issued London, 1980).

O'Casey, Seán. *Drums Under the Windows*. (London, 1945).

O'Connor, Batt. *With Michael Collins in the Fight for Independence*. (London, 1929).

O'Connor, Frank. *The Big Fellow: Michael Collins and the Irish Rebellion*. (London, 1937; re-issued Swords, 1979).

O'Connor, Frank. *An Only Child*. (London, 1961; re-issued London, 1970).

O'Connor, James. *History of Ireland: 1798–1924*. (London, 1929).

O'Connor, John. *The 1916 Proclamation*. (Dublin, 1986).

O'Connor, Ulick. *Michael Collins and the Troubles: The Struggle for Irish Freedom, 1912–1922*. (Edinburgh, 1975).

O'Connor, Ulick. *A Terrible Beauty is Born: The Irish Troubles, 1912–1922*. (London, 1975).

Ó Cuinneagain, Micheál. *On the Arm of Time*. (Donegal, 1992).

O'Donnell, Charles J. *Ireland in the Great War*. (Belfast, 1992).

O'Donoghue, Florence. *No Other Law*. (Dublin, 1954, 1986).

O'Donoghue, Florence. *Tomás MacCurtain, Soldier and Patriot*. (Tralee, 1971).

O'Donovan, Donal. *Kevin Barry and His Time*. (Glendale, 1989).

Ó Dubhghaill, M. *Insurrection Fires at Eastertide*. (Cork, 1966).

O'Farrell, Mick. *A Walk Through Rebel Dublin 1916*. (Cork, 1999).

O'Farrell, Padraic. *The Sean MacEoin Story.* (Dublin, 1981).

O'Farrell, Padraic. *The Ernie O'Malley Story.* (Dublin, 1983).

O'Farrell, Padraic. *The Blacksmith of Ballinalee.* (Mullingar, 1993).

O'Farrell, Padraic. *Who's Who in the Irish War of Independence and Civil War.* (Dublin, 1997).

O'Farrell, Padraic. *Rebel Heart.* (Dingle, 2001).

O'Farrell, Peter. *Memoirs of Irish Volunteer Activity, 1917–1924.* (New York, 1978).

O'Flaherty, Liam. *Insurrection.* (London, 1950, 1993).

O'Hegarty, P. S. *The Victory of Sinn Féin.* (Dublin, 1924, 1998).

O'Higgins, Brian. *The Soldier's Story of Easter Week.* (Dublin, 1925).

O'Higgins, Kevin. *Civil War and the Events that Led to It.* (Dublin, 1922).

O'Mahony, Seán. *Frongoch, University of Revolution.* (Killiney, 1987, 1995).

O'Mahony, Seán. *The Burning of the Custom House in Dublin, 1921.* (Dublin, 2000).

O'Malley, Ernie. *On Another Man's Wound.* (Dublin, 1936, 1979).

O'Malley, Ernie. *The Singing Flame.* (Dublin, 1978).

O'Malley, Ernie. *Raids and Rallies.* (Dublin, 1982).

O'Neill, Brian. *Easter Week.* (1939).

O'Neill, Marie. *Grace Gifford Plunkett and Irish Freedom, Tragic Bride of 1916.* (Dublin, 2000).

O'Sullivan, Michael. *Sean Lemass.* (Dublin, 1994).

O'Sullivan, Michael, and Bernadine O'Neill, *The Shelbourne and its People* (Dublin, 1999).

Osborne, Chrissy. *Michael Collins, Himself.* (Douglas, Co Cork, 2003).

Packenham, Frank. (Lord Longford), *Peace by Ordeal.* (London, 1935, 1972).

Packenham, Frank. (Lord Longford) and Thomas P. O'Neill, *Eamon de Valera, A Biography.* (Dublin, 1970).

Pearse, Padraig. *The Singer and Other Plays.* (Dublin, 1918).

Philips, Alison W. *The Revolution in Ireland, 1906–1923.* (London, 1923).

Pinkman, John A. *In the Legion of the Vanguard,* edited by Francis E. Maguire. (Cork, 1970, 1998).

Plunkett, James. *Strumpet City.* (Dublin, 2006).

Pringle, Peter and Philip Jacobson. *Those are Real Bullets, Aren't They?* (London, 2000).

Purdon, Edward. *The 1916 Rising.* (Cork, 1999).

Purdon, Edward. *The Civil War, 1922–23.* (Cork, 2000).

Purdon, Edward. *The Irish Famine.* (Cork, 2000).

Purdon, Edward. *The War of Independence.* (Cork, 2001).

Pyle, Hilary. *Susan Mitchell, Red-Headed Rebel.* (Dublin, 1998).

Ranelagh, John. *Ireland: An Illustrated History.* (London, 1981).

Reeve, Carl and Ann Barton. *James Connolly and the United States: The Road to the 1916 Irish Rebellion.* (Atlantic Highlands, N.J., 1978).

Roper, Esther, editor. *Prison Letters of Countess Markievicz.* (London, 1934).

Rossa, Jeremiah O'Donovan. *Irish Rebels in English Prisons.* (Dublin, 1991).

Ryan, Annie. *Witnesses: Inside the Easter Rising.* (Dublin, 2005).

Ryan, Desmond, editor. *The Story of a Success by P. H. Pearse, Being a Record of St. Enda's College, September 1908 to Easter 1916.* (Dublin, 1917).

Ryan, Desmond. *Michael Collins: The Invisible Army.* (Tralee, 1968).

Ryan, Desmond. *Remembering Sion: A Chronicle of Storm and Quiet.* (London, 1934).

Ryan, Desmond. *Sean Treacy and the Third Tipperary Brigade, I.R.A.* (Tralee, 1945).

Ryan, Desmond. *The Rising: The Complete Story of Easter Week.* (Dublin, 1949, 1957).

Ryan, Desmond. *The Fenian Chief: A Biography of James Stephens.* (Dublin, 1967).

Ryan, Desmond, editor, *The 1916 Poets.* (Dublin, 1995).

Ryan, Hugh Fitzgerald. *Reprisal.* (Dublin, 1989).

Ryan, Meda. *The Tom Barry Story.* (Dublin, 1982).

Ryan, Meda. *The Day Michael Collins Was Shot.* (Dublin, 1989).

Ryan, Meda. *Michael Collins and the Women in His Life.* (Dublin, 1996).

Sheehy, Jeanne, *The Rediscovery of Ireland's Past: The Celtic Revival 1830–1930.* (London, 1980).

Skinnider, Margaret. *Doing My Bit for Ireland.* (New York, 1917).

Spellissy, Sean. *The History of Limerick City.* (Limerick, 1998).

Spellissy, Sean. *A History of Clare.* (Dublin, 2003).

Stephens, James. *The Insurrection in Dublin.* (Gerrard's Cross, 1978).

Stewart, A. T. Q. editor, *Michael Collins: The Secret File.* (Belfast, 1997).

Street, Major C. J. C. *The Administration of Ireland, 1920.* (London, 1922).

Sturgis, Mark. *The Last Days of Dublin Castle: The Mark Sturgis Diaries* (Portland, 1999).

Taillon, Ruth. *When History Was Made: the Women of 1916.* (Belfast, 1996).

Talbot, Hayden. *Michael Collins's Own Story.* (London, 1923).

Tansill, Charles Callan. *America and the Fight for Irish Freedom 1866–1922.* (New York, 1957).

Taylor, Rex. *Michael Collins.* (London, 1970).

Thompson, William Irwin. *The Imagination of an Insurrection: Dublin, Easter 1916: a study of an ideological movement.* (West Stockbridge, Mass., 1967).

Toibin, Bairbre. *The Rising.* (Dublin, 2001).

Toolis, Kevin. *Rebel Hearts, Journeys Within the I.R.A.'s Soul.* (London, 1995).

Twohig, Patrick, J. *The Dark Secret of Bealnablath, The Michael Collins Story.* (Ballincollig, 1990).

Twohig, Patrick, J. *Green Tears for Hecuba* (Cork, 1994).

Valiulis, Maryann. *Portrait of a Revolutionary: General Richard Mulcahy and the Founding of the Irish Free State.* (Blackrock, 1992).

Van Voris, Jacqueline. *Constance de Markievicz: In the Cause of Ireland.* (Amherst, 1967).

Walsh, J. J. *Recollections of a Rebel: the Fenian Movement, Its Origins and Progress.* (Tralee, 1949).

Walker, Brian. *Past and Present: History, Identity and Politics in Ireland.* (Belfast, 2000).

Ward, Alan, J. *The Easter Rising: Revolution and Irish Nationalism.* (Arlington Heights, 1980).

Ward, Margaret. *Unmanageable Revolutionaries, Women and Irish Nationalism.* (Dingle, 1983).

Ward, Margaret. editor, *In Their Own Voice.* (Dublin, 1995, 2001).

Warwick-Haller, Adrian and Sally, editors. *Letters from Dublin, Easter 1916: Alfred Fannin's Diary of The Rising.* (Dublin, 1995).

Watts, J. F. and Sandra Stotsky, editors. *The Irish Americans, the Immigrant Experience.* (New York, 1996).

Weisser, Henry. *Ireland, An Illustrated History.* (New York, 1999).

Wells, Warre B. and N. Marlowe. *A History of the Irish Rebellion of 1916.* (Dublin, 1916).

White, Jack. *Misfit, A Revolutionary Life.* (Dublin, 1930, 2005).

White, Terence DeVere. *Kevin O'Higgins.* (Tralee, 1948, 1986).

Wilkinson, Burke. *The Zeal of the Convert. The Life of Erskine Childers.* (Washington, 1974).

Williams, Desmond. *The Irish Struggle, 1916–1926.* (London, 1966).

Winter, Ormonde. *Winter's Tale.* (London, 1955).

Yeates, Padraig, *Lockout: Dublin 1913.* (Dublin, 2000).

Yeates, Padraig and Jimmy Wren. *Michael Collins.* (Dublin, 1989).

Younger, Calton. *Ireland's Civil War.* (London, 1968).

Younger, Calton. *A State of Disunion.* (London, 1972).

Younger, Calton. *Arthur Griffith.* (Dublin, 1981).

## *Pamphlets, papers, periodicals*

Akenson, D.H. and J. F. Fallon. 'The Irish Civil War and the Drafting of the Free State Constitution', *Éire-Ireland*, Vol. 5 (1970).

Fr. Albert, O.F.M., Cap. 'Sean Heuston: How Sean Heuston Died', *The Capuchin Annual* (1966).

Bew, Paul. 'Moderate Nationalism and the Irish Revolution, 1916–1923', *The Historical Review*, Vol. XXVI (1999).

Bowden, Tom. 'Bloody Sunday, A Reappraisal', *European Studies Review*, Vol. II, No. 1 (1972).

Bowden, Tom. 'The Irish Underground and the War of Independence 1919–1921', *Journal of Contemporary History*, Vol. VIII, No. 2 (1973).

Bowman, Timothy. 'The Ulster Volunteers 1913–1914: Force or Farce?', *History Ireland*, Vol. 10, No. 1 (2002).Carey, Tim and Marcus de Burca. 'Bloody Sunday 1920: New Evidence', *History Ireland*, Vol. 11, No. 2 (2003).

Carroll, F. M., editor. *The American Commission on Irish Independence 1919: The Diary, Correspondence and Report*, Irish Manuscripts Commission (1985).

Catholic Bulletin. 'Easter Week and After: Eyewitness Accounts and Biographies', *Catholic Bulletin* (1916).

Clifford, Brendan. *The Irish Civil War: The Conflict that Formed the State* (Aubane, 1993).

Clifford, Brendan. *Casement as Traitor Patriot* (London, 2002).

Collins, Lorcan, Conor Kostick and Shane MacThomais. 'Tragedy in the Connolly Family', *History Ireland*, Vol. 12, No. 3 (2004).

Costello, F. 'The Republican Courts and the Decline of British Rule in Ireland', *Éire-Ireland*, Vol. XXV, No. 3 (1990).

Counahan, G. 'The People Backed the Movement 1920', *Capuchin Annual* (1970).

'Cross Border Reflections on 1916', report of a conference organised by Drogheda-Shankill Partnership (2001).

Courtney, D. A. *Reminiscences of the Easter Rising* (Nenagh, 1916, 1980).

Curran, Joseph. 'The Decline and Fall of the I.R.B.', *Éire-Ireland*, Vol. X, No. 1 (1975).

Curtis, Lionel. *Ireland*, with introduction 'The Anglo Irish Treaty and the Lost World of Imperial Ireland' by Pat Walsh (1991).

Davis, Richard. 'Arthur Griffith', *Dublin Historical Society* (1976).

Dowling, Michele. '"The Ireland That I Would Have": de Valera and the Creation of the Irish National Image', *History Ireland*, Vol. 5, No. 2 (1997).

Finch, Bruce-Andrew. 'Birth Pangs of a New Nation: Senator Thomas Westropp Bennett and the Irish Free State', *History Ireland*, Vol. 11, No. 4 (2003).

Fitzgerald, Garret. 'The Significance of 1916', *Studies: The Irish Jesuit Quarterly Review* (Spring, 1966).

Fitzpatrick, David. '"Decidedly a Personality": de Valera's Performance as a Convict, 1916–1917', *History Ireland*, Vol. 10, No. 2 (2002).

Gallagher, Michael. 'The Pact Election of 1922', *Irish Historical Studies*, Vol. XXI (1979).

Gough, General Hubert. 'The Situation in Ireland', *Review of Reviews*, Vol. LXIII (1921).

Harvey, A. D. 'Who Were The Auxiliaries?' *Historical Journal*, Vol. 35, No. 3 (1992).

Henderson, Frank. 'Irish Leaders of Our Time: Richard McKee', *An Cosantoir*, Vol. V (1945).

Horgan, John. 'Fianna Fáil and Arms Decommissioning, 1923–32', *History Ireland*, Vol. 6, No. 1 (1998).

*Irish Republican Digest, Featuring the Rising of 1916, Book 1*, National Publications Committee (Cork, 1965).

Jackson, Alvin. 'Larne Gun Running', 1914, *History Ireland*, Vol.1, No. 1 (1993).

Joyce, Toby, 'The American Civil War and Irish Nationalism', *History Ireland*, Vol. 4, No. 2 (1996).

Kavanagh, Sean. 'The Irish Volunteers' Intelligence Organisation', *The Capuchin Annual* (1969).

Kotsonouris, Mary. 'Revolutionary Justice: The Dáil Éireann Courts', *History Ireland*, Vol. 2, No. 3 (1994).

Kotsonouris, Mary. 'The George Gavan Duffy Papers', *History Ireland*, Vol. 8, No. 4 (2000).

Laffan, Michael. 'The Unification of Sinn Féin in 1917', *Irish Historical Studies*, Vol. XVII (1971).

Lawlor, Sheila. 'Ireland From Truce to Treaty, War or Peace? July to October 1921', *Irish Historical Studies*, Vol. XXII (1980).

Lysaght, D. R. O'Connor. 'The Rhetoric of Redmondism 1914–16', *History Ireland*, Vol. 11, No. 1 (2003).

Lynch, Robert. 'The Clones Affray, 1922: Massacre or Invasion?', *History Ireland*, Vol. 12, No. 3 (2004).

Martin, Francis X., O.S.A. 'Myth, Fact and Mystery', *Studia Hibernica*, Vol. 7 (1966).

Maume, Patrick. 'Lilly Connolly's Conversion', *History Ireland*, Vol. 2, No. 3 (1994).

McKenna, K. 'The Irish Bulletin', *The Capuchin Annual* (1970).

McMahon, Msgr. John T. *The Cream of their Race: Irish Truce Negotiations, December 1920–January 1921* (1970).

Mitchell, Angus. 'Casement's Black Diaries: Closed Books Reopened', *History Ireland*, Vol. 5, No. 3 (1997).

Mitchell, Angus. 'The Casement "Black Diaries" Debate: The Story So Far', *History Ireland*, Vol. 9, No. 2 (2001).

Mitchell, Angus, 'Robert Emmett and 1916', *History Ireland*, Vol. 11, No. 3 (2003).

Mulcahy, General Richard, 'Chief of Staff 1919',

*The Capuchin Annual* (1970).

Mulcahy, Risteard, 'The Mulcahy Tapes and Papers', *History Ireland*, Vol. 8, No. 1 (2003).

Murphy, Brian, 'The First Dáil Éireann', *History Ireland*, Vol. 2, No. 1, 1994.

Nevinson, H., 'The Anglo-Irish War', *Contemporary Review*, No. 667, July 1921.

O'Rahilly, Aodogan. 'The Civil War: A Teenager's Recollections 70 Years On', *Tipperary Historical Review* (1991).

O'Riain, Michael. 'Nelson's Pillar: a Controversy that Ran and Ran', *History Ireland*, Vol. 6, No. 4 (1998).

'Poets of the Insurrection', essays originally published in *Studies: The Irish Jesuit Quarterly Review* (1918).

Shaw, Rev. Francis S.J. 'The Canon of Irish History: A Challenge', *Studies: The Irish Jesuit Quarterly Review* (Summer, 1972).

Stapleton, William J. 'Michael Collins' Squad', *The Capuchin Annual* (1969).

Townshend, Charles. 'Bloody Sunday: Michael Collins Speaks', *European Studies Review*, Vol. IX (1979).

Townshend, Charles. 'The Irish Republican Army and the Development of Guerilla Warfare, 1916–1921', *English Historical Review*, Vol. XCIV (1979).

Trimble, W. D. *The Easter Rebellion of 1916* (1992).

Walsh, Paul V. 'The Irish Civil War, 1922–1923: A Military Study of the Conventional Phase, 28 June–11 August, 1922', paper delivered at the CUNY Graduate Center (11 December 1998).

Ward, Margaret. 'The League of Women Delegates and Sinn Féin, 1917', *History Ireland*, Vol. 4, No. 3 (1996).

Yeates, Padraig. 'The Dublin Lockout', 1913, *History Ireland*, Vol. 9, No. 2 (2001).

## Internet resources

McInerny, Colm. 'The Irish War of Independence and the I.R.A., 1916–1921', www.threemonkeysonline.com (2004).

'Voices of the Easter Rising' www.bbc.co.uk/easterrising/radio/index.

# Index to Historic Locations

Belvedere College: Great Denmark Street
Bennett, Cpt George: Mount Street Upper
Berkeley, George Fitz Hardinge: Howth, St
  Stephen's Green
Bewley's: Grafton Street, Henry Street
de Bhuitleir, Maire (Mary Ellen Butler): Great
  Britain Street
Birmingham, George: Merrion Square
Black and Tans: Middle Abbey Street, Jones
  Road/Croke Park, Seville Place
Blackadder, Brig Gen Charles: Grangegorman
  Road Upper
'The Block': Sackville Street Upper
Bloody Sunday: Airfield Road, Baggot Street
  Lower, Donnybrook, Dublin Castle, Earlsfort
  Terrace, Exchequer Street, Foley Street,
  Gardiner Street Lower, Great Britian Street,
  Great Denmark Street, Jones Road/ Croke Park,
  Lincoln Place, Merrion Square, Morehampton
  Road, Mount Street Lower, Mount Street
  Upper, North Circular Road/Cowley Place,
  Parliament Street, Pembroke Road Upper,
  Sackville Street Lower, Sackville Street Upper,
  St Stephen's Green/Shelbourne Hotel
Blythe, Ernest: North Circular Road/Mountjoy
  Prison, Dawson Street/Mansion House,
  Findlater Place, Harcourt Street, Kildare
  Street/Leinster House
Bodkin, Thomas: Lincoln Place, St Stephen's
  Green
Bohemians Football Club: Phibsborough Road/
  Dalymount Park
Boland, Gerald: Malahide Road, Vincent Street
Boland's Mills/Bakery: Grand Canal Street,
  Mount Street Bridge
Boland, Harry: Abbey Street Middle (tailor
  shop), Capel Street, Clontarf/Marino Casino,
  Cross Kevin Street, Dalymount Terrace (fam-
  ily home), Dawson Street/Mansion House,
  Elm Park/St Vincent's Hospital, Fairview
  Strand, Finglas Road/Glasnevin Cemetery,
  Harcourt Street, Lower Leeson Street,
  Lennox Street, Mary Street (tailor shop),
  Mountjoy Street, Moore Street, Nassau
  Street, Poplar Row/North Strand Road,
  Rutland Square, Sackville Street Lower,
  Sackville Street Upper, Skerries, Synge
  Street, Wexford Street, Whitefriar Street
Bollard, Stephen: North Frederick Street
Bourke, Mary: North Circular Road/Mountjoy
  Prison

Bowen-Colthurst, Cpt J. C.: Baggot Street Upper,
  Camden Street Lower, Rathmines Road
Boyle, Jeannie: Jones Road/Croke Park
Bracken, Peadar: Sackville Street Lower
Brady, Christopher: Beresford Place/Liberty Hall
Breen, Dan: Ashtown/Co Dublin, Church
  Street, Eccles Street, Foley Street, Grantham
  Street, Great Britain Street, Phibsborough
  Road, Talbot Street,Whitehall/Drumcondra
Brennan, James: Bachelor's Walk
Brennan, Dr J. P.: Sackville Street Upper
Brennan, Patrick: Earlsfort Terrace, Harcourt
  Street
Brennan, Robert: Dawson Street/Mansion
  House, Harcourt Street, Molesworth Street
Brennan-Whitmore, Cdt W. J.: Parliament
  Street, Sackville Street Lower
Brien, Vincent: Cullenswood Avenue
Brind, Col J.: Dawson Street/Mansion House
Broadstone Railway Station: Constitution Hill
Brown, Sean: Dawson Street/Mansion House
Browne, Rev Dr Paddy: Kimmage, Pembroke
  Road, Rutland Square
Browning, F. H.: Herbert Park, Northumberland
  Road
Broy, Eamonn (Ned): Arbour Hill, Cabra Road,
  Dawson Street, Great Brunswick Street,
  Westland Row
Brugha, Cathal (Charles Burgess): Beresford
  Place/Liberty Hall, Dawson
  Street/Mansion House, Earlsfort Terrace,
  Eccles Street/Berkeley Road, Findlater
  Place, Finglas Road/Glasnevin Cemetery,
  Frederick Street North, Gardiner Row,
  Gardiner Street Lower, Gregg Lane,
  Harcourt Street, Herbert
  Park/Donnybrook, James's Street/South
  Dublin Union, Jones Road/Croke Park,
  Ormond Quay Lower, Rathmines Road/
  Portobello Barracks, Rutland Square,
  Sackville Street Upper
Budd, Kickham: St John's Terrace/Blackrock
Bulfin, Eamon: Dawson Street/Mansion House
Bullock, Cpl: King Street North
Butler, J. M.: Amiens Street
Butler, Mary Ellen (Maire de Bhuitleir): Great
  Britain Street
Byrne, Charley: Crow Street
Byrne, John: Beresford Place/Liberty Hall, Foley
  Street
Byrne, John Joseph: Manor Place

St Thomas's: Marlborough Street/corner of
Findlater Place
St Werburgh's: Werburgh Street
Union Chapel: Abbey Street Lower
CID, Oriel House: Westland Row
Cinemas
Capitol: Prince's Street North
La Scala: Prince's Street North
The Lyceum: Mary Street
Rotunda Picture House (The Ambassador):
Great Britain Street
Volta Electric: Mary Street
Clancy, Peadar: Dublin Castle, Finglas
Road/Glasnevin Cemetery, Foley Street,
Gardiner Street Lower, Gloucester Place,
Talbot Street
Clarke, Austin: Fleet Street
Clarke, Henry (Harry): Arbour Hill, Francis
Street, North Frederick Street, Grafton Street
Clarke, Joseph: Cullenswood Avenue
Clarke, Kathleen: Bachelor's Walk, Charlemont
Street, College Green, Dawson
Street/Mansion House, Eccles Street,
Exchequer Street, Harcourt Street, Oakley
Road, Richmond Avenue/Fairview, Rutland
Square, Sackville Street Upper, South
William Street
Clarke, Philip: Cork Street, St Stephen's Green
Clarke, Tom: Amiens Street, Dolphin's Terrace,
Findlater Place, Gardiner Row, Great Britain
Street, Hardwicke Street, Herbert
Park/Ballbridge, King's Inns Street,
Mountjoy Street, Richmond
Avenue/Fairview, Rutland Square, Sackville
Lane
Clery's Department Store: Sackville Street
Lower
Clonmel House: Harcourt Street
Clune, Archbishop: Merrion Square, St
Stephen's Green
Clune, Conor: Dublin Castle, Merrion Square,
Rutland Square, St Stephen's Green
Coade, J. J.: Finglas Road/Glasnevin Cemetery,
Mount Pleasant Avenue Upper, Rathmines
Road
Coffey, Denis J.: Earlsfort Terrace
Coffey, Dermot: Howth
Cogan's Green Grocer: Moore Lane/Henry Place
Cogley, Fred: Findlater Place
Colbert, Con: Abbey Street Lower, Ardee Street,
Camden Street Lower, Cullenswood

Avenue, Great Brunswick Street, James's
Street/South Dublin Union, Kildare Street,
Rutland Square
Coleman, Dick: Ashbourne garrison (Rising),
Harcourt Street
Coles, Alderman Walter: Mountjoy Square
Colivet, Michael P.: Amiens Street, Earlsfort
Terrace, Harcourt Street
College of Surgeons, Royal: St Stephen's Green
(West)
Collins, Con: Amiens Street, Dawson
Street/Mansion House, North Circular Road,
Frederick Street North
Collins, Maurice: Cabra Park, Great Britain
Street
Collins, Michael
*Intelligence offices*: Bachelor's Walk, Camden
Street, Cullenswood Avenue, Henry Street,
Mespil Road/Ballsbridge
*Ministry of Finance offices*: Bachelor's Walk,
Harcourt Street, Henry Street, Mespil
Road/ Ballsbridge, Mary Street, Harcourt
Terrace
*Offices:* Bachelor's Walk, College Street,
Great Britain Street, Great Brunswick
Street, Harcourt Street, Harcourt Terrace,
Henry Street, Mary Street, Mespil
Road/Ballsbridge, Portobello Road, St
Andrew Street
*Residences*: Airfield Road/Rathgar, Brendan
Road/Donnybrook, Morehampton Road,
Mountjoy Square, Mountjoy Street,
Richmond Road, Rathdown Road
*Other:* Abbey Street Upper and Liffey Street,
Baggot Street Lower, Berkeley Road,
Botanic Road/Glasnevin, Brendan
Road/Donnybrook, Cabra Road, Church
Street/Howth, North Circular
Road/Mountjoy Prison, Crow Street, Dame
Street, Dawson Street, Dublin Castle,
Earlsfort Terrace, Elm Park, Gardiner Row,
Gardiner Street Lower, Hadden
Road/Clontarf, Harbour Road/Howth,
Herbert Park/Ballsbridge Jones Road,
Leeson Street Lower, Lisburn, Malahide
Road, Marino Casino/Clontarf,
Marlborough Street, Merrion Square,
Mespil Road, Moore Street, Mountjoy
Street, Nassau Street, Parkgate Street,
Parliament Street, Rathgar, Richmond
Road/Drumcondra, Rutland Square,

Dáil Éireann: Middle Abbey Street at corner of O'Connell Street, Brendan Road, Camden Street Lower, Dawson Street/Mansion House, Earlsfort Terrace, Harcourt Street, Kildare Street, Molesworth Street, Mountjoy Square, Ormond Quay

Dáil Loan: Cross Kevin Street, Dawson Street/Mansion House, Harcourt Street, Ormond Quay, Parliament Street

Dalton, Charlie: Crow Street, Pembroke Street Upper

Dalton, Emmet: Bridgefort Street, St Columba's Road Upper/Drumcondra, Sydney Parade

Daly, Edward (Ned): Blackhall Place, Brunswick Street North, Church Street, Four Courts (Rising), Grangegorman Road Upper, Richmond Avenue/Fairview, Sackville Street Upper, Yarnhall Street

Daly, Frank: Dolphin's Barn

Daly, John: Findlater Place

Daly, Paddy: Ashtown/Co Dublin, Gardiner Street Lower, Great Britain Street, Harcourt Street, King's Inns Quay, Phoenix Park/Magazine Fort

Daly, P. T.: Beresford Place

Dalymount Park: Phibsborough Road

'The Dardanelles' area (so-called during the Tan War): Lower Camden Street/Wexford Street/Aungier Street/South Great Georges Street

Davis, Thomas: Baggot Street Lower, College Green (statue)

Davitt, Michael: Military Road/Ballybrack

Deakin, James: Abbey Street Lower, Kildare Street

Deasy, Liam: Dawson Street/Mansion House, Great Denmark Street, Harcourt Street, Wellington Quay

Delaney family home: Heytesbury Street

de Loughrey, Peter: Harcourt Street

Derby, Lord: Sackville Street Upper

de Roiste, Liam: Earlsfort Terrace, Harcourt Street

de Valera, Eamon

   *Command:* Boland's Bakery, Mount Street Bridge

   *Family homes:* Claremont Road/Sandymount, Cross Avenue, Greystones, Merrion View Avenue, Morehampton Terrace/Donnybrook, Munster Street/Phibsborough

   *Offices of the President:* Glenvar/Blackrock, Kenilworth Square, Loughnavale/Strand Road (Merrion)

   *Other:* Burgh Quay, Dawson Street/Mansion House, Grand Canal Street, Grattan Street, Fitzwilliam Square, Harcourt Street, Herbert Park/Donnybrook, Jones Road, Merrion Square, Mountjoy Street, Rutland Square, Sackville Street Upper, Suffolk Street, Tara Street, Wellington Street

de Valera, Sinead: Morehampton Terrace/Donnybrook

Devlin, Pat: Findlater Place

Dicker, Madeline 'Dilly': Mountjoy Street

Dickson, Thomas (*The Eye Opener*): College Green, Finglas Road/Glasnevin Cemetery, Harrington Street, Rathmines Road

Dietrichsen, Cpt F. C.: Northumberland Road

Dillon Family: Moore Street

Dillon, Col Hill: Parkgate Street

Dillon, John: Dawson Street/Mansion House, Earlsfort Terrace, North Great George's Street, Harcourt Street

Dillon, Dr Thomas: Dawson Street/Mansion House

Dillon, Mrs Thomas (nee Geraldine Plunkett): Sackville Street Upper

Doherty, Seamus and Mrs: Connaught Street/Drumcondra

Dolan, Joe: Crow Street, Wicklow Street

Dominicans, Holy Faith School: Dominick Street

Donnelly, E: Harcourt Street

Donnelly, Michael: St Stephen's Green (west)

Donnelly, Simon: North Circular Road/Mountjoy Prison, South Circular Road/Kilmainham Gaol, Earlsfort Terrace, Mount Street Lower, St Stephen's Green (south)

Donovan, Timothy: Larchfield Road/Inchicore:

Doran, William: Wicklow Street

Dore, Eamonn: Dolphin's Barn

Dorrins, Tommy: Church Road/East Wall, Custom House Quay

Douglas, James: Church Street, Dawson Street/Mansion House

Dowling, Maj: Pembroke Street Upper

Dowling, Sean: Gardiner Row

Downe's Bakeries: North Earl Street

Doyle, Archie: Booterstown

Flood, Sgt: King Street North

Flood, Frank: Church Street, North Circular Road/Cowley Place, Earlsfort Terrace, Summerhill Parade

Fogarty, Most Rev Dr Michael: Dawson Street/Mansion House, Merrion Square

Foley, Margaret: Charleston Road

Foran, Thomas: Beresford Place/Liberty Hall

Forester's Hall (Irish National Forester's Hall): Rutland Square

Four Courts: King's Inns Quay
    *Shelling of:* Bridgefoot Street, Winetavern Street, Wood Quay

Fowler Memorial Hall: Rutland Square

France, C.P.: Dawson Street/Mansion House

Franciscan Capuchin Friary: Church Street

Freemason's Hall: Molesworth Street

Furlong, Matt: Parkgate Street, Rutland Square

The Gael Co-Op Society Ltd: Abbey Street Middle

Gaelic Athletic Association (GAA): Dalymount Park, Grafton Street, Sackville Street Lower and Eden Quay, Sackville Street Upper

Gaelic League: Blackhall Street, Frederick Street North (Keating Branch), Great Britain Street, Harcourt Street, Kimmage, Rutland Square (Coisde Gnotha Branch), Sackville Street Upper

Gallagher, Frank (David Hogan): Beechwood Avenue, Charleston Road, North Circular Road/Cowley Place, Fleet Street, Harcourt Street, Molesworth Street, Wellington Road, York Street

Gallagher, Lord Mayor James: Dawson Street/Mansion House

Galligan, Paul: Earlsfort Terrace, Harcourt Street

Gandon, James: Custom House Quay/Custom House, King's Inns Quay/Four Courts, Mecklenburg Street

Gannon, Bill: Booterstown

Garner, Auxiliary Cadet: Mount Street Lower

Gay, Thomas: Capel Street/Municipal Library

Georgius Rex: Northumberland Road

'German Plot', the: Capel Street, Harcourt Street, Mountjoy Street

Gifford, Grace (Plunkett): South Circular Road/Kilmainham Gaol, Dawson Street/Mansion House, Finglas Road/Glasnevin Cemetery, Grafton Street, James's Street, Kimmage/Larkfield, Nassau Street, Oakley Road, Sackville Street Lower Temple Villas/Palmerston Road, Thomas Street

Gifford, Muriel (MacDonagh): Finglas Road/Glasnevin Cemetery, Oakley Road

Gilbey's wine shops: Fairview Strand, Sackville Street Upper

Gill's Confectioners: Middle Gardiner Street

M. H. Gill & Co: Upper Sackville Street

Ginnell, Alice: Oakley Road

Ginnell, Laurence: Dawson Street/Mansion House, Kildare Street/Leinster House

Gleeson & Co: Upper Sackville Street

Glasnevin Cemetery: Finglas Road

Gogan, Liam: Kildare Street

Gogarty, Oliver St John: Abbey Street Lower, Baggot Street Lower, Brunswick Street North, Duke Street, Earlsfort Terrace, Elm Park, Ely Place Upper, Leeson Street Lower, Merrion Square, Richmond Street North, Rutland Square, St Stephen's Green

Gonne, Maud (MacBride): Abbey Street Lower, Charlemont Street, South Circular Road/Kilmainham Gaol, Clarendon Street, Clonskeagh/Roebuck House, Coulson Avenue, Finglas Road/Glasnevin Cemetery, Harcourt Street, St Stephen's Green

Good, Joe W.: Eccles Street, Findlater Place, Gloucester Street, Parkgate Street, Richmond Road, Rutland Square, Sackville Street Lower

Goodfellow, Kathleen: Fleet Street

Gore, John: Cavendish Row, Kildare Street

Grace, James: Longwood Avenue, Northumberland Road, St Stephen's Green (South)

Great Lockout of 1913: Abbey Street Middle, Aungier Street, Beresford Place/Liberty Hall, Bishop Street, Church Street, Clontarf/Croydon Park, Eden Quay, Foley Street, Frederick Street North, Great Britain Street, Great Brunswick Street, Sackville Street Lower, Townsend Street

Green, Alice Stopford: Cullenswood Avenue, Howth, Rathfarnham/The Hermitage, St Stephen's Green

Gregory, Augusta Lady: Harcourt Street

Grenan (Grennan?), Julia: Sir John Rogerson's Quay

Grey, Mrs: Pembroke Street Upper

Baggot Street (customary name for The
     Royal City of Dublin Hospital):
Baggot Street Upper
Bon Secours: Glasnevin
Coombe Maternity: Cork Street/Dolphin's
     Barn, The Coombe
Dr. Steevens': Steevens Lane
'Fever' Hospital: Cork Street at Marrowbone
     Lane
King George V (St Bricin's Military):
     Infirmary Road, Montpelier Gardens
Hardwicke: Brunswick Street North
Holles Street (officially National Maternity
     Hospital): Holles Street
Jervis Street (originally Charitable
     Infirmary): Jervis Street
Mater Misericordiae (Mater Hospital):
     Berkeley Road/Eccles Street
Mercer's: Mercer Street
National Children's: Harcourt St
National Maternity Hospital: Holles Street
     (usually known as Holles Street Hospital)
North Dublin Union: Brunswick Street North
Portobello: Richmond Street and
     Charlemont Mall, overlooking Portobello
     Bridge
Richmond: Brunswick Street North
Rotunda: Great Britain Street
Royal City of Dublin: Baggot Street Upper
Royal Victoria Eye and Ear Hospital:
     Adelaide Road
St Ultan's Children's: Charlemont Street
St Vincent's: Elm Park
St Vincent's Private Hospital: Leeson Street
     Lower
Simpson's: Great Britain Street (William's
     and Woods Factory)
Sir Patrick Dun's: Fitzwilliam Street Lower
South Dublin Union: James's Street
Dr Steevens': Steevens' Lane
Temple Street Children's: Temple Street
Hotels
     Aras na nGael: Mountjoy Street
     Barry's: Great Denmark Street
     Brazen Head: Bridge Street Lower
     Buswell's: Molesworth Street
     Central: Exchequer Street
     Clarence: Wellington Quay
     Crown: Sackville Street Upper
     Doherty's: Bridge Street Lower
     Douglas: Eden Quay

Edinburgh Temperance: Sackville Street
     Upper
Elliot: Harcourt Street
Exchange (Royal Exchange): Parliament Street
Finn's: Leinster Street
Fleming's: Gardiner Row
Grand: Sackville Street Lower
Grand: Skerries
Granville: Sackville Street Upper
Gresham: Sackville Street Upper
Hammam: Sackville Street Upper
Hughes: Gardiner Street
Imperial: Sackville Street Lower
Ivanhoe: Harcourt Street
Metropole: Sackville Street Lower
Moran's: Gardiner Street Lower/Talbot Street
Morrison's: Dawson Street
Munster Private: Mountjoy Street
North Star: Amiens Street
Northumberland Commercial and Family:
     Beresford Place
Ossary: Great Denmark Street
Plaza: Gardiner Row
Royal Exchange: see Exchange
Royal Hibernian: Dawson Street
Russell: Harcourt Street
Shelbourne: St Stephen's Green (North)
Standard: Harcourt Street
Vaughan's: Rutland Square
Waverley: Sackville Street Lower
Wicklow: Wicklow Street
Wynn's: Abbey Street Lower
Howth Rifles: Bachelor's Walk, Cavendish Row,
     Howth, Molesworth Street, Mountjoy
     Street, Ormond Quay, St Stephen's Green
Hoyte's Druggists and Oilworks: Sackville
     Street Lower
Hughes, Michael: King Street North
Hughes, Sally: King Street North
Hume, Walter: College Green
Humphrey, Mary Ellen: Ailesbury Road
Humphrey, Richard: Ailesbury Road
Humphrey, Sheila: Ailesbury Road, South
     Circular Road/Kilmainham Gaol
Hunter, Tom: Harcourt Street, Talbot Street
Hyde, Douglas: Cullenswood Avenue,
     Earlsfort Place, Mount Street Upper,
     Rathfarnham/ The Hermitage, see also
     Gaelic League
Hyland, C. Hanchette: King Street South, Percy
     Place

Oakley Road/Ranelagh, Wicklow Street
Kilcoyne, Tom: Ashtown/Co Dublin
Killeen, Susan: Dawson Street, Harbour
Road/Howth, Mountjoy Street
Kilmainham Gaol: South Circular Road
Kilroy, Michael: Dawson Street/Mansion
House
King, Cpt: Dublin Castle
King, Michael: Crown Alley
King's Own Scottish Borderers: Bachelor's Walk
Kissane, Mrs: Hardwicke Street

Lalor Ltd: Ormond Quay
Lamb Doyle's: Sandyford
Larkin, James (Baker): Meath Street
Larkin, James: Auburn Street, Beechwood
Avenue Upper/Ranelagh, Beresford Place/
Liberty Hall, North Circular Road, North
Frederick Street, Gardiner Place, Great
Brunswick Street, Leinster Road/Rathmines,
North Strand/Creighton House, Oakley
Road/Ranelagh, Sackville Street
Lower,Wellington Road/Ballsbridge
Latchford, Robert: Temple Bar
Lavery, John: Harcourt Street
Lawless, Peadar: King Street North
Lawlor, Fintan: Harcourt Street
Lawlor's: Fownes Street
Lawlor's Candles: East Wall Road
Lawrence's Bazaar: Sackville Street Upper/cor-
ner of Cathedral Street
Legion of Mary: Corporation Street, Francis
Street
Leinster House: Kildare Street
Lenehan, James: Kildare Street
Leonard, Joe: Ashtown/Co Dublin, Baggot Street
Lower, North Circular Road/Mountjoy
Prison
Lemass, Noel: Capel Street
Lemass, Sean: Baggot Street Lower, Capel
Street, Pembroke Road, Suffolk Street
Liberty Hall: Beresford Place
Liddy, Sean: Harcourt Street
Limerick Clothing Factory: Bridge Street Lower
Linen Hall: Linenhall Street
Linenhall Barracks: Lisburn Street, Yarnhall
Street
Little, Patrick J. (Paddy): Abbey Street Middle,
Fleet Street, Kimmage/Larkfield, Rathgar
Road
Lockout of 1913: see Great Lockout

Lonergan, Michael: Kildare Street, Rutland Square
Loreto Convent: St Stephen's Green
Lowe, General W. H. M.: College Green, Great
Britain Street, King Street North, Moore
Street
Lynch, Col. Arthur: Kildare Street
Lynch, Dermot (Diarmuid): Dawson Street/
Mansion House, Jones Road/Croke Park,
Rutland Square
Lynch Fionan: North Circular Road/Mountjoy
Prison, Dawson Street/Mansion House,
Kildare Street, Mountjoy Street
Lynch, John Aloysius: Parliament Street
Lynch, Liam: Dawson Street, DeCourcy Square,
Kildare Street/Leinster House, Parliament
Street, Rutland Square, Summerhill Road,
Wellington Quay
Lynn, Dr Kathleen: Belgrave Road/Rathmines,
Charlemont Street, South Circular Road,
Dawson Street/Mansion House, Oakley
Road, Peter Street
Lyons, Brigid (Thornton): Church Street Upper,
Fitzwilliam Place, King's Inns Quay/Four
Courts (Rising), Marlborough Street

Macardle, Dorothy: South Circular Road/
Kilmainham Gaol
MacBride, John: Abbey Street Middle, Bishop
Street/Jacob's Biscuit Factory (Rising),
Finglas Road/Glasnevin Cemetery, Wicklow
Street
MacBride, Maud Gonne: see Gonne, Maud
MacBride, Sean: Clonskeagh/Roebuck House,
Finglas Road/Glasnevin Cemetery, St
Stephen's Green
MacCormack, Cpt Patrick: Sackville Street
MacCullough, Denis: Findlater Place
MacDermott, (MacDiarmada) Sean: Abbey
Street Lower, Falls Road, Dawson Street,
Findlater Place, Gardiner Street, Great
Britain Street, Harcourt Street, Hardwicke
Street, Herberton Road/Rialto, Kildare
Street, Nassau Street, Rathgar Road, Russell
Place, Rutland Square
MacDonagh, John: Bishop Street/Jacob's Biscuit
Factory
MacDonagh, Joseph: Cullenswood Avenue
MacDonagh, Thomas: Abbey Street Lower,
Beresford Place, Bride Street/Ross Road,
Capel Street, Cullenswood Avenue, Dawson
Street, Hardwicke Street, Herberton

Maguire, Sam: Sackville Street Lower

Mahaffey, Dr J. P.: College Green, Grafton Street/Provost's House

Maher, Daniel: Westland Row

Mahoney, Sean: Gardiner Row, Sackville Street Upper

Malley, Cecil: Sackville Street Upper

Mallin, Michael: Dolphin's Barn, St Stephen's Green (West)/College of Surgeons, York Street

Malone, Andrew: Fleet Street

Malone, Lt Michael: Northumberland Road

Malone, Mrs: Grantham Street

Maloney, Frank: Sherrard Street

Mansion House: Dawson Street

Mannix, Sgt: Donnybrook

Markievicz, Count Casimir: Lincoln Place, St Stephen's Green

Markievicz, Countess Constance (neé Gore Booth):

   *Homes:* Frankfort Avenue/Rathgar, Leinster Road/Rathmines (Surrey House), Mount Street Lower, St Edward's Terrace/Rathgar

   *Offices:* Dame Street, North Frederick Street, Leinster Road/Rathmines

   *Other:* Belcamp Park/Raheny, Beresford Place, Camden Street Lower, Charlemont Street, Clontarf/Croydon Park, Dawson Street/Mansion House, Eccles Street, Fitzwilliam Street Lower, North Great George's Street, Harcourt St, Sherrard Street, St Stephen's Green, York Street

Marrowbone Lane Distillery: Marrowbone Lane

Martin, Eamon: Kildare Street, Rutland Square

Martyn, Edward: Cullenswood Avenue, Hardwicke Street

Mason, Susan (Sinead): Brendan Road

Masonic Lodge: Molesworth Street

Father Mathew Hall: Church Street

Matthews, Mrs: King Street North

'Maudie' (the maid): Upper Pembroke Road

Maunsel & Co: Abbey Street Middle

Maxwell, Gen Sir John: Parkgate Street

Mee, Constable Jeremiah: Frederick Street North, Molesworth Street

Mellows, Liam: Camden Street Lower, North Circular Road/Mountjoy Prison, Dawson Street/Mansion House, Earlsfort Terrace, Harcourt Street, Herbert Park/Ballsbridge, Kildare Street/Leinster House, King's Inns Quay, Wellington Street

Mellows, Mrs: Mountshannon Road

Mendicity Institute: Usher's Island

Meredith, James Creed: Dawson Street/Mansion House, Merrion Square

Merin, Lily: Mary Street, Parkgate Street

'Methusiliers' (Georgius Rex): Northumberland Road

Middleton, Lord: Dawson Street

Military Archives: Rathmines Road/Portobello Barracks

Military Council (IRB): Amiens Street, Clontarf Town Hall, Dawson Street, Dolphin's Barn, Dolphin's Terrace, Rutland Square

Milroy, Sean: Dawson Street/Mansion House, Harcourt Street, Mountjoy Street, Talbot Street

Mitchel, John: Ontario Terrace

Mitchell, Susan: Frankfort Ave/Rathgar, Leinster Road, Lincoln Place, Merrion Square, Rathgar Avenue, Rathmines Road, St Stephen's Green, Wesley Road

Moira, Lord and Countess: Usher's Island

Molloy, Michael: Beresford Place

Molly Malone Statue: Grafton Street/corner of Suffolk Street

Molony, Helena: Belgrave Road, Charlemont Street, Dawson Street/Mansion House, Eccles Street, Oakley Road, Sherrard Street

Monks' Bakery: Church Street Upper

Montgomery, Col: Pembroke Road Upper

'Monto': Montgomery Street

Mooney, James: Rutland Square

Moore, James: King Street North

Moore, Col Maurice: Great Britain Street, Kildare Street, Rutland Square

Moore's Coach Factory: Great Brunswick Street

Moore, Thomas: Aungier Street

Morgue (Dublin City): Store Street

Moran, D. P. (*The Leader*): Abbey Street Lower

Moran, Patrick: Baggot Street Lower, Bishop Street/Jacob's Biscuit Factory, North Circular Road/Mountjoy Prison, Sackville Street Upper

Morris, Auxiliary Cadet: Mount Street Lower

Morrow, Jack: Fleet Street

Mountjoy Prison: North Circular Road/Cowley Place

*The Nation*: Abbey Street Middle
*Northern Star*: Findlater Place
*The Press*: Findlater Place
*The Republic* (Darrell Figgis, editor): Ormond Quay
*Scissors & Paste* (Arthur Griffith, editor): Abbey Street Middle
*Sinn Féin* (Bulmer Hobson, then Arthur Griffith, editors): Abbey Street Middle, Fownes Street
*The Spark* (James Connolly, editor; later Patrick McIntyre was editor): North Great George's Street, Leinster Road
*Sport*: Abbey Street Middle
*Studies*: Leeson Street Lower
*The Toiler* (Patrick MacIntyre, editor, printed by the Western News Company): Ballinasloe, Co Galway
*United Irishmen* (Arthur Griffith, editor): Fownes Street
*The Worker* (James Connolly, editor): Beresford Place/Liberty Hall, Eccles Street
*The Worker's Republic* (James Connolly, editor): Eccles Street, Leinster Road
Noblett's confectioners: Sackville Street Lower
Nolan, James: Beresford Place/Liberty Hall, Foley Street
Noonan, Michael: King Street North
Norgrove, George: Strandville Avenue
Norman, Harry: Lincoln Place
Norway, Arthur Hamilton: Dawson Street, Merrion Avenue/'South Hill'
Nowlan, Alderman: Jones Road/Croke Park
Nugent, Larry: Harcourt Street, Mount Street Upper
Nugent, Mrs Larry: Mount Street Upper

Oates, Col: James's Street, Northumberland Road
O'Brennan, Lily: South Circular Road/Kilmainham Gaol
O'Briain, Liam: Beresford, Place, Fleet Street, Rathgar Road
O'Brien, Art: Dawson Street/Mansion House
O'Brien, Conor: Howth
O'Brien, Dermot: Lincoln Place, St Stephen's Green
O'Brien, Frank Cruise: Lincoln Place, Merrion Square, St Stephen's Green
O'Brien, George: Merrion Square
O'Brien Institute: Malahide Road
O'Brien, James (Constable): Dublin Castle

O'Brien, Nancy: Botanic Road/Glasnevin, Dublin Castle, Harbour Road/Howth
O'Brien, Nora Connolly: *see* Connolly O'Brien, Nora
O'Brien, William (Bill): Belvedere Place, Beresford Place/Liberty Hall, Dawson Street/Mansion House, Rutland Square
O'Byrne, John: Dawson Street/Mansion House
O'Callahan, Kate, Mrs Michael: Eccles Street
O'Carroll Richard (Councillor): Camden Street, Portobello Road
O'Carroll, Ely: Peter's Place
O'Casey, Sean: Beresford Place/Liberty Hall, Camden Street/Bleeding Horse Pub, North Circular Road, Dominick Street Lower, Dorset Street Upper, Eccles Street, Findlater Place, Rathfarnham/The Hermitage, Sackville Street Lower
O'Conaire, Padraic: Fleet Street
O'Connell, Daniel: Merrion Square, Molesworth Street
O'Connell, General J. J. 'Ginger': Baggot Street Lower, Dawson Street, Earlsfort Terrace, Gardiner Row, Herbert Park/Ballsbridge
O'Connell, Sean: Rutland Square
O'Connor, Art: Dawson Street/Mansion House
O'Connor, Batt: Brendan Road, Great Britain Street, Harcourt Street, Mary Street, Morehampton Road, Parkgate Street
O'Connor, Joseph (J. J.): Abbey Street, Dawson Street, Earlsfort Terrace
O'Connor, Rory: North Circular Road/Mountjoy Prison, Dawson Street/Mansion House, Earlsfort Terrace, Fleet Street, Kimmage/Larkfield, King's Inns Quay, Monkstown, Sackville Street Upper
O'Connor, Seamus: Abbey Street Lower/Wynn's Hotel, Kildare Street
O'Donnell, Lily (Private Nursing Home): Eccles Street
O'Donnell, Peadar: Dawson Street/Mansion House
O'Donoghue, Denis: Northumberland Road
O'Donoghue, Florrie: Dawson Street/Mansion House, Sackville Street Lower (GPO)
O'Donovan, Mrs Julia (dairies): Mespil Road, Rathgar Road
O'Donovan Rossa, Jeremiah: Mountjoy Street
O'Donovan, Seamus: Dawson Street/Mansion House

Ormond Hotel: Ormond Quay

O'Shannon, Cathal: Dawson Street/Mansion House, Kildare Street/Leinster House

O'Sullivan, Gearoid: Clontarf/Marino Casino, Dawson Street/Mansion House, Eustace Street, Frederick Street North, Harcourt Street, Mespil Road, Sackville Street Lower/General Post Office, Sackville Street Upper

O'Toole, Luke: Jones Road/Croke Park

O'Toole, Mrs: King's Inns Street

Orange Hall: Rutland Square

Page, Robert: Abbey Street Lower, Kildare Street

Painter's Hall: Gloucester Street Upper

Parnell, Anna: Hume Street

Parnell, Charles Stewart: Dawson Street/Morrison's Hotel, Duke Street, Finglas Road/Glasnevin Cemetery, Temple Street

Parnell, Fanny: Hume Street

Parsons, Dr Alfred: Baggot Street Upper

Partridge, W. P.: Beresford Place/Liberty Hall

Pearse, James: Church Street, Great Brunswick Street, Thomas Street

Pearse, Margaret: Eccles Street

Pearse, Padraig
    *Family homes:* Clarence Street South, Great Brunswick Street, Lisreaghan Terrace/Sandymount, Marlborough Road/Donnybrook, St George's Villa/Sandymount, Sallymount Avenue
    *Other:* Amiens Street, Dame Street, Dawson Street, Earlsfort Terrace, Findlater Place, Finglas Road/Glasnevin Cemetery, Frederick Street North, Great Britain Street, Kildare Street, Parkgate Street, Oakley Road/Ranelagh, Rathfarnham/The Hermitage, Rutland Square, Rutland Street Upper, Sackville Street Lower/General Post Office, Westland Row

Pearse, Willie: Great Brunswick Street, Rutland Street Upper, Sackville Street Lower/General Post Office, Westland Row

'Peter the Painter' (Peter Piatkow pistol): St Stephen's Green (West)

Pilkington, Liam: Dawson Street/Mansion House

Pinkman, John: Findlater Place, Portland Place North

Plunkett, Count George Noble: Abbey Street Lower, Beresford Place/Liberty Hall, Dawson Street/Mansion House, Drumcondra, Kimmage/Larkfield

Plunkett, Countess: Dawson Street/Mansion House

Plunkett, Grace Gifford: *see* Gifford, Grace (Plunkett)

Plunkett, George: Abbey Street Lower, Talbot Street

Plunkett, Geraldine (Mrs Thomas Dillon): Sackville Street Upper

Plunkett, Sir Horace: Foxrock, Lincoln Place, Merrion Square

Plunkett, Jack: Talbot Street

Plunkett, Joseph: Belgrave Road, South Circular Road/Kilmainham Gaol, Dawson Street, Fitzwilliam Street Upper, Hardwicke Street, James's Street, Kildare Street, Mountjoy Square, Rathgar Road, Rutland Square, Sackville Street Lower/General Post Office

Plunkett, Niamh: Rutland Square

Police Stations: College Street, Great Brunswick Street, Kevin Street

Ponsonby Booksellers: Grafton Street

Portal, Col.: Great Britain Street, Moore Street

Portobello Barracks: Rathmines Road (now Cathal Brugha Barracks)

Power, Maureen: Harold's Cross Road, Molesworth Street, Pembroke Road

Powers Distillery: Thomas Street/corner of Bridgefoot Street

Powers Irish Lace: Sackville Street Upper

Price, Lt Leonard: Pembroke Road Upper

Printer's Union: Gardiner Street Lower

Proclamation of the Irish Republic: Beresford Place/Liberty Hall (printed), Capel Street (typeface provided), Henry Street (wording finalised), Sackville Street Lower/General Post Office (proclaimed)

Prostitutes (streets known for): Corporation Street, Mecklenburgh Street, Montgomery Street, Waterford Street

Provisional Committee of the Irish Volunteers: Kildare Street

Pubs
    The Bailey: Duke Street
    Bannons (Bannon Brothers): Abbey Street Upper and Liffey Street
    Bleeding Horse: Camden Street
    Brazen Head: Bridge Street Lower/Bridgefoot Street
    Cummiskey's: Duke Street

Rotunda, The: Great Britain Street
Royal College of Surgeons: St Stephen's Green
   (West)
Royal Dublin Society: Ballsbridge
Royal Hibernian Academy: Abbey Street Lower
Royal Irish Automobile Club: Dawson Street
Royal Lancers: Charles Street
Royal University (National University – UCD):
   Earlsfort Terrace
Russell, George: see AE
Russell, Sean: Dawson Street/Mansion House,
   Earlsfort Terrace, Fairview Strand
Ruttledge, P. J.: Dawson Street/Mansion House
Ryan, Desmond: Rutland Square, Sackville
   Street Lower/General Post Office, Westland
   Row
Ryan, Freddie: High Street
Ryan, Dr Jim: Harcourt Street, Rathgar Road,
   Sackville Street Lower/General Post Office
Ryan, Dr. John: Gardiner Street
Ryan, Fr. Matt: Dawson Street/Mansion House
Ryan, Nell: South Circular Road
Ryan, P.: Harcourt Street
Ryan, Thomas: Jones Road/Croke Park

Sackville Street Club: Sackville Street Lower
Sacred Heart Convent: Leeson Street
St Andrew's Club: Great Brunswick Street
St Enda's School (Scoil Éanna): Oakley
   Road/Ranelagh, Rathfarnham/The
   Hermitage
St Ita's: Howth, Oakley Road/Ranelagh
St James's Brass and Reed Band: Great Britain
   Street
St John's Ambulance Brigade: Northumberland
   Road
St John's Convent: King Street North
St Mary's National School: Dominick Street
   Lower
St Patrick's Park: Patrick Street
St Stephen's Green (duck keeper): see Jack
   Kearney
St Stephen's Parochial Hall and Parish School:
   Northumberland Road
St Teresa's Hall: Clarendon Street
St Vincent de Paul Society: Sackville Street Upper
Sammon, Mick: Jones Road
Samuel Whyte's School: Grafton Street
Saurin, Frank: Crow Street
Savage, Martin: Ashtown/Co Dublin
Scollan, Joseph: Rutland Square

Scott, J.: Jones Road/Croke Park
Scott, Michael: Fleet Street
Father Sebastian, OFM, Cap: Church Street
Scoil Éanna: see St Enda's School
Shaw, George Bernard: Marlborough Street,
   Merrion Square, Synge Street
Sheehy-Skeffington, Francis Joseph Christopher:
   Baggot Street Upper, Beresford Place/Liberty
   Hall, College Green, Finglas Road/Glasnevin
   Cemetery, Grosvenor Place/Rathmines,
   Longwood Avenue, Molesworth Street,
   Moyne Road/Rathmines, Rathmines Road
Sheehy-Skeffington, Hanna: Belgrade
   Road/Rathmines, Belvedere Place,
   Grosvenor Place/Rathmines, Moyne Road/
   Rathmines
Sherlock, Lorcan: Great Britain
   Street/Rotunda
Shields, Arthur: Seafield Road/Clontarf, Vernon
   Avenue, Walworth Road/Portobello
Shields, William Joseph: see Fitzgerald, Barry
Sherwood Foresters: Clanwilliam Place, Moore
   Street
Shiubhlaigh, Maire Nic: Exchequer Street
Shouldice, Jack: Church Street
Sinn Féin: Abbey Street Middle, Dawson Street,
   Great Britain Street, Fownes Street, Harcourt
   Street, Mount Street, Rutland Square,
   Suffolk Street
Skinnider, Margaret: Harcourt Street, Hume
   Street, Waverly Avenue
Slattery, James (Jimmy): Custom House Quay,
   The Squad
Slattery, Liam: Fleet Street
Smith, Det. Cpt Patrick ('The Dog'):
   Drumcondra
Smith, T. H: Morehampton Rd.
Smithson, Annie M. P.: North Circular
   Road/Mountjoy Prison
Smyth, Eugene: Kimmage/Larkfield
Smyth, Lt Col Gerald Brice Ferguson:
   Molesworth Street
South Dublin Union: James's Street
South Staffordshire Regiment (South Staffs –
   176th Infantry Division): Coleraine Street,
   King Street North
Spring-Rice, Mary: Howth
The 'Squad': Abbey Street Upper, Gardiner
   Street Lower; see also Michael Collins
   addresses, appendix 2
Stack, Austin

Abbey Street Lower, Amiens Street, Bridge Street Upper, Dolphin's Barn, Emerald Square, Great Britain Street, Mary Street, Moore Street, Rutland Square

Vyze, Joe: Talbot Street

Walker, Mary (editor of *Honesty*): Mount Street Lower

Wall, Thomas: King's Inns Quay

Wall, Fr Thomas: Dawson Street/Mansion House

Walpole, Harry: Sackville Street Lower/General Post Office

Walsh, George: Kildare Street

Walsh, J. J.: Dawson Street/Mansion House, Harcourt Street, Kildare Street

Walsh, John: King Street North

Walsh, Archbishop William: Drumcondra

Walton, Martin: Frederick Street North

Warnes, George: Grafton Street

Watkin's Brewery: Ardee Street

Watters, Father: Leeson Street

Weafer, Cpt Thomas: Sackville Street Lower, GPO

Weir's Jewellers: Grafton Street

Wellesley, Arthur Duke of Wellington: Merrion Street Upper

Wells, Warre: Merrion Square

Wesley College: St Stephen's Green (South)

West, William Henry: Capel Street

Wheeler, Cpt DeCourcy: Bride Street/Ross Road, St Stephen's Green (West), York Street

Whelan and Son: Ormond Quay Upper

Whelan, Bill: Rutland Square

Whelan, Thomas: Baggot Street Lower, North Circular Road/Mountjoy Prison

White, Cpt J.R.: Beresford Place/Liberty Hall, Clontarf/Croydon park, Summer Street

White, Peadar: Kildare Street

Wicklow Chemical Manure Company: Poplar Row and North Strand Road

Wilde, L. E.: Sackville Street Upper

Wilde, Oscar: Merrion Square, Westland Row

Wilde, Sir William: Merrion Square

Williams and Woods Soap and Sweet Manufacturers: Great Britain Street

Williams Stores: Henry Street

Wilson, Cpt Lea: Great Britain Street

Women's Franchise League: Molesworth Street

Woodcock, Col.: Pembroke Street Upper

Wylie, William: Grangegorman Road Upper

Wyse-Power, Jenny: Abbey Street Lower, Henry Street, Oakley Road/Ranelagh, Rutland Square

Wyse-Power, Dr Nancy: Great Britain Street, Henry Street

Yeats, J. B.: Fleet Street, Harrington Road, Lincoln Place, St Stephen's Green

Yeats, W. B.: Baggot Street Lower, Clarendon Street, Lincoln Place, Merrion Square, Rathfarnham/The Hermitage, St Stephen's Green

YMCA, Abbey Street Middle, Sackville Street Upper